THE SPIRITUAL LITERATURE OF RECOLLECTION IN SPAIN (1500-1620)

THE SPIRITUAL LITERATURE OF RECOLLECTION IN SPAIN (1500-1620)

The Reform of the Inner Person

Angelo J. DiSalvo

Texts and Studies in Religion
Volume 84

The Edwin Mellen Press
Lewiston•Queenston•Lampeter

BX2350.6
.D57
1999

Library of Congress Cataloging-in-Publication Data

DiSalvo, Angelo J.
    The spiritual literature of recollection in Spain, 1500-1620 : the reform of the inner
person / Angelo J. DiSalvo.
        p. cm. -- (Texts & studies in religion ; vol. 84)
    Includes bibliographical references and index.
    ISBN 0-7734-7374-4
    1. Recollection (Theology) 2. Spiritual life--Christianity--History of doctrines--15th
century. 3. Spain--Church history--15th century.4.Spiritual life--Christianity--History of
doctrines--16th century. 5. Spain--Church history--16th century. I. Title. II. Texts and
Studies in religion ; v. 84

BX2350.6 .D57 1999
248' .0946'09031--dc21

                                                                                    99-047829

This is volume 84 in the continuing series
Texts and Studies in Religion
Volume 84 ISBN 0-7734-7374-4
TSR Series ISBN 0-88946-976-8

A CIP catalog record for this book is available from the British Library.

The Edwin Mellen Press
Box 450
Lewiston, New York
USA 14092-0450

The Edwin Mellen Press
Box 67
Queenston, Ontario
CANADA L0S 1L0

The Edwin Mellen Press, Ltd.
Lampeter, Ceredigion, Wales
UNITED KINGDOM SA48 8LT

Printed in the United States of America

Dedication

This book is dedicated to Dr. Azzurra Givens, Professor of Italian and Spanish in the Department of Modern Languages and Linguistics at Florida State University, and to Sr. M. Marcian, S.S.N.D., who taught high school for sixty years and is now retired.

Table of Contents

Foreword

This study originated during the preparation of the book *Cervantes and the Augustinian Religious Tradition*, which is a reworking and expansion of my doctoral dissertation prepared under the direction of Dr. Daniel Eisenberg at Florida State University. It was Professor Eisenberg who suggested that I devote the second chapter to a study of the religious works that Cervantes might have had the opportunity to read. While I was doing the research on this literature of spirituality, I came to realize that it would constitute a study in its own right. A few years later, at a Cervantes Symposium in Cincinnati organized by Dr. Donald Bleznick, I was fortunate enough to meet Dr. Maureen Ihrie who was beginning to work on the *Dictionary of the Literature of the Iberian Peninsula*. She asked if I would write several articles on these writers of devotional literature for this reference work. During the time that I was preparing these articles, I began a more serious study of these works written in Castilian. Various Spanish scholars wrote that very little had been written for the English-speaking world on these works. Thus, I began the arduous task of studying as many of these books of spirituality written and published during the sixteenth and seventeenth centuries in Spain. I limited it to the religious literature of Recollection, since this religious process included all of the stages of the classical concept of the *via mystica* which goes back to the Pseudo-Dionysius, the Areopagite; i.e., purgation, illumination, and union with the Divine Essence. This literature also follows the religious tradition which has been called affective spirituality that can be traced back to Augustine through Francis of Assisi and Bonaventure and includes many Germanic mystics. All of these currents converged in Spain at the end of the fifteenth century inspired by the need to reform the Church and its institutions in Spain. It not only produced writers such as Pedro de Alcántara, Juan de Avila, Bernardino de Laredo, and Francisco de Osuna, but the writings of Teresa de Jesús and Juan de la Cruz. We believe that it is one of the glories of the Spanish people equal to so many of their accomplishments throughout the history of western Europe.

Preface

The complex, intensely spiritual religious activism which characterized so much of sixteenth-century European history has traditionally been seen to follow a quite different course in the Iberian Peninsula. Until the end of the fifteenth century, church leaders in Spain generally followed a course of what historian Henry Charles Lea termed "careless tolerance" toward varieties of faith, quite unlike the practice in other areas of Europe. The political goals of the Catholic Monarchs and their heirs dramatically altered this incurious attitude regarding personal faith and offered the Church, and the Spanish Inquisition, starring roles in setting standards of belief and spiritual behavior, and shaping the religious landscape in Spain. In one sense, the Inquisition's influence has grown over the centuries, for the copious records it kept—records of heresy, blasphemy and deviations—have survived as the primary source for delineating a one-dimensional profile of the Spanish Catholic Church as separate from and actively opposed to spiritual movements in the rest of Europe. The few orthodox luminaries generally studied today, Santa Teresa, San Juan de la Cruz, Fray Luis de Leon, thus have become somewhat surprising exceptions to the general church profile of reactionary, counter-reform activity.

But, as Professor DiSalvo demonstrates, Spain was, at least until mid-sixteenth century, very much an active part of the general European spiritual landscape. His identification of common "seeds" of spiritual reform within and without Spain, and his documentation of the widespread advocacy of interior prayer by ordained church leaders from various religious orders serves to demonstrate that important reforms were supported by the Church. Although they are much less recognized today, reformers such as Juan de Avila enjoyed very widespread influence in their day. Additionally, the sheer number of guides written in Spanish (as opposed to Latin) by churchmen and churchwomen with permission of the Inquisition, attests to certain changes within the church and support for a pervasive spiritual vigor among the populace. Professor DiSalvo's research thus restores for modern readers a valuable, vital part of the picture of sixteenth-century spirituality in Spain and illuminates Spain's relationship to religious currents in other parts of Europe. His lucid explanation of the *Vía del Recogimiento* and its base in the concepts of internalized virtue and a responsive conscience will also enrich our understanding of many other texts of sixteenth-century Spain.

Maureen Ihrie
Associate Professor of Spanish
Kansas State University
June 1999

Acknowledgment

There are various people that I would like to show my appreciation because they are so important in the preparation of this book. First, I would like to thank my colleague and friend Dr. Peter Carino, Department of English at Indiana State University, who proofread and corrected the manuscript. I would also like to thank Marilyn Bisch, Department of Humanities at Indiana State University, who prepared the manuscript for publication. I am also indebted to Dr. Donald Bleznick, Professor Emeritus of the University of Cincinnati, who included an article on the influence of Augustine on Cervantes's *Persiles* in his book *Studies on Don Quijote and Other Cervantine Works*. This was the first article that I had published and it was at the Cervantes Symposium that he organized that I met Professor Maureen Ihrie, who also had an impact on my research when she asked that I contribute to the now published reference work, *The Dictionary of the Literature of the Iberian Peninsula*. I am also indebted to the Spanish scholar Melquíades Andrés Martín, whose two volume study *La teología española en el siglo XVI* and his study *Los recogidos* have been of immense value in the preparation of this study. I would also like to take this opportunity to thank the three people who inspired me to enter the teaching profession, Dr. Michael Miccarelli, Spanish professor and former department chairperson at the University of South Florida in Tampa, Sister M. Marcian, who was my high school teacher in Ybor City (Tampa), Florida, and the late Dr. Victor B. Oelschlager, former Chairperson of the Department of Modern Languages and Linguistics at Florida State University.

INTRODUCTION

Ah, sinful nation,
a people laden with iniquity,
offspring of evildoers,
sons who deal corruptly.
They have forsaken the Lord,
they have despised the Holy
One of Israel,
they are utterly estranged.
(Isaiah 1.4)

THE YEAR 1500 WAS PIVOTAL in the spiritual life of the Iberian peninsula. The important religious reform and revival, which was initiated at that time had its beginnings in the middle of the fifteenth century in the historical context of the Franciscan reform. The Western Church during the Middle Ages had made certain strides within specific communities toward reform. These reforms range from those of St. Bernard of Clairveaux, Francis of Assisi, Bonaventure, Meister Eckhart, Ruysbroeck, Thomas á Kempis and Erasmus up to the Cisnerian reforms of the sixteenth century in Spain. The seeds of a spiritual renewal and reform which produced and nurtured Martin Luther were the same ones that inspired reformers such as Francisco Jiménez de Cisneros, Juan de Avila, Francisco de Osuna, Santo Tomás de Villanueva, San Pedro de Alcántara, the Valdés brothers, Archbishop Bartolomé de Carranza, Bartolomé de Las Casas, the Franciscan houses of retreat, and even the *Alumbrados* and the *Recogidos*. It is not a coincidence that the reform movements in Spain were promoted by members of religious orders that belonged to what can be identified as the Augustinian religious tradition. A. D. Wright in his study of the Counter-Reformation writes:

"The patristic revival of the fifteenth and early sixteenth centuries was thus a common inspiration for both the Protestant Reformation and the Counter-Reformation, since both in fact emerged from the single movement for Christian revival, personal and communal, of the late Medieval and Renaissance period" (3).

Augustinianism and Christian-Platonism were essential in establishing the direction which reformation took in Spain. Although the speculative mysticism outlined in the Thomistic tradition played a crucial role in setting the theological framework for much of the extraordinary output of Renaissance Spanish spirituality in the fifteenth and sixteenth centuries, the Franciscan-Augustinian traditions proffered the foundation of the ascetical, devotional and even mystical literature produced in Spain at that time. Franciscan-Augustinian spirituality looks inward into the depths of the human soul; it ponders life's meaninglessness and nothingness in contrast to the infinite goodness of God. In this mode of Christian spirituality, the soul's will is moved upward or inward by the affections, and in this way the soul commences a journey culminating in its being united to the Divine Essence. This manifestation of Catholic spirituality looks inward as it seeks solitude or recollection. Recollection involves mental prayer, private meditation and later contemplation, which has the effect of cleansing the soul and preparing the individual to practice the Christian virtues. The prayer of Recollection affects the individual's behavior in relation to other human beings in the Christian community. This inner expression of one's spirituality, although it seeks solitude, peace and quiet, recollection, contemplation and union with the Divine Essence, in the Spanish context is never completely passive, for the individual actively participates with the affections as well as with the will.

In this study we shall avoid the term Counter-Reformation at least as far as Spain is concerned. We shall use the expressions Spanish Reform or the Spanish Reformation movement. Throughout this study we shall maintain that the Spanish Reform was principally a phenomenon native to the Iberian peninsula, albeit, with influences originating from the Italian Franciscans, the *Spirituali*, Bernard of Clairveaux and the Victorines in France, and the northern mystics as well as Savonarola and Erasmus. It is important to keep in mind that this Spanish Reform was not a counter-reform movement; neither was it simply a reaction per se to the paganizing tendencies of the Italian Renaissance, as was the case with Savonarola in Florence. The Spanish reform movement had its origins in the Franciscan houses of retreat in Castile and in the reform of Benedictine monasteries, and in particular, Valladolid and Montserrat. The great scholar and expert on Spanish spirituality, Melquíades Andrés Martín, in his lecture *Reforma española y reforma luterana: afinidades y diferencias a la luz de los místicos* (1517-1536), before the Fundación Universitaria Española, stated: "Reforma española, no contrarreforma; nacida en las últimas décadas del siglo XIV se desarrolla a lo largo de todo el siglo XV, principalmente en las observancias y reformas de los franciscanos y benedictinos, dominicos y jerónimos" (*Reforma esp.* 3). He adds that the Spanish reform was a product of an internal, spiritual vitality. Since its origins can be traced back to the late fifteenth and all of the sixteenth centuries, it is safe to claim that it in essence is a native phenomenon. Furthermore, Luther's reform may well be a result of the same or at least similar forces that were widespread in most of western Europe. The establishment of the Franciscan houses of retreat, such as La Salceda, the reforms undertaken in the Benedictine monasteries of San Benito at Valladolid as well as those carried out at Montserrat, the creation of theological schools at Palencia, Salamanca, Lérida among others, the crucial involvement of Cardinal Francisco Jiménez de Cisneros under the auspices of the Catholic Kings, all played important roles in the Spanish Reform and, in addition, bore glorious fruit. In his very important book, *Los recogidos*, Melquíades Andrés makes the valid point that the spiritual current called *Recogimiento* (Recollection), which bore such wondrous fruit in the history of the literature of Spanish spirituality, had its origins in the above mentioned Franciscan houses of retreat in Castile. He writes: "Las casas de retiro, de oración o de recogimiento, son una especie de desierto. . . Se inicia hacia 1483, es codificado por Francisco de Osuna, Bernabé de Palma y Bernardino de Laredo entre 1525-1530" (*Los recogidos* 13). According to Andrés, the spiritual movement designated as *Recogimiento* is the pivotal point around which revolves the entire reform movement in Spain. It is a seed that sprouts into diverse forms of Spanish spirituality which last for two hundred years and produced or inspired some of the greatest masterpieces of ascetical, devotional, meditative, and mystical literature. An important ingredient in the Spanish reform is the Semitic element which in many ways is unique to Spain. We believe that it is this element which differentiates Spanish spirituality from that of the rest of western Europe. It gives a unique quality to the ascetical, devotional, and, most especially, the mystical literature in Spain. When we discuss Semitic elements, both Judaic and Arabic spirituality are implied. Spain included during the fifteenth century large communities of *conversos* and *moriscos* and we believe that, at least in the case of the *conversos*, these people gave immediacy as well as impetus to the reform movements. As *conversos*, these individuals inside the Catholic Church continued to express inner spirituality, a de-emphasis on the purely external manifestations of the faith, and a need to reform many traditional practices of the Church. They eschewed the outer trappings of the established Church, looked inward to find God and united with Him by using very practical and down to earth spiritual exercises wherein the individual's self was never completely lost or absorbed into the Divine Essence. We believe this to be an active participation of the person in contemplation, when individuals once again take an active role in relation to God and even hold Him prisoner in the soul. Spanish spirituality is also practical, and many writers including Teresa de Jesús use references to day-to-day objects to describe their mystical experiences.

Returning to the subject of the Franciscan houses of retreat, the Catholic Monarchs of Spain recognized their importance, as well as the critical need for Church reform. Andrés writes on this subject: "Los Reyes Católicos toman carta definitivamente en el asunto en 1485 'porque en nuestros reinos hay muchos monasterios e casas de religión, así de hombres como de mujeres, muy disolutos y desordenados en su vivir'" (*Reforma esp.* 6). Cardinal Jiménez de Cisneros, himself a Franciscan, sets the stage for beginning the reform in 1493 by, (1) giving proper attention to the naming of bishops, (2) establishing theological schools, and (3) reforming the teaching methods in theology (*Reforma esp.* 6). Cisneros and the Archbishop of Toledo, Bartolomé de Carranza, supported the publication of works that would later make widespread the most important spiritual currents of the time, known as *vías, caminos, guías,* and *montes,* whose purpose was to lead individuals to attain contemplation and, ultimately, union with God. One of the most important of these spiritual ways is called *vía de recogimiento* (Way of Recollection), which originated around 1480 and was codified by important spiritual writers such as Francisco de Osuna in his *Tercer abecedario espiritual* and Juan de Avila in his seminal work called *Audi, filia.* Cisneros nurtured this inner expression of Catholic spirituality which enhanced both the inner and outer practice of the virtues and the avoidance of the vices represented by the writings of Franciscans such as *Caballería cristiana* (1515) by Jaime de Alcalá, *Arte de servir a Dios* (1521) by Alonso de Madrid, and the most important *Exercitatorio de la vida cristiana* (1500) by García de Cisneros, Abbot of Montserrat. These were some of the first books of the spirituality of reform and spiritual renewal to be published in Spain at that time. Although the vast majority of these works were written by monks or nuns, their immense numbers helped to produce a religious literature that was accessible to a large number of lay readers. In this sense, Spanish literature of spirituality was indeed universal; this means that it was read by the common layperson be he/she rich or poor, city dweller or country dweller, noble or bourgeois, laborer or craftsman, man or woman, parish priest, nun, or monk. The essential thing is that the individual know how to read. As a result, the attainment of Christian perfection, the cultivation of the inner life of the soul, the meditative process, recollection, mental prayer and even the mystical experience, had the potential of being accessible to all. This tremendous output not only helped to interiorize Catholicism, but also moderate the outer practices of the Church. It led to the reform of entire communities of monks and nuns, and at the same time brought about the Christianization of the conquest and colonization of the American continents. It also led to the writings of San Juan de la Cruz and Teresa de Jesús, in addition to the founding of the Society of Jesus by Ignatius of Loyola. In fact, these writers were the offspring of the harmonious marriage between Christian humanism and theology (*Reforma esp.* 7).

It must be stressed that although the Spanish reform was a native phenomenon, it was also part of an overall religious environment common to all of Europe in reference to the interiorization of the religious experience and the reevaluation of various rites and ceremonies within the Church. It must also be remembered that the Spanish Reform was a product of the Renaissance in that it sought a return to the spiritual conditions of the primitive (evangelical) Church as well as to Patristic Christianity. Carlo Angeleri in his book *Il problema religioso del rinascimento* (1952) explains the idea of individuals' creativity and their liberty to free it from the shackles of a sterile Scholasticism (Angeleri 44-45). Angeleri adds that this liberation process also rose above the concept of the post-Edenic or fallen condition of humanity common to traditional Augustinianism. Angeleri claims that Francis of Assisi had shown the way for all Christians to free themselves from total, sacerdotal authority so that they could begin to personally enjoy the eternal truths with love, affections and tenderness instead of fear and trembling as they are placed before God in contemplation or union (78). Yet, at the same time, individuals must accomplish this with complete humility and self-denial. These men and women, while remaining active in their communities and societies, deem it necessary to find the time to recollect themselves in meditation, oral and mental prayer, the practice of the Christian virtues, and contemplation in love and humility. They receive illumination to understand God and to perceive Him as He really is, since they have been emptied of all that is material or not God; hence, they become totally unfettered and can contemplate and ultimately unite with the Divine Essence in the innermost depths of their souls. In the process, they are renewed and reformed, and as a result, are ready to set forth from their cells and communities to become involved in the reform of their church and its hierarchy; in addition, they attempt to reform their political rulers, the monarchy, and in the end, their society as well as Spain's policies in the American continents. The Spanish Reform has left humanity a legacy which consists of an incredibly rich and diverse corpus of literature, reformed orders, the Laws of the Indies, and other institutions which continuously serve as a source of inspiration. It is this literature of Recollection and the reform for which it acted as a catalyst that will be the subject of this study. Classical Spanish mysticism is but the full flowering of this religious movement begun in the Franciscan reform.

In the spiritual process known as Recollection, we will find the seeds of the great Spanish mystical writings. This study will not attempt to add anything further to what has been studied about the mystics such as Teresa de Jesús and Juan de la Cruz; it will simply situate these two as part of the long series of writers who continue the spirituality of Recollection in Spain. In other words, their writings fit well within the parameters of the literature of Recollection and the Spanish reform. Many scholars have categorized other writers of this literature as mystics. This study will investigate the works of these lesser known writers within the historical context of the literature of Recollection. It will also study their contributions to the reform of the monastic orders, other religious communities, the institutional Church, the political and even economic system, and to society at large. Most importantly, this reform begins with the spiritual transformation and renewal of individuals in their communities and affects their relations with God and neighbor. We shall note how this manifestation of Spanish spirituality is never absolutely passive, nor does it attempt to free individuals from their social responsibilities, which include their own as well as that of the Church. Neither is it solely an abandonment to God, but contemplation and union with Him, albeit in the center of the soul. This experience is grounded on complete humility as it assists the individual in the attainment of Christian perfection. In spite of the fact that the Inquisitorial examiners became suspicious of many of these works, and, in fact, condemned a few of them, Recollection itself was never declared a heretical movement within the Spanish Church. It came under constant scrutiny, yet at the same time, it was nourished by the orthodox elements of the Roman Catholic Church in Spain. It never renounced participation in the Mass and in the sacraments of the Church, for it was based on the practice of the virtues.

This study will digress from the normal categorization of the works of these remarkable men and women which investigates them under the heading of their respective religious orders. Chapter I is a study of the influences on Renaissance Spanish spirituality from outside of the Iberian peninsula. The study commences with evangelical Christianity, Patristic writings, and in particular, Augustine, together with the Pseudo-Dionysius, the Areopagite. We shall trace the influences of this early Christian spirituality through the renewal of Francis of Assisi and the Italian *Spirituali*, Bonaventure, Thomas Aquinas, Catherine of Siena, Bernard of Clairveaux, the Victorines and even Savonarola, and, finally, to the northern European mystics such as Meister Eckhard, Herp, Kempis, Ruysbroeck and Erasmus. Chapter II will deal with the antecedents of this literature within the Iberian context which begins with Ramon Llull, the early Franciscan reformers, the *recoletos*, different Medieval currents in Spain, the apocryphal texts attributed to Augustine, and various Semitic influences.

Chapter III features a rather in-depth study of this crucial Renaissance manifestation of Spanish spirituality called the Way or Prayer of Recollection. The chapter includes a discussion of the Franciscan houses of retreat (*recoletos*), the reform of important monasteries both in Castile and Aragón, and the study of the works of certain pivotal writers such as Juan de Avila, Bernardino de Laredo, Pedro de Alcántara, and Francisco de Osuna; all of these laid the groundwork for the subsequent ascetical, devotional, meditative, contemplative and mystical literature in Spain, and to a degree, in all of western Europe. Chapter IV studies works which represent the full flowering of the literature of Recollection. These works instruct and guide the reader in the process of meditative reading, prayer (oral and mental), meditation on certain mysteries of the faith, infused contemplation, the practice of the Christian virtues, and the path that will lead to union with God. Prayer and meditation also involve the affections instead of pure speculation.

It is important to note that this study will deal on the whole with the more important or representative works of Renaissance Spanish spirituality in the sixteen and seventeenth centuries. It does not attempt the insurmountable task of studying the thousands of works of spirituality produced from 1500 to 1700 which amount to about three thousand. We will study a limited number of works written in the vernacular that had the potential of reaching the greatest number of readers. The parameters that we have established for this study are the spirituality of Recollection and all of the phases involved in the process which include mental and oral prayer, devotional reading, meditation, and infused contemplation, as well as union or the attainment of Christian perfection. Recollection can also involve ascetical practices as well as training in the practice of the Christian virtues. These works are both a byproduct and the catalyst for Christian reform in Spain. In many ways, they are part of the long Christian tradition associated with the Augustinian-Franciscan tradition, but with large doses of Thomistic speculation. Recollection is also a product of Christian-Platonism. In short, it is affective Christianity with elements of speculative influences learned from the writings of Thomas Aquinas. The synthesis of these various and somewhat diverse elements produced during this period a flowering of religious literature written primarily by Franciscans, Augustinians, Carmelites, Jesuits and a few Dominicans; Juan de Avila belongs to no particular religious order. All of this literature of Recollection looks inward and seeks a certain amount of solitude that transforms individuals within their society. The Dominicans also contributed to the Spanish reform through their novel interpretation of Aquinas's *Summa Theologica*. The Dominican Bartolomé de las Casas defended the rights of the Amerindians by using as his basis the Thomistic concept that all humans are equal because they have a soul and share in the same life of God. Likewise, his fellow Dominican Francisco de Vitoria in his series of lectures at Salamanca supported by the *Summa Theologica* took the position that military conquest, forced occupation of these lands, and Christian evangelization were incompatible with both natural and divine laws.

CHAPTER I

Antecedents of the Spirituality of Recollection and the Reform Movement Outside of the Iberian Peninsula

> *...llegar a la alta*
> *contemplación de la in-*
> *mutable sustancia de Dios,*
> *aprender de él y saber de*
> *su incomprensible sabi-*
> *duría cómo todas las cria-*
> *turas que no son lo que él*
> *no los crió que él.*
> *(Augustine,* Ciudad de Dios,
> *Libro XI: I, 241)*

SPANISH SPIRITUALITY IN THE RENAISSANCE period is the culmination of over two thousand years of spiritual life in western Europe. This spiritual life has been constantly sustained and renewed by evangelical and apostolic Christianity, the Book of Genesis, the Psalms and the Song of Songs, the writings of Augustine, the Pseudo-Dionysius and the long tradition of Christian Platonism (Shahan and Kovach). Augustine is the Church father who most effectively reflects the inward looking tendencies of the affective Christianity that is part of the tradition that bears his name. Augustine teaches that by looking inward into the soul, the individual's intellect will come to the conclusion that the soul reflects the Triune God. Thus, the Church father established the tripartite division of the soul into memory, understanding and will, all of which play such an important role in the development of the meditative and contemplative processes in prayer (Copleston

II: 288). Common to the western Christian tradition traceable to Augustine is also the journey motif: the soul's ascent to God which is also the spiritual peregrination (Chew 175). Thus, already in the writings of Augustine we are able to detect this spiritual tendency to look inward into the very depths of the soul and at the same time effect a spiritual ascent to God. Another very important element of the Augustinian-Platonic-Franciscan traditions of the western Church is that instead of using understanding of or pure speculation on God's essence, the individual's soul is illuminated and divine knowledge is hence infused by the power of the affections, the practice of the Christian virtues, and most importantly, through God's will. Once the intellect is properly illuminated, the will is moved to love. This pure love seeks the contemplation of God and ultimate union with Him.

Historically in the western Church, when there has been a need to reform, religious writers have consistently found inspiration in the writings of St. Augustine. One of St. Augustine's major works, *City of God,* (*De civitate Dei,* 410-13) was written as a response to those who accused the Christians of bringing about the demise of the Roman Empire. Augustine also had to respond to the evident decay and corruption within Rome. In his response Augustine outlines a theological system that was based on a fusion of Pauline Christianity as well as on the *Book of Genesis* with Platonic ideas culled from his readings of Plotinus's *Enneads,* Cicero's *Hortensius,* and Plato's *Timaeus* (Copleston I: 461-63). This most important synthesis laid the foundation for a spirituality that has produced much fruit in the western Church. According to Frederick Copleston, Augustine borrowed from Plotinus his doctrine of the soul, on the transcendence of God, on evil as the negation of good, and the idea of freedom of the will (Turnbull 249).

One of the most important aspects of the Augustinian looking inward into one's soul is in an odd way also connected with the pilgrimage theme that Augustine found in Paul's Epistles. Augustine was himself influenced by reading Paul's Epistles. It is quite probable that Augustine borrowed his image of the pilgrimage theme from reading Paul. Samuel C. Chew in his book *The Pilgrimage of Life* writes: ". . .the Old Testament texts Leviticus 25.23 and Psalm 39.121, which declared that men are 'strangers and pilgrims' was subjected to a new interpretation by St. Paul in Phillipians 3.20" (Chew 175). According to Etienne Gilson, Augustine's spiritual quest which ascends towards God begins with the

Socratic "know thyself" (Gilson 3). Gilson explains further that "the soul may know its true nature and live in accordance with it, that is to say, take its proper place, which is beneath him to whom it should be subject" (3). By looking inside of oneself (inwardly) and knowing oneself first, one is able to recognize that the soul has been created in God's image, and in this way the individual can come to the knowledge of the Divine Essence (O'Connell 14).

What will later be referred to as the ascetical process was already outlined in the corpus of Augustine's works. Love, faith, moral (Christian) perfection and the strengthening of the mind and body by means of spiritual exercises (*ascesis*) are important ingredients in Augustine's theological system. Through *ascesis* (spiritual exercises), the soul's functions (memory, understanding, and will) are properly ordered in order to undertake the spiritual ascent to God. Once the body and particularly the soul have been properly exercised, individuals will receive the grace and other spiritual gifts that will lead to the contemplation of God as He really is, i.e., the very source of wisdom, truth, and beauty. Augustine constantly reminds his readers that in order to contemplate the Divine Essence one must turn away from created objects (O'Connell 29).

During the years 1500 and 1620 Augustine's works were important sources of inspiration for both religious and secular writers of Spanish literature; these include both his Latin works and the major works that were translated into Castilian during this period. The *City of God*, the *Confessions*, and *On Christian Doctrine*, were all translated into the vernacular in the sixteenth and seventeenth centuries in Spain. A popular devotional work called *Meditaciones* was at that time attributed to Augustine. This latter work is a compendium or *summa* of Augustinian theological principles. In the *City of God* the Church Father traces the history of the heavenly and earthly cities from the fall of the rebellious angels to the Second Coming. Augustine argues the fact that the two cities must coexist in this peregrine life. The members of the two cities can be recognized by the objects of their desires. One group lives for the flesh, the other lives for the spirit. One society practices the Christian virtues, the other the deadly sins or earthly vices. The members of the celestial city will only find peace when they reach their destination, God, for they are only travelers or pilgrims in this earthly life. Life lived in the presence of God is perceived to be the real life for the Christian. The Augustinian conception of the earthly paradise reads: ". . .no one, then, denies that

Paradise may signify the life of the blessed, its four rivers the four virtues: prudence, justice, fortitude and temperance; its trees all useful knowledge, its fruits the customs of the godly" (*City of God* XIII: 21, 431).

The *Confessions* were very influential in the Western Church.[1] In the second book Augustine describes his own conversion at Ostia in this way: "We ascended higher yet by means of inward thought and discourse and admiration of works, and we came up to our own minds" (*Conf.* IX: 10). Augustine visualized the descent into his soul in order to begin the ascent to God. In Book X Augustine claims to be an interior man or inner person who has gained knowledge on how to reach God in the very apex of his soul, that is, the deepest or the highest point of his soul (X: 6, 234). He ascertains that by descending into his own soul, he will rise in order to reach God. He compares his mind to a palace, wherein all the physical sensations of light, color, and the forms of the body are separated and classified (234-35). Once again in the *Confessions*, one can find Augustine's comments on love which is that love is a weight: "My weight is my love, by it am I borne whithersoever I am Borne" (XIII: 21, 431).

Love lifts the soul toward God. In Book XII Augustine describes how the soul reflects God's image. In its three functions the soul is, it knows, and it desires or loves. It is divided into three functions or parts: memory (remembering), intellect (understanding, knowledge), and will (desire or love). These three divisions or functions are the basis of all Christian spirituality or the ascetical, meditative process, recollection, mental and oral prayer, passive and active contemplation, and, ultimately, mystical union.

Augustine's important treatise *On Christian Doctrine* was also translated into Castilian during the Renaissance period. In Book I, chapter 10, Augustine describes the soul's cleansing or purgation, an act which allows it to be capable of seeing God's light and thus desire to cling to it once it has seen it. It also unfetters the soul allowing it to make the ascent that will lead it to God. In Book II Augustine writes that the eye of the soul can contemplate God only if it is properly cleansed (purged) by dying to the things of this world. This is all part of the ascetical process which brings individuals to contemplation. Gilson emphasizes the importance that the cardinal or moral virtues play in Augustine's cleansing of the soul to prepare it for contemplating God as He is. These are prudence, fortitude, temperance and justice (Gilson 131). Gilson makes the point that individuals will become virtuous by making the soul conform to the unchangeable rules and the illuminating affects of these virtues which are imbedded in each person who wishes to attain truth and wisdom (131). In Book I of *On the Trinity*, Augustine comments on what he refers to as the art of contemplation: "Contemplation is indeed the reward of faith, and our hearts are purified by faith in preparation for the reward (I: xxv). In this treatise Augustine expounds at great length on the tripartite division of the soul into its respective functions. In Book X he describes the image of the Trinity as it is reflected in the human soul. At this point, he categorizes the three functions, parts or powers of the soul as memory, understanding and will, the will being, according to him, that part of the soul which "disposes of those things that are contained in the memory and understanding" (X: 303-11). Augustine emphasizes that it is within the soul that individuals are renewed in the love and knowledge of God when they reflect on His image contained therein (XI: 315).

The next writer in chronological order who is a pivotal figure in the western Church even though he hails from the Hellenic east, is the Pseudo-Dionysius, known as the Areopagite. In the first chapter of his *Mystic Theology* Dionysius writes:

> Direct us aright to the super-unknown and super-brilliant and highest summit of the mystic oracles, where the simple and absolute and changeless mysteries of theology lie hidden within the super-luminous gloom of the silence revealing hidden things, which in deepest darkness shines above the most super-brilliant and in the altogether impalpable and invisible, fills to everflowing the eyeless minds with glories of surpassing beauty. (I: 130)

Here the darkness is the place where the individual is able to see God's shining light and come to know God's hidden secrets. It is the soul's dark night or nothingness and complete peace, silence or repose where God's light dazzles the soul in contemplation.

Dionysius counsels his disciple Timothy to leave behind "both sensible perception and intellectual efforts, and all objects of sense and intelligence by the persistent commerce with the mystic visions" (130). In this way, Timothy's soul may be raised aloft unknowingly to achieve union with God (130). Dionysius adds: "For by the restless and absolute ecstasy in all purity, from thyself and all, thou wilt be carried on high to the superessential ray of the Divine darkness, when thou hast cast away all and become free from all" (134). Dionysius describes the ascent to the contemplation of the things intelligible "and to the silence when the soul will be wholly united to the unutterable" (135). He describes the negative way which leads to God; in short, the ascent to God becomes a progressive extirpation of every concept and feeling, and the only thing that the individual accomplishes knowing is not what God is but what God is not. The Psuedo-Dionysius, according to Ciriaco Morón Arroyo, gave western spirituality the prototype for the doctrine of the three stages of the mystical or secret way: purgative, illuminative, and perfection or union (78).[2]

Bernard of Clairvaux (1090-1153) was directly involved in France with one of the earliest reforms in the western Church. Much of the influence that Bernard exerted on western Christianity was a result of his eighty-six sermons on the Song of Songs, and on his treatises such as *On Consideration of the Love of God*. In the introduction to Bernard's *The Love of God and Spiritual Friendship*, James M. Houston writes that Bernard's idea of knowledge of God comes only through devotion to God, in poverty, in simplicity, in solitude. . ." (Bernard xvi). Bernard was in effect a reformer of church practices. The religious writers Tauler, Ruysbroeck and Thomas á Kempis were all influenced by him as they in turn directly influenced the Spanish writers of spirituality in the Renaissance. According to Houston the Cistercian reform was a school of love and devotion and he adds the following:

> His (Bernard's) experience of the sweet tasting of the Song of Songs
> was also part of this written revival. Bernard was the herald of this new
> literature of love. He revived the theology of desire from the sermons of
> Origen and Gregory of Nyssa. (xxii)

Bernard, according to Houston, offered an alternative to courtly love literature by creating his own literature of desire and love for God (xii). The treatise form during that period of western monasticism became an extension of the letter form so prized among the members of the monastic communities (xxii). It was also through Bernard that meditation and prayer were added to Sacred Scripture (xxix). The manifestation of his personal spirituality was an affective one in that faith in

God is perceived through the heart and not by reason. This has been referred to as the theology of love (xxix).[3]

The Spanish scholar Antonio Royo Marín in his book, *Los grandes maestros de la vida espiritual,* which is a history of Christian spirituality, states that the point of departure of the ascetico-mystical literature set forth by Bernard is original sin from which the individual rises by love and God's grace. In this ascent to God, Bernard presents several stages or states of love: carnal love, interested (selfish) love for God, and pure love for God (Royo Marín 162-63). Bernard also teaches that individuals in the final stage of love are deified, that is, freed from the prison of the body as the soul is lifted up to the Beatific Vision (164). In the *Sermons on the Song of Songs,* any scholar may encounter some of the sources of western ascetical-devotional-contemplative and mystical literature. These are: (1) personal experience, (2) the influence of the Song of Songs, and (3) the influence of Neoplatonism with its description of the ascent to God. In the image of the kiss, we may perceive the three stages of the mystical way. The kiss on Christ's feet represents purgation or the ascetical process of the penitent in the first stage and initiation or the process of the initiate or incipient. The kiss on the hand represents the illuminative stage of those who are proficient in the mystical way; the kiss on the mouth of Christ represents the unitive stage or perfection, which produces the perfect Christian (Morón Arroyo 89).

Finally, there are two more important contributions that Bernard bequeathed to western Christianity; the devotion of Christ's humanity and the devotion to the Virgin Mary. Bernard enhanced his love for God and for Christ's human nature by meditating on the mysteries of His earthly life (Royo Marín 171). Royo Marín writes that of all of the mysteries of Christ's life, three have special significance for Bernard; the Annunciation, the Nativity, and the death on the cross (172). It is important to note that all three of these mysteries focus on the human aspects of Christ's life on earth. These meditations on Christ's humanity will bear much fruit during the Renaissance in Spain, where the meditation on and devotion to Christ's human nature become a mainstay of this country's spirituality. By meditating on Christ's humanity, the person meditating will be elevated to the heights of Christian perfection (172). After the humanity of Christ, the next most important object of Bernard's devotion is that of the Virgin Mary. Bernard is one of the first to consider Christ's mother as co-redeemer and universal mediator for humankind. Meditation, in addition, is the vehicle through which a person may receive God's grace (173).[4]

The religious crisis of the late twelfth century brought about one of the greatest spiritual renewals and flowering of affective spirituality ever witnessed in the Church. The movement inspired by Francis of Assisi and his Order was based on a return to the apostolic life of the primitive Church, fraternal love, humility, poverty, the example of the Beatitudes, the common life of poverty, preaching and the receiving of alms. It also attempted to harmonize the contemplative and active life of the individual Christian. According to John Moorman in his *A History of the Franciscan Order from its Origins to the Year 1517*, humility, simplicity, poverty, and prayer were the four foundation stones of the Franciscan reform, in other words, a literal obedience to the recorded sayings of Christ (Moorman 3). This series of events in Church history was fortuitous since it is the reform of the Franciscan Order that later became the catalyst for the Spanish reform itself. In effect, the order later had to adapt after the death of its founder for it had to make some compromises with the organized Church. Catholic literature of spirituality was to receive another tremendous boost from Bonaventure who preserved the traditional perspective of Augustinian-Platonic subjectivity together with the Pseudo-Dionysian doctrine of the ascent and the idea of divine fecundity (Shahan and Kovak 7). Bonaventure was born Giovanni Fidanza in Tuscany in 1221. He entered the Franciscan Order and as Professor of Theology at Paris became imbued with the Augustinian and Franciscan traditions but rethought within the parameters of the dominant Neo-Aristotelianism (Copleston II: 245). Bonaventure believed that the philosopher is also guided by the light of faith. He himself was guided by his belief in the supernatural end of human existence, which is the ascent to God as well as eternal felicity in His sight (Copleston II: 246). For Bonaventure, the existence of God is self-evident through the soul's reflection on itself and all creation simply serves as a reminder of this primary fact. When the soul reflects upon itself and its own dependence as well as its desire for wisdom and peace, it recognizes God's existence and also God's presence in it. Thus, it is not necessary for the soul to seek outside of itself; it has only to follow Augustine's advice to enter into oneself (Copleston II: 250). Through divine illumination Bonaventure follows the Platonic-Augustinian belief that the soul receives the idea of the perfect or forms the idea of the perfect in the light of God

(Copleston II: 256). In addition, following the doctrine of exemplarism, God is the exemplary cause of all things, the exemplar of all creation; i.e., there is some resemblance between God and creatures, or stated in another way, the creature is an imitation of God Himself (Copleston II: 266). As a result, individuals contemplate God in themselves (Copleston II: 269).[5]

Bonaventure's most influential work was the *Itinerarium mentis in Deum* (1259), or *The Journey of the Mind to God*. A shorter treatise, *De triplici via, alias Incendium Amoris, (The Triple Way or Love Enkindled)* treats the mystical progression or ascent. This treatise is a seminal work in terms of the literature of contemplation. In it Bonaventure charts the triple way of the mystical ascent; i.e., the purgative, illuminative, and perfective or unitive stages, and each one of these stages is applied in succession to each of the interior exercises which are meditation (reading), prayer and contemplation. According to Joseph de Vinck in his introduction to *The Works of Bonaventure I: Mystical Opusucla*, the end of these exercises is spiritual wisdom, the repose of peace, the splendor of truth, and spiritual sweetness (Vinck 6). When individuals meditate through spiritual reading, mental prayers, and contemplation, they must go through the processes of moral cleansing, asceticism and the practice of the Christian virtues, rational illumination and finally, spiritual elevation. Contemplation should not be confused with the mystical union; this is important in classifying the works of spirituality produced in Renaissance Spain. Contemplation is the "intellectual operation that consists in applying our spirit to the understanding of God, as much as our natural powers permit" (Vinck 62).

Even more influential than the *De triplici* on later Spanish writers is Bonaventure's seminal work *The Mind's Journey to God*. In this treatise Bonaventure is imitating Francis of Assisi, who often turned away from his responsibilities to seek solitude in prayer and in contemplation; in Spain this came to be called *recogimiento*, (recollection). Bonaventure himself at La Verna, just as his spiritual master had done before him, had an experience of mystical union with God. According to L. S. Cunningham in the introduction to the above mentioned work, Bonaventure's contribution to Christian thought was the "reconstruction of the Christocentric mysticism of St. Francis into a coherent whole" (Bonaventure 3). Franciscanism has always emphasized Christ's humanity, and most especially, the events of His birth and passion both of which became objects of meditation and contemplation. Furthermore, for Bonaventure and for Franciscans in general, "the whole world was suffused with the traces of God for the world reflects God. This world gives man some sense of the presence and mystery of God" (Bonaventure 7).

To construct his mind's (soul's) journey to God, Bonaventure makes use of the six wings of the Seraph that Francis envisioned at the time of the stigmata as the different stages of the soul's ascent in which union with God is the final goal (Bonaventure 9). In stage one (purgative-incipient-penitent stage), the mind is still fixed on material objects of creation; it praises God for His marvelous creation. Stage two involves the mind's seeing the righteousness of things; stage three initiates the introspective phase wherein the soul turns in on itself and glimpses its triple division: memory, understanding and will. In stage four, the soul is elevated by God's grace and the practice of the Christian virtues; thus, the soul is purged, illumined and ready to unite with God. This process is assisted by mental prayer, revelation in nature and in the Bible, and God's freely given grace. Stages five and six bring the individual to the contemplation of God (Bonaventure 9). The soul has no need for any further search and it reposes in the "ineffable mystery of God's presence" (Bonaventure 10). In the Prologue to the *Journey of the Mind to God*, Bonaventure informs the reader that reading and speculation are not sufficient preparation for contemplation and union because reading without devotion, research without fear of God, attentiveness without joy, labor without piety, knowledge without love, study without divine grace, instruction without inspiration, do not bring about contemplation (25).[6] Two other works, *Praise of the Holy Cross* (*Laudemus de sancta cruce*) and *The Tree of Life* (*Lignum vitae*) are meditations on the life and resurrection of Christ.[7]

According to Manuel de Castro in a series of lectures presented in Madrid on Bovaventure's influence in Spain, the latter's influence on Bernardino de Laredo and Fray Luis de Granada was considerable. These influences are identified as (1) the process of prayer as dialogue with God, (2) the mystical journey, (3) the contemplation and joy of observing creation, (4) the devotion to the human dimensions of Christ's suffering and passion, (5) the process of mental prayer, (6) spiritual exercises, and (7) prayer as spiritual sabbath or repose (75).

We must also consider the influence of the *Spirituali* and *Fraticelli* in Italy during the fourteenth century. Involved were the Third Order Franciscans' Order of Penance, which was an association of lay persons who were critical and even suspicious of the Catholic Church at that time. They also criticized the temporal power of the Papacy, the worldliness of the religious orders, and certain sacramental teachings and practices of the clergy. They also discouraged their members from attending shows, games, and spectacles. In addition, they practiced abstinence of certain foods, they fasted, prayed, lived in harmony and peace, and visited the sick and dying. Theirs was an active life of devotion, simplicity, and discipline. The Church then, just as in the sixteenth century, was in need of reform and of new inspiration. These religious men and women combined poverty and simplicity with study, and we believe that they became a model that was to be emulated in fifteenth-century Spain (Moorman 52). The *Spirituali* or *Zelanti*, such as Ubertino da Casale and Angela da Foligno, represented this first Franciscan reform which was to bear much fruit in Spain under the guidance of Cardinal Jiménez de Cisneros who had some of the works of these *Spirituali* published at Alcalá. Angela da Foligno, Jacopo da Todi, and, in Spain, Ramon Llull were three outstanding Franciscans who made a notable contribution to the literature of spirituality in Spain (Moorman 265). We shall discuss Ramon Llull when we deal with earlier Iberian works of spirituality. It is interesting to note that all three above mentioned were Third Order Franciscans. One of the most crucial of Franciscan contributions to the literature of spirituality resided in their insistence on using the vernacular language in order to better reach the common people. After the invention of the printing press in the fifteenth century, the literature of spirituality not only extended beyond the walls of convents and monasteries, but it became relatively popular, and in the process, it became truly "democratic" (Moorman 208).[8]

There were several members of the Dominican Order who contributed to devotional, ascetical, contemplative, and, to some degree, mystical literature. Although Thomas Aquinas is considered to be more speculative than intuitive, more outward looking than inward, more intellectual than affective, the great theologian taught a great deal about the essence of God, the parts and functions of the soul, and most importantly, about devotion which would include contemplation. Aquinas insists that knowing is being, and he states that the most perfect and intimate way of possessing a thing is by knowing it, and that the contemplative life is the highest form of life. We possess God and know Him through contemplation. In the first article of Question XII (How God is known by us) in *Summa Theologica* I (1273) he posits the question whether any created intellect can see the essence of God, for he believes that a person's greatest happiness consists in the use of his/her highest function (71). Also, he stresses that any person can "be raised up to such a great height" (78). Aquinas calls this increase of the intellectual power the illumination of the intellect. He adds: "By this light, the blessed are made deiform—that is, like God" (80). This is an extremely important concept which concerns the literature of spirituality in Renaissance Spain. According to Aquinas, those who see the divine essence see what they see in God not by any likeness but by the divine essence itself united to their intellect (88). The fact remains that Aquinas describes contemplation and union but couched in a language that is more intellectual and speculative.

In the reply to Article 4 of Question 44 in *Summa* I, Aquinas establishes that, "all things desire God as their end in desiring any particular good, where this desire be intellectual or sensible, or natural, i.e., without knowledge, for nothing is good and desirable except inasmuch as it participates in the likeness to God (240-41). In Question 75 he treats the essence of the human soul. In Question 77 Aquinas discusses the powers of the soul in this section of the *Summa* in which he relies a great deal on Augustine. Question 79 deals with the intellectual powers of the soul including the fact that every power flows from the essence of the soul or the *synderesis* (343-44). In Question 82, art. 4 Aquinas treats the will where he writes: ". . .the will is higher than the intellect and can move it" (366). In his *Summa contra gentiles*, Book III, chapter 27, Aquinas teaches that an individual's ultimate happiness consists in contemplating God. He adds in Chapter 39: ". . . when the will has obtained its last end, its desire is at rest." Hence, the ultimate end of all human knowledge is happiness. Aquinas adds that this happiness is not achieved through faith (ch. 46), and makes the claim that in this life we are not able to see God in His fullest essence (ch. 47). This leads him to the conclusion that a person cannot achieve ultimate happiness in this life (ch. 48). In chapter 51 Aquinas posits the question of how God may be seen in His essence. This is the response that he gives:

> This immediate vision of God is promised to us in Holy Scripture (1
> Cor. xiii.12). We see now through a glass in a dark manner, but then
> face to face. It would be impious to understand this in a material way,

and imagine a material face in the Godhead, for we have proved that God is not a body. Nor is it possible for us to see God with a bodily face since the eyes of the body, which are situated in the face, can see only bodily things. Thus then shall we see God face to face. (469)

In other words, we are united to God through the intellect or the soul's essence. It is through this vision, according to Aquinas, that we become most like unto God, and participate in His blessedness, "since God understands His substance through His essence" (469). Our intellect must have the assistance of the divine light in order to see God in His own essence (contemplation) (ch. 53).

There were several important Dominican writers that participated and contributed to the reform of Catholic spirituality in western Europe, and, in our case, in Renaissance Spain. Catherine of Siena's *Dialogo della divina provvidenza* (Dialogue of Divine Providence) is a masterpiece of ascetical and mystical literature. She dictated the work in 1378; in essence, it is her spiritual testament in which she attempts to reform fourteenth century Italian society, and, in particular, the Church. According to Angiolo Puccetti, O.P., "ella traccia con chiarezza e continuità tutta la famosa traiettoria della perfezione cristiana che include i tre stati della vita, purgativa, illuminativa e unitiva" (Caterina 16). Catherine terms these as imperfect, perfect, and most perfect. Her ascetical-mystical journey commences with the separation from mortal sin, and it ends with the total union of the will with God by means of the untiring labor of renouncing material things, and through what she calls interior illumination (16). The foundation of her theology rests on the premise that we are nothing and God is everything; "La considerazione della nostra nullità di fronte all'Essere Assoluto..." (16-17). Her work remains a triumph of love, the predominance of God in the individual's soul, and the absolute immersion of the soul into the peaceful sea of God (17). Puccetti adds that the spiritual doctrine which is the essence of the book is an immediate, realistic vision and sense of the spiritual ruin of this world" (17).

In her "Proemio" Catherine describes the typical elevation of the soul whose utmost desire is love for God. This soul, in its desire to attain God, begins by exercising itself in the Christian and moral virtues in the solitude of the cell, which is part of spiritual repose and recollection. Individuals set out to come to a complete knowledge of self in order to better know God's goodness inside of themselves. Catherine teaches that by knowing God's goodness one comes to love

Him (Caterina 25). She adds that this exercise of mental prayer unites the soul to God and it allows the soul to follow Christ crucified. She also teaches that God makes of the soul a vestige of Himself through desire, affection and a love which unites them (25). The *Dialogo* is divided into three parts. In Part I, she discusses the virtues and the importance of Christians knowing themselves. Catherine adds that a virtue cannot of itself be effective if it is not practiced with charity and humility (33). The heading for chapter vii reads: "La carità dà vita a tutte le virtù" (39). In this chapter Catherine puts these words into God's mouth: "L'anima innamorata della mia verità non cessa mai di fare del bene a tutto il mondo" (40). Her ascetical and mystical theology does not separate individuals from society but enhances their treatment of fellow human beings. It participates in both the active and contemplative lives beginning within the very essence of the soul and ascends to God by the practice of the Christian virtues and through God's illumination while never loosing the use of the will.

In Part II, Catherine vividly describes the gradations "scaloni" of truth of which Christ serves as the bridge (72). Christ as bridge has three gradations or steps, which according to Catherine were constructed on the cross (72). The first step is represented by the feet which signify the affections. At the first step individuals rid themselves of the vices and affections for the things of this world. In the second step or gradation, individuals fill themselves with love and with virtues; in the third step the Christian may enjoy the repose of God. The third step rises up to the heavens. Catherine places Christ's mouth in this third step where the soul is carried through love as it is brought together with its three powers. With the eye of the intellect individuals will see and understand God's goodness. On seeing God the soul is illuminated and comes to know Him, and in knowing Him, the will is moved to love Him, as the soul drowns itself in God's essence, and in the process, looses its will (102). The soul is now able to lift itself by leaving behind the weight of the body (102).

Part III of Catherine's *Dialogo* is called "Cammino di perfezione: legge e virtù" (The Way of Perfection: Law and Virtue). In this part she teaches every rational being how to rise above what she calls the sea of the material world and guides them onto the bridge, which is Christ (116). In chapter 65, Catherine writes in a section of the book which she designates as a treatise on prayer and on the states of the soul: "Quando l'anima è rientrata in sè stessa passando per la dottrina di Cristo crocifisso con vero amore della virtù, con odio del vizio, e perfetta perseveranza, e giunta che sia alla casa del conoscimento di sè, se ne sta serrata separata del tutto dalla conversazione del mondo" (135). This segment presents a description of recollected persons whose souls enter into themselves through the doctrine of Christ crucified, as they follow the virtues and acquire knowledge of self. This will later become in Spain the prayer or spirituality of Recollection. She goes on to write in chapter 66 that this particular type of prayer is not necessarily vocal, but is expressed through desire and the affections as the soul raises itself through the individual's knowledge of self (140). According to Catherine, all prayer, whether it be vocal or mental, has as its goal Christian perfection and perfect love of God, as a son or daughter would have, as well as a spiritual friendship (144). Union with God, then, is not a separation of the soul from the body, but a lifting of the soul's powers or functions together with the affections. Using terms that will much later be outlined by Spanish writers of spirituality, Catherine describes how the soul's powers are ingathered ("raccolte" in Italian, "recogidas" in Spanish). These powers are then immersed and drowned in the Divine Essence (162). Those who reach the unitive phase are illuminated in the eyes of the intellect by a supernatural light which is infused with divine grace. The individual then raises the intellect's inner eye into God's darkness where He infuses His light (170-72). This illumination goes beyond that of the light of natural reason. Catherine also describes the dark night of mortal sin, when the soul is totally deprived of God's illumination (378). One could also describe this phenomenon as the dark night of the senses. In her *Dialogo* Catherine presents many of the theological premises that will be significant ingredients in Spanish spirituality of the Renaissance.

This brings us to the last section of the forerunners of Renaissance Spanish literature of spirituality outside of the Iberian peninsula. The representatives of the spirituality are identified by Joaquín Sanchís Alventosa as "la escuela mística alemana", which includes Meister Eckhart, Herp, Thomas à Kempis, Tauler, Ruysbroeck, and, of course, Erasmus. This Germanic ascetical and mystical literature attained an incredible level of influence during the fourteenth and fifteenth centuries. They also followed the religious traditions that had always been nurtured by the Neoplatonists, Augustinianism, the Pseudo-Dionysius, Bernard, the Victorines and Classical Scholasticism (Sanchís A. 7). As was the case in sixteenth-century Spain, the religious writers in northern Europe during the fourteenth century also decried the corruption of the times as well as the relaxation which prevailed both in secular and ecclesiastical circles. These writers also sought Church reform which resulted in a longing for evangelical perfection (Sanchís A. 21). This longing included Christian poverty by following the example of Christ and the earliest apostles. These writers also fostered the inner life of the soul which brought about simplicity in the liturgical practices.[9] To reiterate, these Northern ascetical and mystical writers were seeped in Neoplatonic and Augustinian thought. This involved the innermost or deepest part of the soul, the return to God, and the possession of God within the soul (16). Of all the Germanic mystics there were two who had a profound impact on Spanish ascetical and mystical literature; these were the Dominican Meister Eckhard and the Augustinian Ruysbroeck. We believe that H. Herp, Thomas à Kempis and Erasmus were also influential in Spain. The spirituality of the Low Countries can be described as Christocentric and very practical. In other words, Christ constitutes the center of their Catholic spirituality (24).

The first of these masters is Meister Eckhard (1260-1328), who wrote both in Latin and in German. Although in many ways he remains faithful to Scholasticism and to his master Thomas Aquinas, he still held much in common with the Platonic-Augustinian tradition. Sanchís Alventosa writes in regard to Meister Eckhard's teachings:

> La gracia, el principio sobrenatural que diviniza nuestro ser y nuestra operación se recibe en el íntimo del espíritu, en el fondo o centro del alma y allí se comunica a las potencias. . .se llama amor cuando se apodera de la voluntad, cuando se comunica el entendimiento se llama luz de la fe; cuando se apodera de la parte afectiva recibe el nombre de esperanza. (43)

Sanchís Alventosa also identifies what Meister Eckhard visualizes as God's indwelling in the soul or as the Spanish Franciscan terms it, "la inhabitación de Dios en el alma en gracia" (44). In Meister Eckhard's theological system, the soul remains somewhat passive and Sanchís A. even refers to his "panteísmo" (44). Meister Eckhard teaches that in order for the soul to be transformed into God it must separate itself or seek solitude from all created objects, ". . .de todo lo caduco y terreno. . .hasta del propio yo, hay que recogerse dentro de sí mismo. Ese apartamento y recogimiento es lo que Eckhard llama 'abgeschiedenheit. . . entwerden', el dejar de ser lo que es matando los apetitos de nuestra naturaleza" (46). Eckhard's system is in fact more passive because the soul in transforming itself into God allows God to work in it exclusively (46).

Another German mystic who was heavily influenced by Eckhard belonged to a group that called itself "The Friends of God"; he is Tauler of Strasbourg (ca. 1300-1361), and he attempted to accomplish Christian perfection among the secular or lay people (Sanchís A. 54). Much as in Renaissance Spanish spirituality, Tauler's theological process advocates a practical Christianity wherein the everyday Christian life is more important than the speculative. Sanchís A. culls this passage from one of Tauler's sermons: "Entra en el centro y aprende a conocerte a ti mismo, y no preguntes acerca del misterio de Dios" (56). In the sermon "Dum medium silentium", Tauler establishes that, (1) God is nothing in all created things and, (2) he describes the *"fondo"* or *"hondón"*, the essential part of the soul which participates in the life of God. We do not know if these two crucial aspects of Germanic spirituality were originally created by Tauler or simply reflected Meister Eckhard's influence. Tauler also describes how individuals recollect or gather in all of the soul's powers into its essential or deepest part ("hondón", "fondo", or "centro" in Spanish) (Sanchís A. 63). To return to Meister Eckhard, his most important treatise was called *The Book of Divine Comfort*. He compares a person's relationship to God with the sexual relation in marriage. In the introduction to the monograph *Meister Eckhard: A Modern Translation* by Raymond B. Blarney we read: "God is a procreator, begetter, the Father. The soul is the virgin wife, in whom the Son is begotten. . ." (xx). Blarney adds in the same introduction:

> No one ever expressed more decisively than he (Eckhard) the
> immeasurable difference between God and man. Creatures, of
> themselves, he was never tired of saying, "are nothing. . .it must be
> possible to set free the divine kernel of being in man's innermost self
> by the ever-increasing conquest of his outer self-identity" (xxi).

Meister Eckhard brought the essence of his theology to the common people in his capacity as a Dominican preacher. Blarney writes: "Eckhard told the common people about the unity of God and man, a unity so intimate that there would be no need for kneeling and bowing, no room for a priest in between" (xxiii). Eckhard got himself into a great deal of trouble because of these teachings that gravely threatened ecclesiastical authority. He was a Dominican whom we may conclude had much in common with Catherine of Siena in Italy and Luis de Granada in Spain. All three were Dominicans who followed the Neoplatonic-Augustinian tradition in their writings. In a statement that is pregnant with the spirit of reform, Eckhard writes in the section "On Solitude and the Attainment of God": "But if a man does well, God is really in him and with him everywhere, on the streets, and among the people, just as in church, or a desert place" (Blarney 9). In another treatise on devotion we may read Eckhard's own words in the section that deals with the activities of the inner life and the outer life: "If a person withdraws into himself, with all his powers, mental and physical, he comes at first to a condition in which he has no ideas and no limitations and in which he exists without activity of inner or outward life" (Blarney 36). We may discover this manifestation of spirituality in Molinos's *Quietismo*. In the *Book of Divine Comfort*, we can also read:

> . . .a really perfect person will be so dead to self, so lost in God, so
> given over to the will of God that his whole happiness consists in being
> unconscious of self and its concerns, and being conscious instead of
> God, in knowing nothing and wishing to know nothing, except the will
> and truth of God. (Eckhard 50)

He describes the purgative stage of the ascetico-mystical process in this way: ". . . the soul that is empty of creatures is lifted up to God" (Eckhard 54). Paraphrasing Augustine, Eckhard also describes the spiritual journey of the inner person in whose soul God has planted His seed. This journey is comprised of six grades or gradations; in the last grade, the individual is disformed or transformed into the divine and in this eternal nature achieves full perfection. It is eternal rest and blessedness—the final end of the inner and new man, eternal life (Eckhard 75). One could also describe this stage as a participation in the eternal life of God.

The next Germanic mystic, the Flemish Franciscan Henrik Herp, contributed to the literature of spirituality with his *Theología Mística*. One of the center points of his spirituality was his Christology, which made of Christ the very centerpiece of all spiritual life. Most importantly, it was not the ethical, intellectual imitation of Christ in which the *Devotio Moderna* later developed, but a total emphasis on Christ's human nature that was to bear so much fruit in Spain. In his *Directorio de Contemplativos*, translated into Castilian by Juan Martín Kelly, Herp outlines the spiritual process that contains many similarities with later Spanish writers in regards to the contemplation of the different phases of Christ's human life, in addition to unitive love, the progress in the life of contemplation, the marriage (espousal) of God and the soul, the ascension to God's light and darkness ("luz" and "tinieblas") (31). In addition to the above, Herp's spirituality participates in the active as well as the contemplative life, the discussion of the deepest or essential part of the soul, and the importance of the moral virtues in the process of attaining Christian perfection (Herp 33). Herp, in what is a crucial statement in western European spirituality, writes that all persons, no matter how simple or unlearned, if they are constant (faithful) in the practice of the virtues, will receive directly from God His wisdom not by employing their intellectual powers, but by means of love, the affections, and devotion to God (34). He treats the spiritual espousals and God's direct inspiration (*toques*) (38). We read in the Spanish translation of Herp's masterpiece, *Theología Mística*: ". . .con dicho toque el espíritu se recoge en lo más interior del alma, en íntima función de lo divino hasta el gusto de parecer derretirse y aniquilarse para fundirse en unión con Dios" (*Th. Míst* 2, 57 fol., 189v). Herp adds another important dimension to the unitive process wherein the soul fuses with the entire Trinity and not with any particular person (Herp 39). Herp with his *Espejo de perfeccion* (*Spieghel der Volkomenheit*) influenced the Flemish mystic named John Ruysbroeck. The *Espejo* was one of the many works published at Alcalá together with the *Imitación de Cristo* by Thomas à Kempis, the *Vita Christi del Cartujo Ludolfo de Sajonia* (Valencia, 1496), as well as Ambrosio de Montesinos's edition published at Alcalá in 1502-03. In 1583 Herp's *Theología Mística* appeared in Spanish translation and it included other works by him. There are direct links between the writings of Herp and the works of Francisco de Osuna. The Franciscan reformers were influential in Germany and the Low Countries as well as in Spain and Italy. Their influence, according to Martín Kelly, reached the extent that Lutheranism was their final manifestation in Germany. All of these reform movements had several features in common: (1) a return to a popular piety, (2) the use of the vernacular, (3) a sincere search for God through the cultivation of the inner person by means of mental prayer, (4) a desire for Christian perfection, (5) the prayer of Recollection, (6) the belief in the hypostatic union in Christ, which signifies that in Christ there is only the divine person in which are rooted all of the natural properties, his soul and his body. Other features are, (7) Christo-centrism, (8) the progress in the contemplative life, (9) the ascension toward union with God, (10) the progress of the soul through the ascetical and mystical stages of purgation, illumination, and union in order to accomplish contemplation and ultimately union with the Divine Essence, (11) the democratic element of Augustinian-Franciscan spirituality, i.e., Catholic spirituality extends beyond the walls of the cells and monasteries, (12) the spiritual espousal between God and the soul, (13) the affective more than the speculative aspect of this mode of western spirituality, (14) the model represented by the spiritual life, (15) the practice of the Christian virtues, (16) knowledge of self as a prelude to humility *vis â vis* God's power and magnificence, (17) less emphasis on the outer trappings of liturgical practices, (18) inner reform as well as the reform of the Church hierarchy, politicians, and society at large, (19) a return to a more primitive, evangelical Christianity and to the apostolic life, (20) the renewal of the Church by means of prayer and contemplation, and (21) the importance of well-written and effective sermons with the express purpose of the spiritual edification of the common layperson. All of these are crucial elements of the Spanish reform which, as we have mentioned, had their beginnings in the Franciscan and Benedictine houses of retreat and monasteries during the late fifteenth and early sixteenth centuries in Spain.

Herp's *Directorio de contemplativos* has as its theme the attainment of supreme perfection in the individual and the complete happiness that one may accomplish in this life (244). Herp writes in his prologue: "La sabiduría de que se trata aquí es tan común a los muy devotos y doctos como a los sencillos de buen corazón; pues a veces los ignorantes alcanzan a intuir lo que no son capaces de entender los sabios" (244). These words manifest the democratic nature of this spirituality. He deals with the soul's resemblance to God in that it reaches its own perfection upon uniting with Him. Herp also describes the soul's transformation into God by its participation in His life (248). We read once again from the Spanish translation: "Vuelva el hombre sobre sí mismo y con los ojos de la fe vea la suma inteligencia, es decir, Dios" (254). According to Herp, God penetrates both the individual's soul and the body on the ascent to Him. In a later section of the book, he describes a spiritual exercise similar to those outlined by Ignatius of Loyola, wherein he advocates the individual's bringing to mind the benefits or gifts of God (255). He also advises readers to pause when in prayer and to recollect themselves ("pausa de recogimiento") once per day, according to what his own devotion and time permit. Most importantly, Herp advises that this act of prayer, recollection, should be carried out in the heart and not simply through words: mental and not vocal prayer (250). Herp also describes the mortification of the senses. In addition, he prescribes self-knowledge, and reflection on one's nothingness as compared to the immenseness and infiniteness of God. He also treats the avoidance of temporal things as he encourages his readers to despoil themselves of temporal preoccupations, honors, possessions, sensual appetites, arrogance, and pride. He writes that prayer, recollection and meditation will take his readers to the twelve doors that will lead to the spiritual paradise, the garden of God's delights, which in effect, is the soul (264). Herp also details the stages or grades that lead up to the "intención deiforme", the third degree ("grado"), which is both a union with and a transformation into God (274).[10]

The last three northern European writers of spirituality who had considerable influence in Spain were John Ruysbroeck of Groenendael (1293-1381), Thomas à Kempis (Thomas of Kemp) (1380-1471), and, of course, Erasmus of Rotterdam. Ruysbroeck helped to establish at Groenendael a hermitage and a community of friends of God who practiced spiritual recollection (Sanchis A. 66). In 1349 this small community of hermits were accepted to receive the habit and the rule of the Canons of St. Augustine. Ruysbroeck's teachings also include not only spiritual recollection, but the image of the ingathering of the three powers of the soul and the unity of the spiritual powers into the very center. Sanchís Alventosa describes it as "fondo simple del espíritu, esencia del alma." Rusbroeck defines this as "synderesis", the simple essence of the soul, "chispa del alma, suprema unidad del espíritu y el sumo fondo esencial de las fuerzas humanas, ápice de la intimidad desnuda, simplicidad de la mente y quietud ociosa de nuestra alma" (Sanchís A. 75). He also describes this phenomenon as the culminating point of one's intelligence and as "anchura del alma." (75). This is the same language that will be encountered in almost all of the writings of the Spanish writers of spiritual Recollection, meditation, mental prayer, contemplation, and unitive love.[11]

Ruysbroeck's major contribution to western European literature of spirituality is his book *The Spiritual Espousals* (ca. 1351). In this work he condemns the complete passivity of the quietist Brethren of the Free Spirit, because they discourage "all conscious practice of virtue" and they cultivate the absolute passivity of the individual in contemplation (Ruysbroeck 28). Ruysbroeck advises his readers not to attempt to understand God's mysteries, but to accept them through simple faith (35). He establishes the doctrine of the not-knowing, which is also referred to as the negative way. In Book One Ruysbroeck teaches his readers the manner in which they may see with the spiritual eye assisted by the light of God's grace; the will here is freely turned to Him, and the person's conscience is not afflicted with deadly sins (47). Ruysbroeck describes Christ's second coming into the individual's soul in the spiritual marriage between God and the human being (57). This second coming of Christ into the soul will bring new virtues to it; these include charity, humility, and justness. Humility, in essence, is the foundation and origin of all virtues for it fosters obedience, patience, meekness, mercifulness, and compassion (64).

Ruysbroeck entitles Book Two "The Life of Yearning for God." In this section of his work, Ruysbroeck describes what he calls the inward coming of Christ as well as a spiritual going out to the meeting with Christ (87). He also describes this spiritual phenomenon as "an inward exercise of yearning which many achieve through the life of virtue and through interior devotion" (87). In Part II of Book Two, Ruysbroeck finds "three manners of special coming in men who exercise themselves with devotion in the interior life, and each of the three comings of Christ which raise each person into an exalted state of being (94). As is most evident, Ruysbroeck's spirituality is indeed Christocentric. He also defines for the reader the devotional process of the interior life in the spiritual process of the Threefold coming of Christ. The first is comprised of interior exercises which help to raise the individual through the use of the senses "from within upwards to heaven and urges him to have unity with God" (94). According to Ruysbroeck, this coming touches and moves individuals in their lowest nature, for that nature must be purged in order to be spiritually adorned. These comings of Christ in fact take place in three stages (grades, degrees, scales, steps) as part of the ascetico-mystical process common to the spirituality of Recollection. The second coming of Christ involves greater gifts (graces) and illumination. These graces or gifts flow into the highest power ("synderesis") of the soul; this is also called the apex ("ápice") (95). The third manner of the inward coming of Christ is an inner stirring or touching ("toque") in the unity of spirit. Ruysbroeck teaches that this coming creates the innermost and at the same time the highest existence of the soul's life. Ruysbroeck writes that the effect of Christ's coming is inner devotion with the result of a "new inward consolation, and a heavenly dew of divine sweetness" (101).[12]

Ruysbroeck offers analogies to bees, ants, and the soul which is "wounded by love", which according to him, "is the sweetest sensation and the most grievous pain that man can bear" (105). He compares the gathering of the fruit of the virtues in the soul to the autumn harvest: "This is the gathering-in of the corn and of every timely fruit, on which man shall live and in which he shall be rich with God. . .Thus are all virtues made perfect and mistrust is turned into an everlasting wine" (114). In his discussion of the second manner of Christ's coming, Ruysbroeck visualizes Christ as "the living fount of water with three streams." He adds that this fount from which the three streams flow forth is the abundance (*hacimiento* in Spanish) of God's grace in the unity of the soul (121). He conceives the first stream as the gathering of one's recollection; the second, the illumination of our understanding; the third, the enkindling of the will, with God's touches, for the soul is touched by God in love, and the spirit is wounded by this love (122-41).

Ruysbroeck's book sets forth many of the spiritual images that will be common to many writers of Spanish spirituality, such as Francisco de Osuna, Bernardino de Laredo, Teresa de Jesús and Juan de la Cruz. In chapter VII of the *Spiritual Espousals*, Ruysbroeck treats the subject of divine darkness. He writes: "Now understand that in this turning inward again, the delectable unity of God is as it were a darkness and a lack of manner and an incomprehensibility" (16). He continues: "And out of the unity of God there shines in him a single light, and this light reveals to him darkness, nakedness and nothing. In the darkness, he will be seized, and he will fall into a lack of manner, as it were into a trackless waste."[13] Book Three, we believe is also crucial to the development of Spanish literature of spirituality; it is called "The Life of Contemplation of God." In this section Ruysbroeck describes the individual's inner possession of God: "The inward lover of God who possesses God in delectable rest, and himself in a compelling and active love, and all his life in virtues with justness and due proportion" (179). He refers to God as the Bridegroom and considers his coming as a new birth and a new illumination without cessation (183). It is our conclusion that Ruysbroeck's contribution to Spanish spirituality is of considerable importance because of his Christocentrism, the cultivation of an inner devotion, the recollection of the soul, the active participation of the individual in contemplation, his use of everyday agricultural and natural analogies, and, most importantly, his description of the negative spiritual way of nothingness, darkness and the incomprehensibility of God.

The next important writer of Germanic spirituality is Thomas à Kempis (ca. 1380-1471). In his *Imitation of Christ* (1413-1436), a seminal work in Roman Catholicism, Kempis calls the individual to spiritual perfection by imitating Christ. Book II is a discussion of what the interior or spiritual life entails. It includes the classic exposition of that interior life where he describes one as following the "royal road of the Cross" (Kempis, *Imitation* xi). Book III consists of a discussion of the consolation that accompanies a well-developed spiritual life for the soul that desires to become more like Christ (xi-xii). Thomas à Kempis, according to P. G. Zomberg's introduction, became the most important publicist for the renewal movement known as *Devotio Moderna*, which took root in the Netherlands at the end of the fourteenth century. During the fifteenth century it spread to Saxony, northern France, and then, to Spain (xiii). Although Thomas was born in Kempen, Germany, near Cologne, it was in Deventer in Holland that he came under the influence of the Brothers of the Common Life, who were the promoters of a religious devotion inspired by the example of the earliest Christians (xiv).[14] In the imitation of Christ's life of humility and love, the person could come to the contemplation of God and union with Him. This spiritual movement in essence was a call to reform oneself and also the Church at large. However, it must be stressed that it followed a strict Roman Catholic orthodoxy even though it promoted spiritual renewal and the reform of certain practices and abuses in the Church.

The essence of Thomas à Kempis's spirituality as a follower of the *Devotio Moderna* was a regeneration in response to the laxity of the Church hierarchy. He, as a follower of that religious movement, promoted a spirituality founded on the example of Jesus; this included a devotion to the passion and to the Eucharist, a formal plan of meditation, self-mortification, and an insistence that divine and human goods be rightly ordered. It also promoted a withdrawal from all attachments to earthly and material possessions, devotional reading of the Bible and a skeptical attitude toward the worth of an excessive emphasis on scholarship or human culture (xiv-xv).

Book I of the *Imitation* is called "Counsels for the Spiritual Life." One of these in fact involves imitating Christ and learning to despise the vanities of this world: its riches, honors, esteem, desires, and selfishness (4). He advocates the cultivation of the virtue of humility for "if a man knows himself well, and truly, he sees and admits his weakness and faults and he will begin to become humble" (5-7). He adds that the way to find God is not through advanced studies, but through humility of heart and through a sure knowledge of our own weakness (8). In chapter XX he admonishes the reader to learn to love solitude and silence. He directs the individual to set aside some time for meditation: "You will find that you have a great deal of time for quiet meditation if you simply keep away from idle chatter and visits, and not gossip" (30). Kempis adds that if it is one's aim to imitate Jesus in loving the spiritual life, one must go apart from the crowd (30). At the end of Book I he writes: "A Christian believer who meditates attentively on the holy life of Jesus, especially his passion and death, will learn all that anyone needs to know about spiritual goods" (47). Book II is dedicated to the cultivation of the interior life, and the preparation of the heart for union with Christ. He advises the reader to place no value on external things and to pay close attention to what is within each one (53). In chapter VII he demonstrates how one can follow the royal road of the Cross. In order to do this, one must cultivate the virtue of patience (76). He continues:

> To carry the cross. . .to love the cross. . .to do bodily penance. . .to
> bring the body to subjection. . .to flee honors. . .to accept the contempt
> of others without anger. . .to think little of ourselves and to wish others
> to do the same . . .to accept patiently adversity or loss. . .to desire no
> prosperity in life. (78)

It is in fact this contempt for the things of this world that led to this book's being called *Contemptus Mundi* in Spain. In spite of love for God, the devotion to Christ's cross, and love for contemplation, no matter how closely one imitates

Jesus, there will always be a time of spiritual dryness and desolation together with a lack of true devotion. This will become an important aspect of the second or illuminative stage of the ascetical-mystical-meditative-devotional-contemplative and mystical process which leads to God (95).

We shall close this chapter of our study with Erasmus's *Institutio principis Christiani* (*Education of a Christian Prince*) (1516), for this book takes many of the precepts of the *devotio moderna* and applies them to the training of a Christian prince. The early sixteenth century was a time of turmoil and wars, and Erasmus disapproved of the warlike policies of his age (Erasmus 8). In Erasmus's world view, reform must begin at the very top of the social and political ladder. In other words, the prince should be like God, and in particular, Christ. Just as many monks and priests who opposed the practice of the conquistadors and soldiers in America, Erasmus, much like Thomas More, rejected wars that enhanced the policies of empire-building. The Spanish Dominicans' important contribution to reform (in the case of Francisco de Vitoria, Bartolomé de Carranza, Domingo de Soto, and Bartolomé de Las Casas) was in the area of politics. In the case of Erasmus, as was the case with Juan de Avila, the prince (monarch) was supposed to be the initial impetus for reform (19). Lester Born in the introduction to his translation of the *Institutio* writes:

> The important point is that he (Erasmus) did appreciate the need of
> reform in church and state, and in the hearts of his fellow men. This
> reform he sought wholeheartedly and unceasingly to accomplish
> through the means that he knew and understood, the application and
> development of critical insight and the power of human letters. (25)

According to Erasmus, the prince must develop the idea of the "unity of Christian ethics and ruling authority" (32). Erasmus promotes a sound Christian education not only for the prince but for the sons of the idle rich (37). The prince should be like a shepherd to his people, or like a father to his children; he must embody the Christian virtues, most importantly, justice, together with self-control, temperance, physical endurance, and serve an example to all his subjects (50). In other words, the good prince will be the very image of God since justice is the measure of royal greatness and true happiness consists in the possession of true virtue (72-73). He ought to be just, merciful, virtuous, simple in dress, devoid of greed for worldly wealth, controlled in his emotions and pleasures, self-disciplined, for his true nobility comes from being virtuous and not from his bloodline. He must be prayerful and mindful of God, chaste in his personal life, humble of heart, ready to correct evils in his state, charitable and moderate (103).[15] Erasmus also teaches that the lessons of Christ apply to no one more than to the prince (148). He writes: ". . .do not think that Christ is found in ceremonies, in doctrines. . . Who is truly Christian? Not he who is baptized or anointed, or who attends church. It is rather the man who has embraced Christ in the innermost feeling of his heart. . ." (153). As any other citizen does, Erasmus asks the prince to carry the cross of Christ.

The works discussed in this chapter, although outside of the territorial confines of the Iberian peninsula, significantly influenced Spanish literature of spirituality in the Renaissance. The majority of the works which make up the literature of spiritual Recollection including ascetical, meditative or devotional literature, the literature of contemplation, spiritual exercises, and mystical literature, forms in effect a long continuum that stretches from the earliest days of the Church through the Church Fathers, and in the west, Augustine, and later to the Neoplatonists, especially Plotinus, and the Pseudo-Dionysius, the Areopagite. The literature of spirituality is revived as a result of conditions existing in Europe at the end of the twelfth century with the foundation of the mendicant orders, and, most especially, Franciscan spirituality. Similar social, political, and religious conditions existed in Spain in the late fifteenth century which led to the reform that produced one of the most extraordinary outpourings of literature of spirituality in the history of Europe. With the unification of the Spanish kingdoms, the defeat of the Moors, the impetus of Ferdinand and Isabel, and the invention of the printing press and its introduction into Spain, there was now a better opportunity for people to have more access to the Bible as well as to the already existing literature of spirituality. This gave religious men and women, who at the same time were actively promoting the reform of the major religious orders, access to a veritable wealth of religious literature, including the Bible itself. The reformers were anxious to translate, produce and disseminate the religious literature among the lay people, and the printing press facilitated the publication of these works in the vernacular. As a result, Spanish literature of spirituality was able to leave the walls of the monasteries and convents; at the same time that the reform inspired a return to a more evangelical form of Christianity, and it led preachers and missionaries to spread the Christian message throughout all parts of the Iberian peninsula as well as thoughout the lands under Spanish rule. However, before we can commence a study of the more important works of Renaissance Spanish spirituality it is important that we look at its antecedents within the historical context of the Iberian peninsula.

CHAPTER II

Antecedents of Recollection and the Spanish Reform in the Iberian Peninsula

Blanquerna dice a sus padres:
Voy a los bosques a contemplar a
mi Señor Jesucristo y a su gloriosa
Madre la Virgen María. Llevo por
compañeros la fe, la esperanza, la
caridad, la justicia, la providencia, la
fortaleza y la templanza. Necesito la fe
para creer, los artículos de nuestra santa
fe católica apostólica romana, para
encer las tentaciones que causa la
ignorancia. (Ramon Llull, Libro del
amigo y del amado*)*
. . .mas ara som en temps esdevenguts
que cor hom no n'usa tan fort como
deuria, de la intenció per que los oficis a
les ciènces són, por aÇó es, lo mon en
error e en treball, e Deus és ignorat
desamat, desobeit per aquells qui són
obligats a amar e coneixer e obeir Deu.
*(*Llibre d'Evast e Blanquerna, *Cap. cxv)*

IN THE LATTER PART OF the fifteenth century conditions in Spain, as in the rest of western Europe, were ripe for reform. These conditions prevailed in all of that part of the continent; in Italy they led to Savonarola's reforms, and in Spain, to Jiménez de Cisneros and the Franciscan houses of retreat. Hence, we have come to the conclusion that the reform in Spain was a native movement, and thus we avoid the term Counter-Reformation. This movement is not isolated since it is common to the rest of western Europe from the middle of the fifteenth century.[1] The religious phenomenon that led to the reform of the Spanish religious orders, which also supplied the initiative for the production of ascetical-devotional-meditative-contemplative and, ultimately, mystical literature, had its roots in that century. In Spain, it was to a great extent given impetus by Cisneros's having founded the University of Alcalá de Henares and by the setting up of a printing press there that led to the publication of the works of important writers of spirituality, such as Bonaventure, Bernard of Clairvaux, the Victorines (Hugo and Richard of St. Victor), Catherine of Siena and Angela da Foligno, as well as Ruysbroeck, Llull, Meister Eckhard and Erasmus. This is the reason why we designate the extraordinary output of religious literature written in Spanish during the sixteenth century as principally products of the Spanish Reform. The reforms that were initiated in the fifteenth century also produced Luther, Erasmus, as well as the Spanish literature of Recollection. These reforms were part of the cross-currents that affected most of the countries of western Europe. This does not take away from the fact that the Spanish Reform with the literature that it produced was a native religious phenomenon, which shared many Medieval influences with the Protestant Reformation.

We shall not classify the works produced in Spain during its Renaissance as simply Spanish Mysticism even though several writers, including Juan de la Cruz and Teresa de Jesús, produced mystical works. The lives and works of these two writers of classical Spanish mysticism have been thoroughly studied, and we have little to add other than the fact that we have placed their works within the parameters of the literature of Recollection. Juan de la Cruz and Teresa de Jesús do not appear onto the scene of Spanish religious literature as if they had existed in a vacuum; in fact, they are part of a continuum. They are indeed the full flowering of the type of literature that we shall be investigating in this study. The purpose of our study is to investigate certain works of Spanish literature of the Golden Age, or the literature of spirituality inspired by and a product of the reform of the Spanish Church, its orders, and civil as well as ecclesiastical society. This led to an inward reform of individuals by means of an ascetical process that would prepare them for meditation, mental and vocal prayer, ascetical exercises, as well as the exercise of the Christian virtues, contemplation, and in the end for some, union with God. Although the term used to designate this type of prayer and meditation is Recollection (*recogimiento*), this religious process never loses sight of the individual's own responsibility to the community, be it monastery, convent, parish church, or town. It attempts to recollect persons to prepare them to set out on the spiritual path which will ultimately lead to contemplation and/or union with God. The spiritual journey comprises the practice of the Christian virtues, humility, and love and compassion for one's neighbors. It is a spiritual path that looks inward into the deepest part of the soul in order to arrive at the contemplation of God. As it renews and regenerates the person, it then moves outward to the practice of the Christian virtues and to the love of neighbor. Although it begins with the renewal and renovation of the individual person, it also involves the outward person in the practice of these Christian virtues and this affects the individual as a member of a community. This renewal also involves the church hierarchy, and the religious, political, social and economic reform of the society at large. It even involves the rethinking of the way Spain organized its overseas empire.

This manifestation of an inner spirituality in fact is a product of the Augustinian-Franciscan-Platonic traditions, but is imbued with the results of a reinterpretation of Aquinas's *Summa Theologica*, accomplished by members of the Dominican Order in Spain, who were instrumental in changing imperial policies in America and in the process led to the creation of modern international law and the universal rights of all people. Thus, it led to a complete reform of the social, economic and political system that the conquerors and explorers had brought to the American continents. The product of this vast output of spirituality was the above mentioned reform of the important religious orders, the creation of the Jesuit Order with the introduction of the Ignatian spiritual exercises, the establishment of universities and schools of theology, and the reforms in the education of children, and most importantly, the literature of Recollection, which also included the ascetical-devotional works together with works of prayer and meditation, and the development of the art of contemplation and of achieving union with God. It also includes the reform of the art of preaching or sermonology, as well as the above mentioned political, social and economic reforms. The Spanish Reform produced some of the most wonderful literary creations in the history of all religious literature.

There were several social and religious conditions that prompted this need for renewal and reform in the latter part of the fifteenth century in Spain. These include: (1) abuses together with the loss of prestige of many members of the hierarchy, (2) rampant superstition and ignorance, (3) religious ignorance among the clergy, (4) belief in witchcraft, (5) sexual licentiousness and promiscuity, (6) social abuses, (7) corruption of the nobility and laxity among priests and within the convents and monasteries of the realm, (8) public and private immorality, (9) exclusive cultivation of the exterior in liturgical practices, (10) excessive commercialization of the religious life, (11) serious lack of pastoral sense among priests and bishops, (12) economic abuses among the same, (13) priestly abandonment of duties and responsibilities to the faithful, and (14) excessive individualism in contemporary piety that led to the decrease of spiritual devotion (García Oro 6-7). In other words, it was essential that the established church take the lead in sanctioning and promoting piety. It was also very important that the Catholic Church properly channel this overflow of spirituality within its sphere of influence.

The catalysts for the great Spanish Reform were the Franciscan Observants, the reform of the Benedictine monasteries of San Benito (Valladolid) and at Montserrat, and, most importantly, the reforming efforts of Cardinal Francisco Jiménez de Cisneros during the years 1492 and 1517. The time between 1492 and 1500 was crucial for the developing reform and for Renaissance Spanish spirituality. Cisneros was already Archbishop of Toledo in 1495 and in 1500, when his relative, García Jiménez de Cisneros, published his *Exercitatorio de la vida espiritual* at Montserrat which became the forerunner of the Ignatian spiritual exercises. The Spanish literature of spirituality published beginning with the watershed year of 1500 was a result of a reform movement that originated at the highest levels of civil and ecclesiastical authorities; i.e., the Catholic Monarchs and the primate of Spain (Sanchís A. 96). In fact, Queen Isabel herself was the promoter of this reform movement that bore such wondrous fruit in Spain. The renovation of inner religious life and also of the monastic life authorized by the queen herself was manifested by the vast production of ascetical, devotional, meditative and mystical tracts, some of which we shall be investigating in this study. This literary production, although rooted and steeped in western European religious currents going back to Augustine himself, reflected its own Iberian characteristics. These are, according to the Franciscan scholar Sanchís Alventosa, the following: the exaltation of Christ's human nature, which it shares with Italian Franciscans and their Germanic counterparts, human individualism, an avoidance of pantheistic qualities, the defense of the doctrine of freedom of the will, avoidance of extreme passivity and quietism, with the exception of the sixteenth century *alumbrados* and seventeenth century *Molinismo* or *Quietismo*. It is most active and preserves the individual's identity in the contemplation of and union with God. It also stresses the importance of the active life, presents the individual as a whole person composed of body and soul, maintains a practical, active and realistic religious posture, advances the ascetical practices on the path to Christian perfection, blends asceticism and mysticism with psychological elements, and represents the image of the spiritual life as a struggle or battle to be won (*lucha, conquista, triunfo, batalla*). Finally, it is seeped in Semitic manifestations of the spiritual life (Sanchís A. 97).

When Cardinal Jiménez de Cisneros founded the University of Alcalá de Henares, what transpired through its Schools of Theology and its chairs was a harmonious marriage between humanism and theology (Andrés Martín 7). This opened the door to the publication of numerous works of spirituality both from inside of as well as outside of Spain. The books published by Cisneros at Alcalá set the stage for the subsequent publication of works that set in motion the dissemination of religious literature. This led to the development of the different spiritual ways or paths such as *via de recogimiento, via de los beneficios de Dios, vía de cristianismo evangélico, ejercicios de la oración mental, vía de la contemplación infusa, ejercicios espirituales, guías, caminos, vías, espejos,* and other spiritual tracts, guides, guidebooks, handbooks, and ways (Andrés Martín 6-9). Spaniards were now able to read works by Augustine, Bernard, Hugo and Richard of St. Victor, Tauler, the *Mistica Theología* of Hugo de Balma, a Carthusian who wrote this commentary on the works of the Pseudo-Dionysius. They were also able to read Spanish works such as *Teología natural* by Sabunde, *Lumbre del alma* by Juan de Cazalla, the *Caballería cristiana* by the Franciscan Jaime de Alcalá, the *Guía del cielo* by the Dominican Pablo de León, the crucial *Arte de servir a Dios* by the Franciscan Alonso de Madrid, and the *Loor de virtudes* by the Hebraist Alfonso de Zamora. In addition, the printing press at Alcalá also made available works such as the seminal *Tercer abecedario espiritual* by Francisco de Osuna, which in fact codified the process of spiritual Recollection in 1527. It must not be forgotten that it was at Alcalá that the *Biblia Políglota* was published, a fact that gave many Spaniards the opportunity to have direct access to the sacred scriptures in addition to devotional literature in their own tongue. To reiterate, the role of the printing press, that of Cardinal Cisneros and the founding of the University of Alcalá, together with the reform of the chairs of theology at the university and the monastic communities were all pivotal in the development of the literature of spirituality in the sixteenth and seventeenth centuries in Spain.[2]

Before we initiate the investigation of the different works produced in this period, it is crucial that we identify and define the different spiritual paths and currents that were viable in the context of Spanish Catholicism. Pedro Sainz Rodríguez identifies three spiritual currents that were prevalent at that time. He classifies the first one as affective because it involves the affections over and above the use of intellectual speculation (Sainz Rodríguez 229). As we have studied in the previous chapter, this current involves the imitation of Christ, the humanity of Christ, and Christ as an instrument through which one may reach God. It is a spiritual current that is common to the Augustinian-Franciscan tradition with the possible exception of Luis de Granada, who is a member of the Dominican Order, but can be placed within the above mentioned tradition. Sainz Rodríguez identifies the second religious current as Scholastic and Intellectualist. According to this Spanish scholar, this religious tradition "busca el conocimiento de Dios mismo por la elaboración de una doctrina metafísica" (229), and it involves both Dominicans and many Jesuits. The third spiritual current he classifies as the eclectic school, or the Spanish school represented by the Carmelite mystics (229). The problem, in our opinion, is where to classify the spiritual paths or currents which Melqíades Andrés M. identifies as "recogimiento", "oración mental", "oración metódica", "beneficios de Dios y de cristo", and the classical works of pure asceticism as well as contemplation, which most probably participate in all three of the above mentioned currents identified by Sainz Rodríguez. It is also our opinion that Dominicans, such as Luis de Granada and Bartolomé de Carranza, also participate in the affective current of

Spanish spirituality. Other Dominicans, such as Francisco de Vitoria and Domingo de Soto, base their works on Aquinas's *Summa Theologica*, as they reinterpret this crucial work and apply their interpretation to novel historical, political, economic, and social theories that could be considered a part of Neo-Aristotelianism. Since our study will deal with the spiritual paths of Recollection, the practice of the Christian virtues and the law of love, mental prayer, the art of contemplation, and, mystical union, we shall place more emphasis on the affective and contemplative writers.

When the process of what we have come to know as Spanish mysticism is outlined, we become aware that it is somewhat restrictive for it is the culmination of a very complicated spiritual process that includes several stages, in addition to several kinds of exercises, prayers, devotional readings, and meditation. It also involves physical as well as spiritual ascetical practices, physical and spiritual recollection, a certain amount of solitude and quiet, vocal as well as mental prayers, methodical spiritual exercises, the practice of the Christian virtues including humility, the art of contemplation, all of which prepare the individual for the final stage which involves pure love and union with God. It is a long and arduous journey and ascent to God. Mystical union is simply the last stage of the spiritual journey and ascent to God. In fact, once mystical union is attained the individual may return to the other stages of the process. In addition, mystical union assists the individual in attaining Christian perfection, which also involves love of neighbor and one's responsibilities within the Christian community. Recollection includes all of the stages of the mystical way with its three stages that are part of the spiritual ascent to God. These are the purgative, which involves purification or the end result of *ascesis*, the illuminative stage with the practice of the Christian and moral virtues, in addition to the meditation on Christ's human nature. The third or unitive stage involves the direct contemplation of God leading to union with Him through the will's power to love, which will lead to Christian perfection. The different works produced in the sixteenth and seventeenth centuries in Spain include in varying degrees all of the various stages and practices involved in the spiritual ascent to God. These works focus on one particular element of the spiritual journey, or they include all of them. Some works focus on ascetical practices, others on the practice of the virtues and avoidance of vices, on methodical prayer or spiritual exercises, on the art of prayer and meditation or spiritual reading, on the art of contemplation, on the art of loving or the law of the love of God and neighbor, and, finally, several deal with the ways and means to achieve union, or they may be a description of the mystical union.

There are works which deal principally with spiritual exercises and/or methodical prayer. Others deal in essence with the process of Recollection, which is a term that may include the entire spiritual journey or ascent to God. In the process of what is called the prayer of Recollection, the soul is prepared little by little for the contemplation of and union with God in the very center or essence of the person's soul in solitude and apart from all daily activities. The majority of the religious works which have come to be defined as mystical, including those earlier ones that treat the process of Recollection in prayer, outline extensively all of the stages of the spiritual process (way) that lead to contemplation and union; these would include the works of Classical Spanish Mysticism. There are even a few works that deal with all of the above, but in the context of the life of a particular saint, such as Mary Magdalen or the life of the Virgin Mary. However, there are a number of features that all of these works have in common. One is the attempt to reform the individual from within by placing emphasis on an interior, affective Christianity. Second, the writers of these works quote extensively from the Bible (Old and New Testaments). Most of these works are replete with direct citations or paraphrases of Biblical texts. Their readers will also note extensive quotes from or references to the works of Augustine, the Pseudo-Dionysius and all of the religious writers that we have mentioned up to this point. Third, many of the works, if not in fact a majority of them, have as their end not only the reform of the individual, but also of Church, community, and the nation at large including Church hierarchy and civic leaders and even the nobility and royal family. Most of the works are written by monks, priests, nuns, and even in one or two cases, archbishops. However, most are meant to be read by the common person; i. e., they are meant to reach a more extensive readership. Finally, they allow individuals to participate in the contemplative life, but they never abandon the active life. It is never intended that the individual be at all times in the meditative or contemplative state. Recollection means retiring from one's responsibilities and duties for a limited period of time. However, one can never lose sight of the fact that one lives in a community and has responsibilities to fellow human beings.

This is never ignored and, in fact, is a very important element of Spanish spirituality, which constantly holds the individual responsible for actions before God and community.

Angel L. Cilveti in his important study *Literatura mística española*, presents the mystical experience, but always accompanied by ascetical practices. According to Cilveti, the term ascetical signifies the spiritual efforts or the exercises that prepare a person for illumination, in addition to the practice of the Christian virtues and avoidance of the vices. It also predisposes the individual to receive God's gifts, one of which is contemplation, as well as the right to live a life of Christian perfection. The mystical phenomenon (in Greek, secret) involves not only union with the Divine Essence, but also a superior knowledge (*gnosis*), which is secretly communicated by God to those who have been predisposed through the ascetical process. The latter involves the purgation of the individual's body and soul, the spiritual exercises, and meditation together with mental prayer. It is infused knowledge or wisdom that is communicated directly by God within the very essence of the person's soul. At the end of this long process, the soul is divested of all that is not God, and in this state of nothingness and complete quietness (spiritual repose) is then permitted to glimpse the Divine Essence as it really is. At the moment the person is allowed to see with the eye of the intellect God as He really is, the soul's will is moved by a burning desire to have union with God, and when God allows the individual to share in His divinity, and it is this that we call the mystical union.

Cilveti refers to the individual who commences this spiritual journey (*vía, camino, proceso*) and is still in the purgative stage as a "principiante." The "principiante" is the beginner, learner, novice, or a spiritual apprentice. The second stage of the spiritual journey or ascent to God is identified as the illuminative phase, and the individual who had entered this stage of the journey to God is identified as an "aprovechado" (advanced, proficient, more experienced). Finally, individuals enter the contemplative phase of the spiritual ascent which culminates in union. Each individual here is called "perfecto" (complete, consummated, perfected Christian), who now may participate in the life of Christian perfection (Cilveti 11-12). These different phases of the spiritual ascent to God can be described as follows; the initiate in the ascetical life, the meditative, and the contemplative in the life of attempting to attain Christian perfection. The ascetical stage, as well as the meditative stage, involve an active process in which the individual employs all of the powers of the soul to develop and make progress in the spiritual journey to God and Christian perfection. However, illumination, contemplation, and the sharing in the divine life of God are always deemed to be gifts. The writers of the literature of spirituality always stress that few are chosen (*escogidos*) to advance into these stages of the spiritual life. This is the reason that the Spanish Church eradicated the *alumbrados*, because the manner in which they manifested contemplation and union was completely passive. They saw no need for vocal prayer, the sacraments, the practice of the virtues, meditation, and the active participation of the individual. The clergy was of no importance to them because their communication with God was direct. Many were also known by the name of *dejados*, because they abandoned themselves exclusively to God or they would lose themselves in this union, for they felt themselves to be directly enlightened by the Holy Spirit and thus did not need the clergy, the sacraments, nor the Church. Although a few of the classical writers of this type of literature of spirituality in Spain describe union with God as a river flowing into the immensity of God's sea, the majority of them, in their description of the mystical experience, refer to the phenomenon as a contemplation, or as a sharing in the divine life, where the soul and God commingle. The soul at no time loses its active role before God, nor does it lose its own identity. It shares and participates in God's life as it unites with Him, but it almost never loses itself in God's immensity; most important, the person remains humble.

Cilveti differentiates between meditation, mental prayer and contemplation which he states are always intuitive:

> La meditación describe los defectos que se oponen a la unión, el modo
> de desprenderse de ellos, y al mismo tiempo excita sentimientos de
> amor a Dios, rasgo que la distingue del mero entrenamiento intelectual
> . . . sustancialmente esos defectos se reducen a los apetitos, a apego
> desordenados de los sentidos de las potencias espirituales, a las
> criaturas, buscando satisfacción en ellas y no en Dios. (12)

The individual's body and soul are weighted down by their attachment to physical objects and worldly pleasures. The period of ascetical exercises, methodical prayer, and meditative reading is meant to cleanse individuals in body and soul, and at the same time, redirect their desires for spiritual things, as well as the practice of the virtues. At the end of this first stage, every deadly vice and sin is replaced with the Christian virtues. Once individuals are cleansed or purged of their earthly attachments, God then infuses in the soul a spiritual light which illumines the intellect. The soul is now enlightened or illuminated with this infused light, and it is moved through contemplation ("conocimiento infuso"). Contemplation moves the soul in the love for God. This infused knowledge is by its very nature somewhat passive only in that at this particular juncture it is God who is infusing the soul with divine light, wisdom, and understanding. This is not the same as the acquired knowledge that the individual had gained through reading, meditation, and mental prayer. It is infused by God Himself and not necessarily acquired through personal industriousness and diligence (Cilveti 12-13).

Cilveti distinguishes various spiritual phenomena that may all be included in the contemplative and unitive stages of the spiritual journey to God. Between meditation and what is called "unión de desposorio", there may be included a number of spiritual phenomena. These are: "recogimiento" which is, as we shall study in more detail, an ingathering of all the three spiritual powers or functions of the soul into its very essence ("sindéresis", "hondón", "fondo"), much like a tortoise or sea-thistle, as Teresa so aptly describes it in *Moradas* IV, 3. The other spiritual phenomenon is termed "quietud", which is the condition of the soul in the presence of God. It is the will that is in repose and not the intellect nor the soul's memory and imagination, as Cilveti notes. The other spiritual phenomenon in the latter stages of the spiritual journey to God is called the "sueño de las potencias"; the soul's intellect and will are in a spiritual sleep. Cilveti quotes from Teresa's *Vida* to describe this particular phenomenon: "las potencias no saben cómo obran, estando el entendimento y la voluntad unidos con Dios" (Cilveti 13). Finally, Cilveti describes complete union replete with "éxtasis", "visiones", "locuciones", "toques", "estigmatizaciones", "transverberaciones", "levitaciones", "revelaciones", "profecías" and "escritura automática", which accompany it. These are rare and frowned upon by many of these writers. Cilveti quotes from a Spanish-Arabic Sufí named al-Hallaj in describing the active role of the individual's soul in union: "El espíritu se mezcla con mi espíritu como el vino con el agua pura" (16). Cilveti then goes on to describe the effects of the contemplation of and union with God within the individual's soul. These are: abandoning oneself to God, innocence, complete peace, and, very importantly, works done in the service of God and of one's fellow human beings (Cilveti 17).

Cilveti also studies the interrelationships between the three religious communities in Spain: Christians, Moslems and Jews prior to the edicts of expulsion. During the Medieval period, all three groups produced works that described the intense experience of God. These writers also outlined methods of spirituality and the religious practices of these three communities within Spain. The Spanish scholar makes the observation, and we concur, that the Spanish literature of spirituality of the Renaissance was nourished by the commingling of these Semitic influences within the traditions that were inherited by the Spanish Church. In addition, we cannot overlook the influence of the Song of Songs on Spanish spirituality, and also the historical fact that Augustine himself was of Semitic origin. Neither can it be overlooked or dismissed that centuries of sharing a common land by three of the world's great religions would have had a profound impact both on the secular and religious literature of the Spanish people (Cilveti 7). In the Semitic spiritual experience, the deeply rooted consciousness of the individual's own personality is always predominant. The preservation of the "I" of the individual's own identity is evident even in the presence of the Godhead. This tradition was inherited by the Spanish writers of spirituality, who at the same time were also descended from the fiercely individualistic Celts and Iberians. Cilveti adds: ". . . por muy íntimo que sea el grado de unión con la divinidad, los místicos españoles, en particular los cristianos, afirman resueltamente su propia personalidad" (8-9).

The other Semitic trait that can be detected in Spanish ascetical-devotional-meditative-contemplative and mystical literature is the practical end of the contemplative and unitive experience. We must not forget that this religious experience leads to the life of perfection, and in the end, service to God as well as to one's neighbors. It is mystical, but also leads to the practice of the virtues in community, where the individual is constantly regenerated and renewed by means of spiritual recollection, meditation, contemplation, and the actual participation in the divine life. These spiritual exercises are not aimed at separating individuals from their own society nor at inducing them to lead a hermetical existence, but to perfect them as a part of the Christian community so that they may better serve

God and neighbor. These members of the community would include the religious communities, the Church, the poor, the society at large, and, members of one's families and one's closest neighbors. The spirituality of Recollection does not attempt to make individuals holier than their fellow human beings, but simply to predispose them through humility to love and serve their community as well as God. This, in our opinion, is the essence of the beauty of this spirituality of Recollection and the works that it produced.[3]

The entire spiritual journey can also be conceived as a spiritual growth or advancement through several stages, phases or even periods that are not limited to any particular time period. In effect, the initial (purgative and ascetical phase) can last for a very long period of time, even years. It is also possible that a person who has at one point reached Christian perfection may relapse into periods of spiritual sterility or dryness; this is common during the illuminative or meditative stage or phase. This first phase begins with some form of conversion, and this is the reason that this literature can be directly linked to reform. One is spiritually awakened to a new consciousness of the reality of God and of one's own imperfection or insignificance before Him. This always involves the Socratic knowing of oneself (in Spanish *conocimiento de sí mismo*), which leads an individual to the practice of humility when compared to the wondrous beauty, immensity, bountifulness and eternity of God (Cilveti 17).

The spiritual journey to God begins, as we have already seen, as a looking inward into one's insignificance, when one can perceive not only God's perfection and beauty, but also the beauty of creation. When individuals look at their own imperfection and nothingness compared to God, they are literally humbled. Individuals become new persons who must work extremely hard carrying out spiritual exercises, mortifying the senses, practicing good works, involving oneself in discursive prayer or meditation, practicing the Christian and moral virtues, and imitating Christ's human life, in order to free themselves or leave behind "el hombre viejo." When the old person is left behind, the new one is free and unencumbered to begin the spiritual ascent to the contemplation of God (Cilveti 18).[4] This is the reason why so many of the works include as a part of their title the following designations: *guías, caminos, artes, vías, reglas, montes.* Works, which concentrate on the meditative and illuminative processes, employ the terms *vergel, monte, castillo, llama, triunfo, meditación, oración, lumbre,* and *contemplación*. Others will use the term *examen, conversión, manual, ejercicios, exercitatorio,* etc. There are other terms such as *comentario, conquista, lucha,* and others including the very standard *tratado* and the more specific *abecedario espiritual*. In effect, all of these terms are used to describe some aspect of the spiritual journey to God as well as to different phases of the process that ultimately will achieve Christian perfection in the service to God and to other people.[5] In the words of Robert Ricard, taken from his *Estudios de literatura religiosa española*, the aim of this particular type of religious literature, and more specifically the Ignatian spiritual exercises, is to create the necessary conditions for salvation which in effect are: "la lucha contra la concupiscencia y las malas tendencias, la penitencia, la mortificación, el amor a Dios y al prójimo, la adhesión a la Iglesia, la frecuencia de la oración y de los sacramentos, las grandes prácticas de piedad" (Ricard 153). We would add obedience to confessors and to the Church hierarchy together with conforming oneself to the Inquisition.

A. Tanquerey, in his study translated into Spanish with the title *Compendio de teología ascética y mística*, also makes clear that the object of ascetical-mystical theology is indeed the perfection of the Christian life (Tanquerey 7). He states that the sharing of the supernatural life in this earthly existence is the participation in God's life by means of the gift of grace, which allows one to participate in His life. Our life is in constant need of being perfected, and it gradually perfects itself as it struggles on its spiritual journey to reach God. Absolute perfection, according to Tanquerey and indeed to most theologians, can only be achieved at death: "que únicamente en el cielo alcanzamos donde poseeremos a Dios por la visión beatífica y el amor puro. . ." (7). He stresses that on earth one may only reach a relative perfection when we strive to reach an intimate union with God. Tanquerey defines the ascetical process as "la educación física o moral del hombre" (8).

One of the important points that Tanquerey makes in his study is the contribution of Thomas Aquinas's *Summa Theologica* with its three parts. In *Summa* I Aquinas expounds on the points which aim to provide evidence that God is the first principle of all creation. In *Summa* II he outlines the points that demonstrate how God is the ultimate end for all human beings. In *Summa* III Aquinas presents Christ as the Word Incarnate, who is the path or way by which Christians may reach God (Tanquerey 9). Tanquerey goes on to describe the ascetical process as a primary component of moral theology. He writes the following concerning this subject: "la moral nos enseña cómo hemos de corresponder el amor de Dios, cómo hemos de evitar el pecado y practicar las virtudes y deberes de nuestro estado. . . La ascética nos da las reglas de la perfección" (9). He adds: "La ascética es la parte más excelente de la moral cristiana por ser la que tiende a hacernos perfectos cristianos" (9). It is important to note, as all of the writers of ascetical literature will stress, that the ascetical process is a true art or skill that must be practiced under the guidance of an experienced spiritual director (12). This is an essential feature of this manifestation of Spanish Catholic spirituality, since recollection and union have always had the potential of leading to heresy if not carried out under some guidance. Tanquerey adds: "La ascética tiene por objeto la teoría y la práctica de la perfección cristiana desde sus comienzos hasta los umbrales de la contemplación infusa. . .la ascética guía al alma a lo largo de las vías purgativas e iluminativas hasta la contemplación adquirida" (12). He states that the mystical process is part of a spiritual science, or "cienica espiritual", that has as its aim the theory and practice of the contemplative life, from the initial dark night of the senses to the repose or "quietude" of the same until the individual attains a spiritual marriage (espousal) with God. He differentiates the ascetical-devotional-meditative phase of the spiritual ascent as "vías ordinarias de la perfección" and the contemplative-mystical stage as the "vía extraordinaria", wherein God's graces are freely proffered. He divides contemplation into two categories; one is a simple and affective vision of God and of divine things which may be acquired as the fruit of our own activities guided or assisted by grace. This is called "contemplación adquirida." "Contemplación infusa" goes beyond these activities, exercises and efforts, for it is operated by God with our consent and participation (12-15). It is important to take note that there is a definite continuity between the ascetical and mystical phases of this spiritual journey, since one is always a kind of preparation for the other.

The ascetical-meditative-contemplative literature of Spain is based on reason that is not only illuminated by faith, but also by personal experience and by revelation. This is the reason why so many of these works also contain elements that can be considered studies of personal psychology (Tanquerey 18). In his discussion on contemplation, Tanquerey defines it as "el elemento esencial que es la fijación prolongada y amorosa de la mente en Dios por impulso de una gracia especial" (20). He adds that there are references in the Bible that will confirm this fact. In the Christian tradition, we can deduce of what Christian perfection consists and then from meditating on this, progress toward and achieve contemplation. In addition to this, the soul will also have undergone the mortification of the senses or "noche oscura de los sentidos", and the exercise of the moral and theological virtues (21).

It is through the reading of spiritual books that one increases the desire to achieve Christian perfection. Not only is there a struggle at the initial phase of the spiritual journey between the soul and the body, but also between God and the soul. In this battle ("lucha"), there is always in the individual's will a thirst for independence and autonomy from God, which is in essence a type of spiritual arrogance or pride that must be subjugated. Once the senses are subdued, by knowing ourselves in comparison to God, we are emptied of all sensible desires and acquire true humility. This is an important step in the process that leads to conversion, for it allows one to ascend in the spiritual journey (Tanquerey 39-40). Once individuals reach the illuminative stage of the spiritual ascent, they not only receive God's sanctifying grace, but also the gifts ("dones") of the Holy Spirit.[6] These persons having rid themselves of the vices of the soul, and having commenced to practice the Christian virtues, are now assisted by God's special graces and by the gifts of the Holy Spirit to fight spiritual dryness and sterility and ward off temptations, so that the soul is illuminated and is at this point able to achieve infused contemplation.[7] Union then is a participation in the divine life within each person and "no es más que una participación, una semejanza, una asimilación, que no más hace dioses, sino deiformes. . . .es una vida semejante a la de Dios" (60). This is a most crucial point in understanding Spanish ascetical-mystical literature. The soul participates in the life of God, it shares His life and in the process, comes to resemble Him. One does not become God; neither is one equal to God, but there remains a certain similarity between the two, for God speaks through the Holy Spirit to the soul in its deepest or most essential part, and in the process, engenders or begets Christ in the soul (58-60). Thus, one's soul becomes literally the temple of God in Triune form as each Christian believes (63). In this last phase of the inner and spiritual journey to God, each individual will see or contemplate God as He really is. At this point, the Divine Essence will come to join itself to the soul (69).

The union of the soul with its body is termed substantial or "hipostática" because the two entities form one nature only or one person (Tanquerey 72). Thus, in the union between the soul and God, individuals at all intervals conserve their nature and personality and, because of this, their souls continue to exist as a distinct entity from God. This is an important element common to many of the writers that we shall study subsequently. They refer to this phenomenon as "unión hipostática." The Spanish writers also refer to the "unión hipostática" of Christ, since they affirm that His human and divine natures are one, albeit different forms; they are one person (73). They refer to the union of the individual's soul with God as accidental because it does not cancel one's own personality. Tanquerey also makes the important point that at the moment of justification, God infuses the theological and moral virtues (76).[8] The gifts of the Holy Spirit perfect the theological virtues as the exercitants make the ascent to God (77). Justification is, in effect, the infusion of ordinary or habitual graces, which is part of the soul's illumination since it prepares it for subsequent contemplation and ultimately union.[9]

As we have discussed above, two very crucial ingredients of Spanish spirituality of the Renaissance are Christ's role in the perfection of an individual's life, and devotion to the Virgin Mary. Christ is the exemplary cause for each Christian's life. Christianity is seen by these individuals as an imitation of Christ's human life, for He is the perfect model, the paragon of all the virtues which recollected persons are working so arduously to acquire in both their relation to God and in their responsibilities to other humans (Tanquerey 85-86). An important part of spiritual or devotional reading and meditation involves Christ's life: Incarnation, Nativity, Passion, Death, and Resurrection. In fact, the Christian believes that Christ, through his death, resurrection and ascension, has earned for each person the right to practice the virtues, plus the right to receive God's gifts and earn salvation. The life of Christ offers various examples of a life of abnegation of self, the horror of sin and vice, humility, patience, fortitude, love for neighbor and for God, responsibility to society, and devotion to family and friends. By means of a devotion to Christ's human nature, Christians will consider others to be their brothers and sisters (90-91).

Fundamentally, the Virgin Mary functions as mediator between her son and ordinary persons because of her intimate relationship to Him. She is seen as the mother of all human beings, thus further reinforcing the ideal of the brotherhood and sisterhood of all humans (Tanquerey 96-97). In the Christian tradition, after Christ, she becomes the most perfect model for all Christians to emulate. Through her life, she reflects all of the virtues which Christ possessed (97). Among the virtues which Marian devotional literature outlines are her virginity, her profound faith and willingness to suffer, her humility, her own inner and profound spirituality, her love for God and her friends, her patience, obedience, poverty, and her role as mediator for those who will receive God's gifts and graces (98). In other words, the individual may honor God and Christ through her.[10]

Another manifestation of Spanish spirituality is its devotion to the sacraments, the Eucharist, its devotion to Christ crucified, and the performing of good works such as almsgiving ("limosna") to the infirm and poor, in addition to the practice of evangelical poverty (*Beati pauperes Spiritu*). Another important element of Spanish spirituality is the place of oral prayer alongside that of silent or mental prayer. Oral prayer and the outward liturgical practices are an important part of the spiritual journey to God, especially in its initial phase, wherein the individual is counseled to pray to God orally as well as mentally. Mental prayer is part of a more advanced spiritual stage, for it is considered to be superior to vocal or oral prayer.

In sum, oral prayer, frequent participation in the sacraments such as communion, and formal attendance at Mass are integral parts of a spiritual experience that also includes an inner spirituality that does not necessarily exclude an outward form of Catholic spirituality. This is an important feature in understanding Spanish ascetico-mystical literature. Individuals at all times remain an integral part of their monastery, parish, and are members of the community at large. Individuals, justified by God's grace, are free to practice the theological and moral virtues, which lead them to the love of God and neighbor, and will assist them in becoming contributing members of their community; in other words, faith in God and good works are essential elements of this form of spirituality. Good works also include one's responsibilities to other members of the community, especially the helpless and the poor. It is a purer form of Christianity, but it keeps constantly in mind that the individual exists in and shares a community whether it be convent, monastery, parish, town, city and nation. These writers even teach that meritorious works increase the potential for God's offering His graces (Tanquerey 138). However, even though each person has an obligation to advance in the Christian life, in the Post-Edenic, fallen condition of humanity, Christians cannot maintain themselves in the state of grace forever if they do not work hard to proceed further in the spiritual life (194). Through self-abnegation, the imitation of Christ, and keeping the laws of love, one does advance toward spiritual perfection (197).

Prayer, as we have mentioned, is an integral part of the inner, spiritual journey to God. It is a constant desire to perfect oneself; it presupposes a certain knowledge of God and of oneself, as well as the type of prayer that always conforms one's will to God's (Tanquerey 271). It has been perceived as the elevation of the soul toward God, in order to better praise Him and to ask Him for the graces that will enable one to become a better human being. This metaphor of the elevation of the soul has been employed for hundreds of years to describe prayer because it involves the effort that persons make to disengage themselves ("desasirse"), or become free from all that is created and this includes oneself. The person is unfettered and thus free to ponder God, who completely surrounds the individual, and in addition, exists in the innermost section of the soul. The difficulty in describing prayer resides in the fact that it leads inwardly and at the same time it ascends toward God. In various spiritual exercises, especially in the Ignatian ones, prayer is termed a colloquy ("coloquio"), or a conversation with God (272). There are different ways to pray and there are several manifestations of prayer. It may take the form of the colloquy, it can also be a petition for some favor; it may also be an expiation for some wrong. It may be, as we have mentioned above, mental or vocal. It can be expressed in the most interior or inner part of the soul, or it can move outwardly in the form of a request or a simple act of devotion. The ascetico-devotional-contemplative and mystical writers of Spain devote numerous pages to mental prayer, which they describe as a form of inner conversation with God; it is never manifested externally, because it is an interior action whose end is union with God by means of knowledge of what He is truly like, and also through the act of love. The prayer of Recollection is one of the most important forms of mental prayer. The consideration of what God is, spiritual discursiveness, the examination of conscience, the loving gaze of the soul, contemplation, the heart's impulse to attain God's presence, can all be considered different forms of mental prayer, and all these acts prepare the soul for God (276).

Vocal prayer, as is evident by its very name, is manifested through spoken or whispered words, and also through certain gestures: genuflection, sign of the cross, recitation of the rosary, etc. Oral or vocal prayer may be private or public or part of Catholic liturgy. It may be recited in the name of one individual, or in the name of an entire congregation or community. It also includes the Mass, public prayer, stations of the cross, novenas, public recitation of the rosary, the reading of the divine offices, and other liturgical practices common to the Catholic Church. If one studies carefully the works of these writers of ascetical-devotional-mystical literature, one will consistently find references to and commentaries on the Our Father, since this prayer is perceived to be the most perfect one of all, as well as the most beautiful (Tanquerey 277). Prayer is seen as a most efficacious way to reach perfection in the Christian life. It allows individuals to ponder God in a very personal way, and to love Him as we forget ourselves as well as the rest of created things. Prayer assists individuals in perfecting their union with God, as it recollects or gathers in all of the soul's faculties in order to permit the person to concentrate solely on divine matters and on the contemplation of God (280).

Another important contribution of the Spanish writers of spirituality is the outlining of the spiritual exercises, meditation, and methodical prayer ("oración metódica"). These writers distinguish between prayer and meditation. Prayer and meditation are referred to by these writers with the following Latin terms: *lectio, oratio, meditatio, contemplatio*. In many instances "*oración*" and "*meditación*" are used indiscriminately. In the process of meditation, mental activity always predominates. This involves mental prayer and discursive meditation ("consideración discursiva" or "meditacón discursiva") (Tanquerey 359). Meditation needs a longer period of time than simple or short prayers ("jaculatorias"). Meditative prayer is also effective in that the affections and the will are involved. There are numerous topics on which to meditate, especially in the first stages of the spiritual journey to God; some examples are the end for which humans have been created, the horrors of sin, God's benefits in creation and within each person, hell, the Final Judgment, the vanity of earthly things, the joy of heaven, etc. There are numerous works of an ascetical and devotional nature which are in essence books of meditation ("libros de piedad", "lectura meditada") (Tanquerey 369). The books of methodical prayer and devotional-meditative works share some common points: (1) careful reading of the material on which one is to meditate divided into the different parts of the day: vespers, matins, afternoon, night, etc., (2) recollection to a private place or a secluded area, (3) mortification of the senses, (4) humility, (5) deep concentration with confidence, trust and humility before God, and (6) placing oneself in God's presence and especially within one's soul (371). An ancillary part that is included in great detail in numerous books of meditation are the spiritual exercises, and more specifically, Ignatius's *Spiritual Exercises*, together with its predecessor, García de Cisneros's *Exercitatorio de la vida espiritual* (1500), which the latter wrote in order to carry out the reform of the Benedictine Monastery of Montserrat. One of the most characteristic features of the Ignatian meditative process is the "composition of place", wherein one places oneself mentally precisely where the topic on which one is meditating took place. The individual applies all three powers of the soul to accomplish this. This meditative process is rather structured and very practical. As individuals proceed to the illuminative stage of the spiritual journey to God, they commence with a genuine imitation of Christ through the positive practice of the Christian virtues.[11] In the proficient or illuminative stage of the spiritual journey to God, affective mental prayer receives spiritual consolations, which prepare the soul for contemplation, spiritual peace, joy, and a spiritual sweetness that precedes the presence of the Divine Essence.[12]

The last form of prayer to which many Spanish writers devote portions of their treatises is the prayer of quietude (repose, stillness, silence), in Spanish, "la oración de quietud." It is in this type of prayer that the image "dark night" can be found. The "oración de quietud" commences with an arid, dry, or sterile phase, and ends in a quiet, peaceful, restful, or tranquil stage of spiritual repose. The phase of dryness and sterility is called the dark night of the senses wherein God attempts to test the individual. In the first (purgative stage) exercitants free themselves from everything that is sensory. At this initial phase of the spiritual journey persons will feel no spiritual consolations. There is in fact a purifying sterility and emptiness which is caused by God. There is another form of spiritual dryness brought about by our own carelessness, lukewarmness, and negligence (Tanquerey 752-54). As individuals become more proficient in the advancement of their spiritual life, they begin to enter the prayer of peace and quietude ("oración de la quietud suave"), which can also be referred to as the prayer of divine pleasure when one feels the presence of God through a definite spiritual pleasure ("gusto espiritual"). Teresa calls it "oración de quietud y oración de silencio" (Teresa de Jesús ch. xiv), because the soul ceases to think or reflect and only feels. Tanquerey describes this passive recollection in this way: "una dulce y amorosa absorción del entendimiento y de la voluntad en Dios, producida por una gracia especial del Espíritu Santo. . .la parte superior del alma, el entendimiento y voluntad es cautivada por Dios que le da a gustar un sosiego muy suave y un gozo muy vivo de su presencia. . ." (762). The contemplation of the Divine Presence is always associated with sweetness, joy, pleasure, and tranquillity or spiritual calm. The important point to keep in mind when we discuss the Spanish religious writers and this prayer of repose and silence is that it is not completely passive. Complete passivity of all three spiritual powers of the soul most often led to serious problems with the Inquisitorial powers and established Church hierarchy. In the classical Spanish concept involved with the prayer of silent repose, only the will with its understanding is captivated by God; however, thought, reflection and the imagination remain free.

The prayer of silent repose and contemplation of God is followed by the prayer of complete union ("oración de unión plena"), where all three powers of the soul unite and share in the life of God. This union brings about the suspension of all of the soul's spiritual powers, together with the total absence of every distraction, the absence of tiredness and an abundance of complete joy (Tanquerey 768). The Spanish writers of spirituality use the terms "*unión extática*" or "*desposorios espirtuales*" to describe the culmination of the spiritual journey to achieve union with God. There are also various physical phenomena that accompany this ecstatic union of the soul with the Divine Essence, which these Spanish writers call "*éxtasis simple*", when the soul receives a wound that is painful and delightful at the same time. There is also what is termed "*arrobamiento*." The rapture or trance occurs in the spiritual espousal (marriage), where at times the soul experiences such bliss that it wishes to leave the body ("el vuelo del espíirtu"). At this juncture, the individual may envision images from Christ's human experience. Most of these images and terms are already familiar to most students of Spanish mysticism through the numerous studies already done on the works of Teresa de Jesús and Juan de la Cruz. However, these works can be placed within the proper historical context as the culmination of the spirituality of the inner way of Recollection, with its accompanying asceticism, devotional-meditative and contemplative literature.

Andrés Martín, in his excellent two volume study of Spanish theology during the Golden Age, classifies the spiritual literature that we are investigating as "teología positiva", in contrast to the "teología escolástica o puramente especulativa" (Andrés Martín I: 42). According to Andrés Martín, one of the outstanding features of this positive theology is the study of the Bible in addition to an ascetical, moral, practical, affective, and pastoral orientation (42). Andrés Martín makes the valid point that this positive theology was the one promoted and practiced by the Church reformers and the religious men and women of the strict observance in the different orders (42-43). The reform of theology carried out at Spanish universities, and most especially at Alcalá de Henares in 1508, helped to further promote the different forms of affective spirituality in Spain. At the University of Alcalá in 1508, there were established three new chairs: the Chair of Nominal Theology, the Chair of Duns Scotus, and the Chair of Thomas Aquinas. The *cursus theologicus* was also instituted at both Salamanca and Alcalá as well as at Valladolid and later at Lérida (Andrés Martín I: 50-52). These schools helped to produce and nourish a generation of theologians, which included Francisco de Vitoria, Domingo de Soto and Luis de León, and also led to the reforms among Spanish Franciscans, Augustinians, Dominicans, and ultimately, the Jesuits and Carmelites. Thus, the theological currents were at this point in history reinforced by this reform and restructuring of theological studies at the major Spanish universities. Many writers of religious literature derived inspiration and spiritual nourishment from the spiritual currents coming out of the theological circles of these universities. The establishment, reform, and restructuring of the theological schools were occurring congruently with the reform of the Franciscan, Benedictine, Dominican and Augustinian Orders. At the same time, the reform and reorganization of their convents and monasteries energized numerous monks, nuns, secular clergy, and certain members of the hierarchy as well as the common folk. According to Andrés M., the Spanish reform movement led religious men and women directly to an inner spiritual life of recollection, and also to the study of the sources of Christian thought and tradition: the Bible, Church Fathers,

Bonaventure, Bernard, etc. (I: 84). By the middle of the sixteenth century, the return to a strict observance on the part of the above mentioned orders led to one of the pinnacles of spiritual life and literature which the western Church had witnessed in one country. The final product of this native reform movement in Spain is this literature of the spirituality of Recollection.

It is a reform movement that has its origins in the plains, hills and mountains of Castile: in the *recoleto*, which was a house of retreat where members of a religious order lived a life of austerity and spiritual recollection. The members of these houses were known as *descalzos*, discalced or reformed monks.[13] Andrés M. writes: "Los reformadores querían ir a Dios más por la vía del corazón que por la de la razón. Preferían la vía afectiva a la racional, la piedad sencilla que busca a Dios sin preocuparse por las fórmulas racionales. . . " (I: 94). This reform, in addition to a wondrous, varied, and beautiful body of religious literature with its positive theology, the practice of evangelical and pastoral Christianity, the Dominicans' novel interpretation of Aquinas's *Summa* concerning the equality of all humans before God, prepared the way for the redirection of Spanish colonial policy with the evangelization and Christianization of the Americas and the Philippines (Andrés Martín I: 101). The Spanish Reform in effect was more than a religious movement that produced two or three great mystics. It was indeed an extraordinary, complex, extensive and all-encompassing spiritual output that affected every stratum of the political, social, economic and religious institutions of Spain, and even filtered down to the common folk, as well as the indigenous peoples of the American continents. The earlier works, inspired by the renewal of the spiritual life brought about by Recollection, later formed and nourished the great writers such as Teresa de Jesús, Juan de la Cruz, Juan de Avila, Ignacio de Loyola, Luis de Granada, Bartolomé de Carranza, Archbishop of Toledo with his catechism, and even missionaries such as Bartolomé de las Casas (Andrés Martín I: 114-15).

Besides the Franciscan houses of retreat and the reformed convents in Castile, there were other focal points that contributed to the Spanish reform movement. One was the Dominican *Colegio de San Gregorio*, where there existed an affective current of spirituality, albeit Dominican, which led to the writings of Bartolomé de Carranza and Luis de Granada. It is in fact at this *Colegio* that the Dominican Felipe de Meneses wrote the spiritual tract mentioned in the prologue to *Quijote* I called *Luz del alma cristiana contra la ceguedad y ignorancia en lo que pertenece a la fe y a la ley de Dios*, published at Valladolid in 1554. Even though the *Colegio* was a Dominican institution, it nonetheless produced two great writers of positive theology and affective, inner spirituality: Carranza and Luis de Granada. Andrés Martín comments on this famous *Colegio*: "En Valladolid se encontraron en feliz confluencia la ascética tradicional, la humanista, la afectiva, la erasmista y la de la oración metódica" (I: 135). He adds this cogent piece of information: "De ese encuentro había de nacer el más importante manual de oración metódica popular que produce España en esa época, *El libro de la oración y meditación* de fray Luis de Granada completado por la *Guía de pecadores*" (I: 135). Another important *Colegio* was the *Colegio de San Esteban* at Salamanca. In fact, it was another Dominican house where priests were trained, although it was more traditional in its emphasis on the Scholastic tradition; yet, Francisco de Vitoria and Domingo de Soto were formed in this convent school. Andrés says of this particular *casa de formación*: ". . .más escolástica, más tradicional, más medieval, más abierta a América, más preocupada por los grandes problemas dogmáticos y morales que los espirituales (I: 137). Another focus of reform was the Benedictine monastery of Montserrat under the direction of its famous Abbot García de Cisneros. Montserrat was the focal point of the Benedictine reform in the kingdom of Aragon and in particular in the Principate of Cataluña. Also, the Augustinian *Colegios de humanidades* contributed to the Spanish reform by cultivating moral theology and the study of the Bible. This made a contribution to the humanistic preparation of its monks through the study of Greek, Hebrew and Latin. These Augustinians became the champions of the vernacular tongue in the composition of their religious tracts (I: 138).

The final section of this chapter will deal with Iberian writers who contributed to this Renaissance of spiritual literature in Spain. One of these very influential Medieval writers was Ramon Llull (1230-35 to 1315-16), born in Palma de Mallorca. Llull was a lay Franciscan who composed various books that were to have a profound impact on subsequent Spanish spirituality. These were the *Libre de Contemplació en Deu* (Book of the Contemplation of God), *Blanquerna*, (a philosophical-religious novel), *Los cent Noms de Deu* (The One Hundred Names of God), *Libre del Orde de Cavallería* (Book of the Order of

Chivalry), which spiritualizes chivalry and outlines Llull's system of reform, *Libre de amic e amat* (Book of the Lover and the Beloved), *De decem modis contemplandi* (On the One Hundred Ways of Contemplation), and the *Libre de oracions et contemplacions del enteniment* (Book of the Prayers and Contemplations of the Mind). Llull's spirituality is in essence Franciscan and evangelical since he devoted himself to studying Arabic in order to bring about Islamic conversion to Catholicism. Interestingly enough, Llull was an anti-Averroist (Aristotelian-Islamic synthesis), who defended the Neoplatonic-Augustinian synthesis. Much as in the sixteenth century, thirteenth-century Europe was also in need of spiritual renewal because of heresies, corruption in the Papacy and in the hierarchy, a decline and decadence in the monastic life, the failure of the Crusades, useless wars, the decline of the feudal system, and the growth of cities with growing capitalist enterprises. Europe was ripe with movements the Church judged to be heretical: *Spirituali*, Beguines, Illuminists, Albigensians, Waldensians, and others. This is the social and religious milieu in which Llull lived and worked. Adding to his personal experience was the historical fact that he had close contacts with Arabic speaking Moslems.[14] Llull, much as the writers of Spanish spirituality during the sixteenth century, wrote and worked in a civil and ecclesiastical society in need of a return to a more simple and evangelical form of Christian practice.

According to Miguel Hernández Cruz, the extraordinary influence that Llull's *Libre del Orde de cavallería* had on Hispanic literature of spirituality is based on the fact that he attempted to transform the violent and secular state of contemporary chivalry, which he knew rather well as a page in the court of King Jaime II of Aragón, into a type of *caballería a lo divino* (Cruz 223). The true Christian knight evolves in his station by means of a rigorous, pedagogical system, which imposes on him a strict code of obligations and responsibilities that involve the practice of all of the Christian and moral virtues. The Christian knight must be exercised in truth, justice, loyalty, simplicity, spiritual nobility, patience, humility, and mercy or compassion for others (224). In Chapter I of the *Libre del Orde de Cavallería* called *Del començament de Cavallería* (The Beginning of Chivarly), Llull opens with these words: "Defallí caritat, lleialtat, justícia e veritat en lo mon. Començà enemistat, deslleialtat, injúria e falsetat. E per açò fo error e torbament en lo poble de Deù, qui era creat per ço que Deù sia amat, conegut, honrat, servit e temut per home. . ." (*Orde* 41). All of the Christian virtues had failed so God created the order of Chivalry so that He could be loved, honored and known. Llull sets the stage for the need to establish a Christian knighthood based on affective Christianity, Franciscan simplicity and the practice of the theological and moral virtues in a society in which all of these were lacking. In the second chapter of the book the knight's responsibility is to maintain the Catholic faith. This profession of Christian Chivalry in fact is meant to preserve justice among God's people.[15] In order to become a true Christian knight a man must love and fear God as well as possess nobility of heart. Possessing nobility of heart requires faith, hope, the search for justice, and loyalty, as well as the other Christian virtues. Nobility of heart belongs more to the soul than to the body (*Orde* 59-61).

Another very influential work composed by Llull is the *Book of the Lover and the Beloved* (*Libre de amic e amat*). We read in the English translation of the Prologue that the book is divided into as many verses as there are days in the year, and "each verse suffices for the contemplation of God in one day" if one follows the *Art of the Book of Contemplation* (410). Verse 11 reads: "Long and perilous are the paths whereby the Lover seeks his Beloved. They are peopled by considerations, sighs and tears (*Blanquerna* 412). The *Libre de amic e de amat* forms chapters vi and vii of the longer *Blanquerna*, a religious-philosophical romance. The *Libre de contemplació* (*Arte de contemplación* in Castilian) is also attached to the *Blanquerna*, and continues with these words in Verse 34: "The Lover set forth over hill and plain in search of true devotion and to see if his Beloved were well served" (416). In Verse 46 we read: "The Lover longed for solitude and went away to live alone that he might have the companionship of his Beloved. . ." (418). Verse 56 reads: "The heart of the Lover roared to the heights of the Beloved, so that he might not be impeded from loving Him in this abyss, the world, and when he reached his Beloved he contemplated Him with sweetness and delight. But the Beloved led him down again to this world, that he might contemplate Him in tribulations and griefs" (419). Verse 79 reads: "And what did Love bring thee? The wondrous ways of my Beloved, His honors and His exceeding worth. How came these things? Through memory and understanding. Wherewith didst thou receive them? With charity and hope. Wherewith dost thou guard them? With justice, prudence, fortitude and temperance" (423). Verse 241 states: "The Lovers said: 'The infused science comes from the will, devotion and prayer, and acquired science comes from study and understanding'" (448). Finally, in verse 265 Llull writes: "The Lover contemplated his Beloved in the greatest diversity and harmony of virtues" (451). *Blanquerna*'s full title in the Castilian translation is *Blanquerna: maestro de la perfección cristiana en los estados de matrimonio, religión, prelacía, apostólico señorío y vida eremética.* Blanquerna is the quintessential Christian knight, whose personal efforts attempt to restore justice to his society. He feels that the world's salvation can be accomplished through an individual whose heart is filled with love. Humble charity will be the conquering virtue that will dominate humans' fierce nature and thus allow people to coexist in harmony. In this fifth book on the art of contemplation, Blanquerna separates himself from the world and becomes a hermit in order to raise his understanding up to God in solitude and silence, and to spend his days in contemplation and devotion to God (*Blanquerna* 201-02). Blanquerna divides this book of contemplation into twelve parts according to the subjects to be meditated or contemplated: divine virtues, the essence of God, the unity of God, the Trinity, the Incarnation, the Ten Commandments, the Lord's Prayer, the Virgin Mary, the Sacraments, and the Christian virtues with their opposites, the worldly vices or the deadly sins (203). One of the essential ingredients of Llull's art of contemplation or meditation is that the individual be free from all cares and attachments to material things within the three powers of the soul (memory, understanding and will) at the particular moment of entering into contemplation (204). We read in the Castilian translation of Llull's text: ". . . no sería tan Grande Bien que pudiese mi alma llenar en Ti a su memoria, y en Ti a su entendimiento de entender, y en Ti a su voluntad de amar, pero siendo Tú bien infinito y eterno puedes llenar mi alma, y todas las almas racionales de gracia infusa . . ." (205). In chapter xiii Llull describes Blanquerna in contemplation: "Contemplar quiso Blanquerna la Santísima Trinidad de Nuestro Señor Dios, y por eso en el principio de su oración rogó a Dios le exaltase las potencias de su alma para poder ascender a contemplar sus divinas Virtudes y Dignidades . . ." (221). Blanquerna then applies his intellect to the contemplation of Christ's Incarnation and Passion. Chapter xvi is called "De la oración del Pater Noster": "Recordó Blanquerna las Divinas Virtudes y Dignidades y quiso por ellas contemplar a Dios en la oración del Pater Noster en su memoria, entendimiento y voluntad" (242). One important feature of Llull's art of contemplation and meditation are his colloquies which are in effect Blanquerna's colloquies with God. One example is the following: "¡Oh Justicia Divina! Entre nosotros se dice, de justo, Justicia en Ti, Justo y Justicia, son una misma cosa" (266). Another example is: "Amor divino, que tienes en tu amador infinito y eterno en amar" (265). We believe that Llull taught subsequent Spanish writers the art of contemplation, as well as the art of conversing with God. His is a major contribution to the Spanish literature of spirituality which follows, and blossomed three centuries after the tragic death of this extraordinary lay Franciscan.[16] To conclude this section on Ramon Llull, we quote from the end of the English translation of the *Art of Contemplation*: "Once more is born a fervent zeal / Once more an apostolic love." The last line reads: "Blanquerna! Who can show thy all? / Where art thou gone? / fain would I be where thou dost dwell / With God above!" At the end of *Blanquerna*, there are poems added to the *Art of Contemplation*.[17]

Another important work of Spanish spirituality written prior to the Golden Age is a Castilian translation of a book attributed to Hugues de Baume (Hugo de Balma) carried out at Toledo in 1513, which in turn is a commentary on the *Mystica Theologia* by the Pseudo-Dionysius, the Areopagite. In essence, it is a popular version of Dionysius's mystical theology. For Dionysius the spiritual phases of purification, illumination, and perfection are the three degrees of the highest contemplation and the result of the "spiritual elevation achieved by human effort (*hierarchia*) in cooperation with God" (Valdés 71). According to José C. Nieto in his study on Juan de Valdés and the origins of the Spanish and Italian reformation, Dionysius writes that human cooperation is the essential driving force which "elevates itself at the level of its proper human powers seeking divinization and union with the One as its goal" (72). The Spanish title of this work is *Sol de contemplativos compuesto por Hugo de Balma de la Orden de los Cartujos nuevamente romanzado y corregido*. In the prologue to this seminal work, we read about, "la consolación en esta triste vida del hombre justo; no hallan los siervos de Dios otra consolación sino subir con los deseos a contemplar las cosas soberanas" (Balma fol. i). Apparently, in the same prologue the reader is informed that the translation carried out by "un religioso del monasterio de San Juan de los Reyes de la ciudad de Toledo de la Orden de San Francisco queriendo aprovechar a las ánimas devotas, mostrarles camino para alcanzar tan preciosa margarita" (fol. i). The Franciscan continues in the same prologue: "Trata de enseñar cómo el alma puede venir a la perfección" (fol. ii). The monk is not sure if the original work was written by Hugo de Balma or Bonaventure. The prologue also continues with an allusion to Jacob's ladder and the ascent to God: "la escala para subir a Dios" (fol. iii). He also declares that the perfect thing about contemplation is the soul's arriving at the presence of God (fol. iii). The Franciscan monk outlines the three phases of the *via mystica* as "vía purgativa", "vía iluminativa" and "vía unitiva."

The author opens with these words: "Aquí comienza un tratado que compuso Hugo de Balma, monje cartujano: de tres maneras de contemplación o oración por las quales se puede el hombre en esta vida llegar a Dios" (Balma fol. iv). In chapter I the original writer admonishes all souls to avoid natural science, which is an impediment to attaining true wisdom (fol. iv). The souls free themselves from earthly things: "suben a Dios y {a} aquella ciudad Jerusalén celestial, alzándose sobre toda razón y entendimiento humano aun morando en aquesta casa del cuerpo terrenal" (fol. v). Making an allusion to St. Paul and to the Areopagite that he erroneously believed was the former's disciple, he describes this "sabiduría", which is an understanding of love that allows one to reach God (fol. vi). According to the author of the text, "esta sabiduría es escrita en el corazón por alumbramientos divinales y por destellos celestiales" (fol. vi). This divine knowledge enlightens the soul's understanding: "alumbra el entendimiento."

In chapter II the writer presents three "carreras" that will help one attain spiritual wisdom ("sabiduría espiritual") (fol. vi). He guides the soul so that it will rise by means of the ladder of love ("la escalera de amor") to the fountain of all goodness, which is God. This divine knowledge will not be attained through human discourse: "el que quiera entrar a esta escuela celestial poderla-ha alcanzar quanto quiere que sea rudo, sabiendo sobre todo entendimiento con deseo de amor" (fols. vi-vii). The unknown author designates each of the stages, degrees, levels, phases, or ways as "carreras." He explains: "La primera carrera es para alimpiar el corazón, la segunda para lo alumbrar y la tercera para lo ayuntar con Dios" (fol. vii). He then goes on to name what he considers to be the components of this "carrera": "purgativa", "iliminativa", and "unitiva." The author writes that when the heart (soul) begins to grow in love, it is lifted and rises with its thought or understanding (fol. ix). He then reminds the reader that individuals must learn to become accustomed to "bien obrar", if they wish to understand the science of spiritual wisdom (fol. x).

The author, in writing about the "primera carrera", suggests that the person must practice humility. One must be just and the virtue of justice must be imbedded in the heart as well as the virtue of charity and goodness or kindness (Balma fol. xiii). He then adds: "El hombre debe humillarse acordándose de sus pecados en algún lugar muy apartado, mayormente de noche en secreto, en silencio, no se deteniendo sino brevemente en la memoria de los pecados carnales" (fol. xiii). Once individuals are purged of all sin, and have sought a secluded, silent and secret place, they will begin "orando con la continuación y devoción de su corazón. . .así alimpian los suspiros y gemidos la orín de los pecados, y de grandes vicios" (fol. xiiii). The author then asks his readers to bring to their memory all of God's benefits: "acordarse de los beneficios que ha recibido de la fe, pensar cómo lo crió de la nada" (fol. xv). Readers are then presented with this form of colloquy which will later form part of the Ignatian system of meditation: "Criaste me Señor, de nonada tan noble criatura a la tu imagen y semejanza" (fol. xv). He then asks his readers to remember or bring to the memory, which is the first power of the soul, Christ's Incarnation and human nature, the Passion and Death, His suffering and wounds, and finally the sufferings to be endured in hell (fol. xvi).

Chapter VIII is called "De la segunda carrera que es llamada iluminativa." The soul is now illuminated and sees (visualizes, contemplates) God's face (countenance, presence). The soul sees itself as in a mirror and by knowing itself commences to know the One in whose image it was created (Balma fol. xxiii). The writer adds: ". . .y cuando es alumbrada la oscuridad del alma responde; luego la alumbra aquel sol espiritual con los rayos de su gran bondad" (fol. xxiii). In chapter IX he writes about how that divine ray of light enlightens the will in three ways. The ray of the spiritual sun in effect shines and radiates in the heart or in the deepest part of the soul. He then adds: "Así como el ojo corporal se alza a ver el sol material en el aire, no por otra luz veíble, no por los rayos de ese mismo sol que resplandece en el aire. . .así el ojo del entendimiento se alza al conocimiento de las cosas secretas. . . por los rayos enbiados del sol divinal" (fol.

xxiii). In other words, the eye of the intellect does not arrive at the understanding of God's secrets through study and speculation.

Chapter X is entitled "Tres son los sesos anagógicos", which signifies a mystical interpretation of a word, passage or text, especially in scriptural exegesis that identifies allusions to heaven or the afterlife (Gr. *anagoge*—to lead up). The author states: "Noche es llamada aquesta corteza de la letra de la santa escritura porque es oscura y aun puede ser aquella llamada noche cualquier criatura corporal por la qual es alumbrado dentro el corazón para se allegar espiritualmente al amor que ayunta al hombre con Dios (Balma fol. xxvii). The Spanish word "seso" in this context we believe signifies wisdom; the author of *Sol de contemplativos* employs the expression "seso anagógico" and "seso celestial" in reference to the superior wisdom or "soberano seso" that one acquires from studying Holy Scripture. He continues:

> Anagógica quiere decir palabra enderezada arriba y puede ser, dicha en la nuestra lengua, *seso soberano celestial* porque habla de las cosas celestiales y en esto es señalada la diferencia que es según la razón entre el que es alzado el alma entre aquel a quien es alzado ca, no es alzamiento corporal entre Dios dador de la bien andanza y entre aquella que hace bienaventurados con la su paz verdadera. (fol. xxix)

In Chapter XII entitled "la declaración espiritual de la oración del Pater Noster que ordenó el Salvador", he explains that this art of anagogic wisdom is reached by the joining of the soul with God through love, and it is enclosed within the readings of Holy Scriptures as well as in praying the *Pater Noster* (Balma fol. xxx). This prayer involves our friendship with God expressed through filial love; it attempts to procure God's love as well as the attainment of God's kingdom, which "viene al hombre quando el hombre desea al sólo placer y no halla refrigerio y sosiego sino en sólo El" (fol. xxx). Chapter xxvii discusses the fact that through this special wisdom the virtues are affirmed within the soul (fol. xxxi). Finally in chapter xlviii we read: ". . .que quanto el hombre más se acostumbra a alzar el corazón tanto se hallará más presto a subir a se ayuntar con Dios" (fol. cxxiv). When the union ("ayuntar") with God is achieved, "la parte más alta de la voluntad es movida" (fol. cxxxi, ch. liii).

This brings us to the last work published in the early part of the sixteenth century that we believe had an impact on the Spanish literature of spirituality during the Golden Age. It is a work spuriously attributed to Augustine, but in effect is a compendium of Augustinian theological-ascetical and even mystical principles. The work is called *Meditaciones y soliloquio y manual* (1511-12). Its popularity rests on the fact that many editions existed during the period running from 1511 through 1611. In the first book of these meditations there is an admonition to avoid "codicia, riquezas, lisonja, embidia", in other words, the deadly sins or vices of the soul. Furthermore, the reader is urged to "huyr de los malos y abraçar las virtudes y desechar los vicios" (*Meditaciones* 92). The unknown author counsels individuals to place their faith in God, and, at the same time, flee from the things of the material world. The writer employing beautiful language meditates on the wondrous beauties of paradise, and at the same time, deprecates material objects together with the desire to attain these (92-93). In Book II the pseudo-Augustine compares "la miseria y flaqueza del hombre", when compared to God's wonders and greatness (95-96). The book is fraught with ascetical elements including the continual warning to look beyond the transitory nature of human existence on earth. This life is finite and nature is limited when compared to eternity (121). Readers are reminded that they must look upward toward God and place their trust and faith in Him; faith must be accompanied by the "hervor del alma y caridad" (113). The author explains the importance of God's grace in the vitiated condition of a fallen human nature: "la voluntad humana no tiene eficacia para las buenas obras sin la gracia divina" (132). The writer then proceeds to describe "la profunda predestinación y presciencia de Dios" (135). These meditations also focus on the inner way of the spiritual journey to God: ". . .que ni por los sentidos esteriores ni interiores puede ser hallado Dios" (148). God is to be found in the inner recesses of the soul without the use of the inner or the outer senses (148-49). These meditations also assist in the meditation on subjects such as the glories of the Celestial City, and it describes God in terms of light and love. The work concludes with the writer's longing to attain "la delectable fruyción de Dios", together with the "gozos de la vida eterna, esperança mía y gozo de mi corazón" (180).

Thus, we conclude this second chapter of our study on the inner path that Spanish spirituality took to attain a sharing in the life of God. We have discussed the different elements that inform the works of most of the religious writers that will be discussed in subsequent chapters. These include: the prayer of Recollection, the various stages of the spiritual journey to God that commences in the deepest, highest or essential part of the soul, the expression of an affective rather than a purely speculative form of spirituality, the movement to renew and reform oneself, as well as one's immediate community, which not only includes the convent or monastery, but also the Church with its hierarchy, and even the society at large together with the state and its imperial agenda in the overseas colonies. Other manifestations of this mode of spirituality are the place of prayer in one's spiritual life, the function of the spiritual exercises, self-abnegation, humility, the practice of the Christian virtues, the proper blend of contemplative and active lives, the different purposes of oral and mental prayer, methodical prayer, and the art of acquired and infused contemplation, which bring about spiritual repose, silence, and joy leading up to a sharing in the life of the Divine Essence. These writers exult human nature, humility, patience, the earthly mission, passion and sufferings of Christ and His mother. They champion the virtue of humility, as well as spiritual simplicity, a frugal lifestyle, spiritual and bodily discipline, the love of God's creation with all of its creatures, a burning love and hope, obedience, and simple prayers such as the Lord's Prayer. Many of these works attempt to return members of religious orders to the simplicity of communal life, as well as recollection and silence in the individual cells. They promote prayer, silence, and also unselfish work and self-sacrifice, which is part of expressing one's love for fellow members of the community and the search for a more simple, less-complicated lifestyle of persons who wish to eschew lavish riches and luxury, palaces, worldly honors and position. They exhort priests and bishops to return to their pastoral responsibilities in their relations to their flock. This literature is written in the vernacular in a relatively uncomplicated Castilian which any layperson can read. This type of inner spirituality was a vast outpouring that, in our opinion, is one of the glories of the Spanish people; it is a body of literature of which every Spaniard should be proud. Much of this literature is virtually unknown in the English-speaking world, and we have attempted to take on the task of investigating as many of these works as we have been able to study. The works that we shall investigate in the remaining chapters of this study have been selected the following the subsequent criteria: (1) the works which were written in the vernacular (Castilian); (2) they are representative, seminal, unique or influential works in the context of the spirituality of Recollection; (3) we were able to study them directly either through inter-library loan or they were available to be studied in the rare book room of the Bibliotica Nacional in Madrid. Unfortunately, there are hundreds of these works of spirituality that we did not investigate because they are part of private collections or in monastic libraries.

CHAPTER III

The Initiators of the *Vía del Recogimiento*
(The Way of Recollection)

> *El recogimiento no es pura interioridad al servicio del hombre que se una personalmente con Dios. Es también un proyecto de hombre nuevo, un servicio al ideal de reforma ristiana. No se queda en lo exterior y estructural, sino que llega al contenido esencial cristiano. Es un proyecto de hombre nuevo que se integra en sí mismo, aunando lo exterior, interior y superior, la persona y el espíritu purificándose del mundo de los sentidos y potencias superiores y llegando a la parte suprema o fondo del alma. Luego se une con Dios. Pero esa unión le obliga a darse a los demás. En la cima de la vida contemplativa descubre, ante todo, su armonía con la vida activa, el nexo de caridad y solidaridad con los demás, la necesidad de la reforma de las estructuras.*
> *(Andrés Martín* Teología esp. *II: 226)*

THE SPIRITUALITY OF RECOLLECTION IS a spiritual path to God that looks inward, but it also thrusts renewed individuals outward to the love and presence of God as well as of their fellow human beings. This type of spirituality is not simply an ingathering of the soul's spiritual powers, nor is it solely a mystical or secret union with God, but is a compendium or series of spiritual processes that ultimately lead to a sharing in the life of God. This inner way of Recollection, which had begun in the Franciscan houses of retreat or in a few reformed convents and *colegios*, ultimately led to the mysticism of Teresa de Jesús and that of Juan de la Cruz (Andrés M., *Teología esp.* II: 198). This particular manifestation of the spirituality of the inner way was initiated to a large extent by writers such as Juan de Avila, Francisco de Osuna, Pedro de Alcántara, and Bernardino de Laredo. It reaches its fruition in the *Noche oscura*, *Camino de perfección* and *Castillo interior* of the two greatest masters of Spanish mysticism. This chapter will deal in a more in-depth manner with those works which have been identified as contributing to what we define as the spirituality of Recollection; yet, in reality the inner path on the journey to God and Christian perfection involves other processes such as: "oración mental metódica", "caminos o métodos de oración", "exercitatorios de la vida espiritual" ("ejercicios espirituales"), "contemplación imaginativa", "arte de amar a Dios" or "amor puro." These have been identified in Melquíades Andrés's *Teología española en el siglo XVI* as "las vías del espíritu."

This inner mode of Catholic spirituality is a part of what is termed "la nueva espiritualidad" that was born in the Franciscan convents and houses of retreats (*recolectorios*) around 1480 (Andrés M., *Teología esp.* II: 118). There are allusions to this type of spirituality in the early works such as the *Carros de dos vidas* (1500) by Gómez García, the *Exercitatorio de la vida espiritual* (1500) by García de Cisneros, and the *Vía spiritus* by Bernarbé de Palma. Hispanic asceticism first attempts to reform the individual as a means to reform the entire Church and the society as a whole (Andrés M., *Teología esp.* II: 116). According to Andrés, "la vía del recogimiento es expuesta por {Francisco} Osuna en cuatro *Abecedarios*: tercero (1527), cuarto (1528), segundo (1530) y quinto (1540). . . por Bernarbé de Palma en *Vía spiritus o de la perfección espiritual del alma* (1532)." Andrés includes Francisco de Ortiz's writings and Bernardino de Laredo's *Subida del monte Sión* (1535 y 1538) (*Teología esp.* II: 201). Bernarbé de Palma (1469-1532) was another lay Franciscan born in Palma del Río, who described his rich ascetical and mystical experience in his work *Vía spiritus* published in Sevilla in 1532. It was included in the Inquisitor Valdés's *Index* of prohibited books in 1559, and apparently was a very influential work as far as the literature of Recollection was concerned. His influence was greatest in Seville, central Spain, Valencia (Gandía) and Barcelona (Andrés M., *Teología esp.* II: 203).[1] We shall once again use M. Andrés Martín's synthesis of this work since we were not able to have access to the manuscripts which still exist in private libraries.

The *Vía spiritus* is divided into five parts. De Palma devotes the first section to the preparatory exercises involved in mortification or self-abnegation, as well as to that of mental prayer and the difference between the contemplative life and the active life. In the second part, he treats what Andrés M. calls "lo puro corpóreo"; in the third, "lo corpóreo y espiritual" above all, "aniquilamiento o conocimiento de nuestra propia nada", or as other writers call it, *nonada*. The fourth section of the work deals with "la pura espiritualidad", or the spiritual powers of the soul in which the author describes the "el ejercicio de la aniquilación" from the Latin *nihil*. This particular exercise is in fact a coming to terms with our defects, imperfections, and nothingness when considering God's benefits. In the fifth section which deals with the supernatural powers of the soul, we read: "El alma en este estado debe saber no obrar, quedarse quieta y sosegada, a manera de uno que oye y escucha, pero no pregunta nada, ni hace demostración alguna de que entiende lo que se dice, `Procede por vía de recepción, no de aprehensión'." Palma describes this phenomenon as "divina condescensión" (Andrés M., *Teología esp.* II: 204).[2]

Francisco de Ortiz was also one of the earliest catalysts in Spain for the literature of Recollection. He was yet another Franciscan who lived from 1497 to 1546. Ortiz was a convert who had dealings both with the *recogidos* as well as the *alumbrados*. According to Andrés, Ortiz was the first to separate in his sermons the "vía del recogimiento" from that of the *alumbrados* in 1523. Andrés laments the historical fact that the sixteen volumes of his spiritual, moral, dogmatic and exegetical works have never been found. Francisco de Ortiz was sentenced by the Inquisition. According to Professor Andrés, two very brief *Abecedarios espirituales* (Cortes, leg. 2388 fol. 125) were found at the Academia de la Historia, and these actually form part of a Christmas greeting sent by Ortiz to a gentleman (Andrés M., *Teología esp.* II: 205).[3]

Another important early work is the *Carro de dos vidas* written by Gómez García, a priest from Toledo. It was published in the important year of 1500. It exists only in manuscript form and is now stored in the Biblioteca Nacional (Andrés M., *Teología esp.* I: 490; I: 372). The work consists of two treatises ("tratados"), the first of which is a spiritual tract dealing with the contemplative life; it is composed of 96 chapters. The second part, composed of 173 chapters, deals with the active life that involves the theological and cardinal virtues, in addition to prayer and its different categories. In introduction we read: ". . .así sobre este carro de dos vidas contemplativa y activa, estibado y cargado el ejercicio del ánima cristiana, ella va e procede seguramente fasta el término de su salida de este mundo, mediante el don e lumbre de la gracia, . . . la verdadera vida contemplativa que es el otro mundo. . ." (Andrés M., *Teología esp.* I: 372). This is one of the first works written in Castilian that deals with this inner way of Spanish spirituality. According to Andrés this work is, "digna de estudio, su concepción sobre la meditación, imaginación, y contemplación, sabiduría sabrosa, recogimiento, modo, materia y tiempo de meditar el exceso del alma sobre sí misma, subir sobre sí y abajo de sí descender. . . (I: 372).

In short, present here are all of the themes that we shall be investigating that appear in the works which are a product of sixteenth and seventeenth century Spanish spirituality and spring forth from this inner way of attaining God and Christian perfection. The *Carro* is a work that contains in nucleus all of the spiritual processes common to the ascetical-devotional-meditative-contemplative and mystical literature subsequent to 1500 in Spain which is part of the inner way of Recollection.[4]

Lastly, we shall here present Andrés Martín's definition of the way of Recollection prior to commencing our investigation of the Spanish writers who contributed to this most important of spiritual processes. Professor Andrés posits this definition: "La vía del recogimiento es una espiritualidad metódica, una oración o arte de amor. Exige, pues, trabajo y técnica. Es una vía completa. Trata de llevar al hombre desde la profundidad del pecado a la sublimidad de la mística" (II: 202). It comprises three processes or phases of the spiritual journey to God "conocimiento propio" ("aniquilación") (self-knowledge), imitation of Christ's human nature, and union or transformation ("deiforme") (II: 202).

Individuals are to know themselves not in a Socratic fashion but as a process, path, or way that will lead in the end to God. It incorporates the tradition of devotion to Christ, in both human and divine natures, and, most especially, to the

Incarnation and Passion ("Cristocentrism"). Finally, it involves first the contemplation and then the union or transformation or sharing in the divine life not through the understanding, but through pure and selfless love ("amor puro") (Andrés M., *Teología esp.* II: 202). This section on Recollection will also deal with the theme of quietude (silence, stillness, spiritual peace) ("quietud", "sosiego", "silencio") within the soul before achieving union, which is the culminating point or climax of the prayer of Recollection. This is the idea inherent in the phrase "no pensar nada", or what is defined as the "vía negativa" as many religious writers and mystics have called it since the time of the Pseudo-Dionysius (II: 123). The spiritual process that will be discussed in this study involves all of the three spiritual powers or functions of the soul; discursive meditation involves the intellect, and the prayer of Recollection involves the human will with its contemplation and union. However, the soul becomes still in spiritual inspirations ("aspiraciones") and the desire for union and love for God (II: 197). These "aspiraciones" also involve a loving or burning desire to achieve union with God. Imaginative meditation is also an important part of this spiritual process in that it embodies the function of not only knowing oneself, but comprises meditations at different intervals during the course of the day. These meditations include all of the mysteries of Christ's life, especially His birth, passion, death, and resurrection (II: 197).

In his other important study called *Los recogidos: nueva visión de los místicos españoles* 1500-1700, Andrés reminds us that the process of "recogimiento" (recollection) is accessible to every individual within the community. It does not differentiate between ascetical, meditative, and mystical practices, for in fact it includes all of these. Mystical union is the end result of the process of Recollection, not a spiritual phenomenon that is separate from it. It can be compared to climbing a mountain starting from a deep valley and ultimately arriving at its peak (pinnacle). The image is ancient but still applicable to describe the arduous process involved in the spirituality of Recollection. Neither does Recollection divide the contemplative life from the active life of an individual in community. Most importantly, it even drinks from the fountains of speculative theology as well as mystical, interior or secret manifestations of Christian theology (*Los recogidos* 13). Recollection involves all of the spiritual processes that we shall be studying. It integrates the entire human being and reduces one into an essential unity or center found in the deepest or highest part of the soul ("hondón" or "ápice") (14).

In commencing the study of the religious writers who contributed to this inner spirituality of Recollection, and these would include the writers of Spanish classical mysticism, it is important that we have a definition of the term "vía" as well as give the names of the various "vías" which these writers employ in their works. According to Andrés, "Vía es un camino seguro, orgánico completo, para alcanzar la unión con Dios." Those who participate in these spiritual ways are called "incipientes", "progredientes", and "perfectos", as they pass through the different phases, stages, or steps ("estados") of the spiritual journey or ascent to God. These stages are also called "vías" or "estados" and are thus termed: "purificativo", "ilumnativo", "unitivo" (*Los recogidos* 29). Andrés also identifies other processes or "vías" as the "vía tradicional de la lectio divina", the attendance at Mass, the reading of the breviary, vocal prayer, the methodical practice of the virtues and the cleansing or purging of the vices or deadly sins (*Los recogidos* 31). Other "vías" that we have already mentioned in several occasions are the "oración mental metódica", "vía de recogimiento", "vía de la consideración de los beneficioes de Dios", "vía de los beneficioes de Cristo", "vía de la nueva espiritualidad de la Compañía de Jesús", "vía de los alumbrados o de los dejados", etc. (31). Throughout this study we shall use the Spanish terms with the accompanying English translations. Andrés informs us that it is in effect Francisco de Osuna who invents the term "recogimiento", at least in Spain and in the context that we will be using the term in this study (36). The Spanish scholar also identifies different periods (epochs) of the spirituality of Recollection. He considers the Golden Age of the spirituality of Recollection to be represented by the works of Ignacio de Loyola, Juan de Avila, Francisco de Osuna, Juan de los Angeles, Diego de Estella, Luis de Granada, and Teresa de Jesús; I would add Juan de la Cruz. The latest period of the spirituality of Recollection is represented by Miguel de Molino's "quietismo", which belongs to the seventeenth century. "Recogimiento" encompasses all the spiritual processes that we have already outlined above. We also accept Andrés's classification of these works. However, we shall devote this chapter to the more specific "vía de recogimiento", but at the same time acknowledge and in fact demonstrate that it is a most complex and involved spiritual process that includes ascetical-devotional-meditative practices, the arts of vocal and mental prayer, methodical prayer as well as spiritual exercises, imaginative and contemplative exercises, pure contemplation and mystical union and transformation, which lead to Christian perfection. It is in fact the literature that describes or outlines parts or all of these spiritual processes. Most of the works that we shall investigate in this study contain at least one of these processes; some contain several.

Thus, we begin the study of the writers who contributed to the Spanish literature of Recollection. This chapter will include the *Caballería espiritual* by the Franciscan Jaime de Alcalá (1515), the *Arte de Servir a Dios* (1521) by Alonso de Madrid, Francisco de Osuna's *Tercer abecedario espiritual* (1525), the *Subida del Monte Sión* (1535-38) by another Franciscan Bernardino de Laredo, and Pedro de Alcántara's *Libro de la oración y meditación*.

Jaime de Alcalá first published the *Libro de la caballería cristiana* in 1515 at Valencia. The 1570 edition, which is the second, was published in Alcalá and is housed in the rare book collection of the Biblioteca Nacional in Madrid.[5] In the introduction addressed to the "lector", he posits his reasons for composing this work by prefacing the fact that so many people devote their idle time to the reading of secular books of chivalry. Many writers of spirituality decried the fact that so many people were reading the romances of chivalry in addition to pastoral literature. These writers aimed at providing the secular, as well as religious reading public, with a body of literature that would offer an alternate and more edifying corpus of reading material. In his most important book called *Místicos agustinos españoles*, the Augustinian scholar Ignacio Monasterio quotes one of these writers of spirituality, Luis de Alarcón, who wrote:

> Los libros que deben usar e frecuentar las personas no letradas ni
> latinas son los que en nuestro vulgar romance traducidos no solamente
> alumbren el entendimiento para conocer las cosas de Dios, mas
> justamente inflamen el afecto, el temor e amor divino. (*Camino del
> cielo* in *Misticos agustinos esp.* 106)

In the prologue to his *Conversión de la Magdalena*, the Augustinian Malón de Chaide also refers to the deleterious influence of these types of books on a vitiated humanity prone to sin by its fallen nature:

82

Así la ceban con libros lascivos y profanos a donde y en cuyas rocas se rompen los frágiles navíos de los malavisados mozos, y las buenas costumbres padecen naufragios y van a fondo y se pierden y malogran. Porque , ¿qué otra cosa son los libros de amores y las Dianas y los Boscanes y Garcilasos y los monstruosos libros y silvas de fabulosos cuentos y mentiras de los Amadises, Floriseles y Don Belanís, y una flota de semejantes portentos como hay escritos puestos en manos de pocos años sino cuchillo en poder del hombre furioso? (*Conversión* 58-61)

Jaime de Alcalá expresses the same concern:

Visto que algunas personas ocupaban su tiempo en leer historias de romana caballería, y de algunas ficciones y sueños como Amadís y otras semejantes, no por eso condenando los cavalleros y personas que con la lanza en la mano son obligados y su linaje y virtud los conbida y fuerza para morir por la justicia . . . (Alcalá fol. i).

He goes on to exhort the reader to be a Christian knight who has been armed at confirmation with, "arma de cavallero do recibieron especial esfuerzo de gracia para vencer otros fuertes enemigos" (fol. vii). This life is conceived as a battle or war and the spiritual enemies of the soul are the devil and the flesh. Christians must battle against these enemies by arming themselves with the Christian and moral virtues. For the Christian who does this, God will then proffer His light, "y con la lumbre de la fe, la qual lumbre muestra entendimiento para conocer sus engaños y después de conocidos para alcanzar la buen andanza según la ordenación divina es necesaria la gracia para enteramente resistir y vencer" (viii).

In his prologue Jaime de Alcalá informs the reader that the work is divided into three "Tratados": "La obra tiene tres tratados. El primero de los encuentros y golpes con sus remedios. El segundo el combite que haze el rey de la gloria al cavallero después de su vencimiento. El tercero del premio y satisfacción de sus trabajos" (viii). The first "Tratado" deals with how Christ, the King, arms the Christian knight. At the time of one's baptism God infuses into the soul the theological virtues of faith, hope, and charity. The arms which will be employed to fight one's spiritual enemies are given at the sacrament of confirmation (ix). Paraphrasing Bonaventure, a fellow Franciscan, Alcalá places faith and charity as the foundations of the strength of his spiritual edifice. He adds: ". . .quanto al entendimiento y voluntad y pues en la fe está la primera elevación y levantamiento en las cosas divinas y en la caridad la manera de abrazarse el alma y unir se con Dios. . ." (x). The practice of the virtues cleanses the soul and strengthens it to make the ascent to God. At confirmation, the soul is also fortified by means of God's grace; this grace "que en él (the soul) se nos comunica y mayormente conviene a aquellos que están en la delantera de la batalla espiritual" (x).

Jaime de Alcalá visualizes life as fraught with "espirituales enemigos y peligros", and it is at the time of baptism that the person receives these arms in order to do battle and fend off the enemies of the soul; in other words, the soul is knighted in the spiritual sense to do battle. According to Alcalá the soul needs the graces to combat these spiritual enemies because "es tanta la flaqueza de nuestro libre albedrío que nunca estaría firme en la batalla si el Señor no le dava gracia de confirmarlo y confortarlo" (xii). Jaime de Alcalá even sustains that without this grace a person cannot be saved because without God's grace a person will not have the spiritual armament necessary to wage battle against the enemies of the soul, and thus, will be prevented from entering into God's kingdom.[6] Fray Jaime compares the knight's horse with the Christian knight's intellect or understanding "que sube al cielo a contemplar las cosas divinas. . .agora se abaja presto a la tierra a ver y considerar las humanas y terrenas" (xiii). The person who has ascended in the spiritual journey to God and contemplates the divine things must also return to live among his fellow men and women in society.

Jaime de Alcalá also emphasizes the importance of the moral virtues in the life of a Christian. He writes: ". . . los servidores de este cavallero y mozos de espuelas son las virtudes morales" (xiv). Accordingly, the "servidores" and "mozos de espuelas" of the soul fight against the spiritual enemies such as the flesh, earthly pleasures and Satan himself. These spiritual enemies which are in counterposition to the virtues are the vices of the soul, and the deadly or capital sins. Jaime de Alcalá lists them as "soberbia", "avaricia", "lujuria", "ira", "gula", "envidia", "pereza" (xv). Armed with the spiritual armament of the theological and the cardinal or moral virtues, individuals in the first phase of the spiritual ascent will fend off the vices and purify themselves in the constant battle against them. Chapter one of Jaime de Alcalá's work reads: "Capítulo primero de cómo deve resistir el cavallero de Cristo a su enemigo el qual con armas de la mundana prosperidad deste engañoso mundo viene a pelear contra los otros que no son desta cavallería" (xvi). The Christian knight must forego all earthly prosperity by keeping in mind at all times the example represented by Christ's life on earth, "la cual fue muy agena desta vana buenaventuranza" (xvi). It is interesting that the tribulations, persecutions, torments and the feeling of desolation and estrangement are brought about not by God to the individual, but are perpetrated by the "maligno enemigo para ver si con las adversidades podrá vencer a aquel el qual con las prosperidades mover no pudo de su santo propósito de ir al paraíso" (xxii).

The following chapters of the book deal with all the arms which the enemies of the soul hurl at it, such as sadness, spiritual anguish, temptations, tribulations, desperation, spiritual afflictions and lashings ("azotes"), the pursuit of earthly glory, vainglory, honors, love of riches and delights, idleness, fineries, and lust for sexual contact (fols. xxvii-ix). He exhorts his readers to meditate on the poverty and humanity of Christ at His birth (xli). Alcalá warns the reader not to be deceived by false joys and consolations: "no deben recibir pena si les faltan los gozos y consolaciones exteriores y humanos. . .por estos gozos y placeres muchas veces se pierde el entrañable gozo del ánima" (xlvii). In order to avoid sin, Jaime de Alcalá suggests that the reader meditate on death: "acuérdate de la muerte y no pecarás que aquel que cada día se le acuerda que ha de morir menosprecia las cosas presentes y aquéjase por alcanzar los que están por venir en el cielo, sin duda el menosprecio de la presente vida hará la persona ser segura y reposada" (xxxviii).

In the Second Book's subtitle we read: "Del combate que el rey de gloria ha hecho a nuestro cavallero en el Santísimo Sacramento del altar el cual contiene trece capítulos" (clxx). Fray Jaime outlines the history of the sacrament of the Eucharist from Melchisedec to Christ as the Paschal Lamb. Without communion the Christian knight cannot fight against sin (ch. 5). The fruits of this sacrament are grace, and the increase of charity; in addition, communion brings to the memory Christ's passion and our redemption. It also increases one's devotion and faith and advances the inner life of the soul. This Second Book contains elements of what we have studied as the second stage of the spiritual ascent to God, even though Alcalá uses the benefits of frequent communion to explain it. Individuals advance in the practice of the virtues in their devotion to God. There is also an increase in the reception of God's graces, the remission of sin, the experience of certain peace and spiritual consolations, including an increase in charity for God and for fellow humans. This book also deals with the meditation on Christ's passion, the incorporation of each person into the Mystical Body, the mitigation of temptations, and the "mala inclinación que tenemos a pecar" (cxcix).

Book Three includes, "la forma como el rey eterno corona nuestro cavallero después de las victorias y vencimientos que esforzadamente ha habido de su enemigo en esta vida presente" (ccxix). It contains 33 chapters, the first of which informs the reader that one will not find God's glory in earthly goods, honors and riches, worldly glory and fame, and bodily pleasures. Fray Jaime clarifies the fact that the full possession of the glory of heaven will never be achieved in this life; however, this glory is the ultimate end to which all humans must strive (fols. cxlv-ccli). The heavenly kingdom will have no end and, in addition, it consists of "la perfecta unión y ayuntamiento con aquel bien -el qual ayuntamiento es buena venturanza" (ccli). In chapter 12 the reader is told that seeing God is the ultimate happiness for all human beings, and it is an act which our soul operates for itself. The action of union, then, is operated solely within the soul. He adds that this joining of the soul with God is achieved through the function of the will together with that of the intellect, but more especially that of the will. This union is conceived by Alcalá as a spiritual crown attained by the Christian Knight which will be greater after the Final Judgment. Although Fray Jaime's ascent is totally eschatological in the sense that it reaches its fruition only after death, the terminology he employs is similar to the other writers of the inner way of Recollection. For example, chapter 22 deals with how the soul's intellect is illuminated, and how this will enhance the attainment of the beatific vision, which is the crowning point of the Christian knight's mission. His union with God is strictly spiritual by dint of the fact that it takes place solely after death. The body of the blessed will be involved only after the Final Judgment (chs. 23-30), when their bodies will become "cuerpos claros y resplandecientes" to the point of being "cuerpos muy ligeros" (cccvii). The beauty of many of the remaining works that we shall investigate in this study rests in the fact that the individual writers develop a similar spirituality that Jaime de Alcalá does, but the process of spiritual Recollection is meant to be carried out in this life. Employing the same spiritual armament that Alcalá describes in his book, the individual in the spiritual ascent to God, which is part of the process of Recollection will not only reach the state of contemplation of God and of spiritual things, but also share in the divine life itself through union or transformation. In Jaime de Alcalá readers may glimpse only traces of the spirituality of Recollection, wherein Christians must look into their own soul in solitude and peace in order to prepare themselves to fight the enemies of the soul that will weigh it down and prevent the ascent to God.[7]

It is not a mere coincidence that almost all of the early writers who first defined and outlined the spirituality of Recollection were Franciscans. In addition to Jaime de Alcalá, there is another Franciscan in whose important work, *Arte de servir a Dios* (1521), we may glimpse early traces of this particular mode of spirituality. In the introduction to the collection *Místicos franciscanos españoles* (Gomis I), Juan Bautista Gomis explains the term "arte" and in particular "arte de amor": ". . .sólo por amor se alcanza y con ella más que con otra arte o industria alguna se multiplica el amor" (9). "Arte" involves skill and effort whether it be in loving or in serving God. Some of these spiritual processes are labeled "artes" for example, the art of serving God in this case. The manuals or books which have been prepared are meant to guide each person in perfecting the art or skill which is to be acquired. These "artes" are in essence guidebooks or manuals, which will serve individuals who wish to dedicate themselves to the service of God. It should be made abundantly clear that when persons are serving God, they are also serving the community at large and its members. In other words, we serve God and by serving God we also serve our fellow human beings. Everyone, in effect, is called to serve God regardless of their station in life.[8]

According to Fray Gomis in his introduction to the *Arte de servir a Dios*, this work is "una concepción unitaria de la vida espiritual racional, afectiva y sensitiva" (60). He adds that "arte" implies that, "la invención y exposición ordenada de estos métodos aplicados a la vía voluntarista y afectiva es propriedad y gloria de Alonso de Madrid" (62). He considers Fray Alonso's work a crucial book, for this Franciscan posits "una ciencia ordenadora de nuestras actividades espirituales y sensitivas" (60). It involves the whole person which includes the body, the affections, the intellect, and, most importantly, the function of the will. Thus, it is referred to as "unitiva", "afectiva", and "voluntarista." Gomis adds that in his work Alonso de Madrid offers, "arte y manera para mover el entendimiento y la voluntad a saber cómo habemos de poner en obra las grandes cosas de que todos los libros están llenos" (62). According to Gomis, Alonso de Madrid, "disponía su alma en tres meses para venir al perfecto amor de Dios" (63). Melquíades Andrés Martín writes that Alonso de Madrid's work is the first that transformed service to God into an art (*Los recogidos* 76). This "arte" will later culminate in the Ignatian spiritual exercises, where all the bodily and spiritual functions of the person will be called into action. Spanish spirituality beginning with Isidore of Seville (ca. 556-636) and later enhanced by the rule of Benedict has always stressed self-abnegation, poverty, reading, prayer (liturgical as well as private), and manual labor in addition to some intellectual work, as Isidore stressed in his *Regula Monachorum* (*Los grandes maestros de la espiritualidad*).

Alonso de Madrid, as his name suggests, was a native of Madrid. He was a prominent theologian and known for his asceticism as well as his mysticism. He is considered to be the first master of the ascetico-mystical Spanish school. According to Gomis in his introduction to the *Arte*, this work "expone la ciencia del gobierno de sí mismo y del recto vivir cristiano con claridad meridiana" (85). For Gomis the *Arte* contains a logical order as well as a psychological one. Alonso de Madrid evidently believed that people conduct themselves with skill (art) and reason, and that they can employ this skill and reason to obtain perfection, which is the object of the book. In addition to skill and reason, love also becomes an important means to obtain Christian perfection. In serving God as a means to Christian perfection, one must know that Christian love is an all-encompassing affection. Once again in Gomis's text, where he defines the crucial place that love holds in existence, we read: "La filosofía de amor, hispánicamente sentida, es una sinfonía de amores que se levanta desde lo bajo y humilde de las criaturas hasta lo alto, sublime y secreto de Dios" (6). Love flows from the self, to created nature, to fellow humans, on to the universe and to God. Alonso de Madrid opens his "Prólogo del autor" with these words: ". . .poco podría aprovechar saber todo lo que está escrito para servir a Dios si no supiésemos qué manera y orden debemos tener para ponerlo por obra. Será, pues, para esto provechosa la breve forma o arte se siga para poner en obra las grandes cosas que la Santa escritura nos enseña" (97). It is most interesting to note that these "ejercicios del alma", as he calls them, are meant to set in motion the teachings that one learns from reading the Bible.

He continues explaining that he will outline in his book "reglas comunes que nos enderecen en todo lo que hiciéremos" and "otras cosas necesarias para el servicio de Dios" (98). In "Notable" I he posits several suggestions for those who wish to take advantage of his book. The readers themselves in effect become both the teacher and the disciple, "con la ayuda del soberano Maestro" (99). Fray Alonso writes that everyone is born in this perishable world not to rest and repose in the enjoyment of the goods that the earth's bounty has to offer, but "que ocupemos toda la vida en entender en las muy altas riquezas de aquel gran Dios" (99). He establishes his thesis based on having studied the Doctors of the Church that each human being's soul is created in the image and likeness of God" (100). He quotes Matthew 5.48 where we read in the Spanish version: "Sed perfectos como nuestro Padre que está en los cielos" (101). He advises each one to seek Christian perfection by moving one's heart away from all that is earthly. The important message he wishes to communicate here is that each person must strive to be like God in spirit and in desire; "ser un espíritu y un querer con Dios" (100). In common with the other writers expounding on the inner way of Recollection, Fray Alonso writes that the above may be accomplished by taking the path of all the virtues written about in the Scriptures. Following this "Notable" he adds a "Sumario" where he establishes that since each individual is created with the potential to become "hombres divinales", each one should try to "hacer una mudanza en nuestro ánimo tal que sintamos que ya nuestra voluntad no sirve de querer nuestras cosas en cuanto nuestras, sino de querer a Dios, y cuanto bien tiene su Majestad" (100-01). Individuals can become "divinales" and attain such a supreme good and ascend to God.

Prior to presenting the reader with six more "Notables", he composes this "Exclamación": "¡Oh doloroso estrago de nuestras almas, que tan bestializadas están del pecado. . .pero si oyen o ven o leen otras cosas terrenas y bajas, están muy llenos" (103). He concludes that his book "disporná más perfectamente su alma en tres meses para venir al perfecto amor de Dios el que se guiase según las reglas deste Arte, sacadas del Santo Evangelio" (104). He claims that by following the rules, which he admits are taken from the Bible, an individual can come to the perfect love of God in three months.

In "Notable" (notice, comment, exposition) II, Fray Alonso states that this section speaks about the end that will move each one to do the things mentioned above. He adds: ". . .el siervo de Dios que a su señor desea aplacar debe plantar en su alma una fuerte voluntad o hábito" (104). He then comments that, by implanting in one's soul the desire to love God, His joy will be planted within the soul (105). Exercitants employ all the inner and outer forces of their being in order to render this service to God. In a section of "Notable" II entitled "Comparación", Fray Alonso expresses a very important element of the inner way of Recollection that we can also find in Juan de Avila's *Audi, Filia*. In the famous poem "El soneto a Cristo Crucificado", the anonymous author writes that if one's will is inflamed in devotion to God, that every good work that one does, or every Christian virtue that one possesses, will be done with ease and in a short time-lapse (106). Fray Alonso writes concerning this: "El verdadero siervo de Dios debe obedecer a aquel mandamiento no por huir de la pena, pero porque el Señor Dios, que amenaza, quiere y es servido que hagamos penitencia" (111). A person should practice virtue to please God, and not to avoid punishment.

In "Notable" III Fray Alonso presents two ways in which one can serve God. First, one must always keep the commandments. Second, one must abandon the desire for earthly things, and follow the example of Christ on earth. The commandment to which Fray Alonso is alluding is the one that admonishes humans to love God with all one's heart and strength (112). He adds that one can serve God as "con amor sirve un page que quiere bien a su señor; pero no por amor, porque no le servirá sino por lo que dél espera. Con amor y por amor serviría si sirviese sólo porque aquel señor quiere y huelga de su servicio, porque ama la bondad y compañía de su señor sin otro respecto" (113). Following Christ, Fray Alonso explains, "obrar lo que El obró para nuestra doctrina y en la manera que El obró" (113). Christ lived his life with love and through love, because this is the loftiest way to live. Thus, each individual should "obrar con amor y por amor" (113).

"Notable" III deals with the ravages brought about in the soul as a result of sin. The ravages of sin, though, can be repaired by meditation on our own disposition to sin and by recognizing the sin which is impeding our becoming servants of God (114). These sins have the effect of debilitating and damaging the soul through what Alonso terms a spiritual illness. Sin brings about anguish and loathing to the soul, which leads one to covet "cosas groseras, dañosas y viciosas", making one forget the infinite goodness for which each person is born.

The soul is now separated from the things of God and wallows in its own desires for what Fray Alonso calls the vitiated and damaged things that are not capable of bringing sweetness, delight, and consolation. The soul is indeed vitiated, for it feels loathing and despair as a result of sin.

In "Notable" V Fray Alonso presents the "instrumentos que nos son dados en el cuerpo y en el alma" in order to repair the sick soul. Since the body has feet in order to walk and hands in order to obtain what one desires and a tongue with which to speak, the soul has the will to love and an intellect (understanding) so that it may know and learn, together with various spiritual desires (115). One may use the soul's understanding, and by exercising this understanding, one can become aware of "cuánta poquedad son las honras deste mundo . . ." (115). Fray Alonso mentions the works of the soul and those spiritual exercises that will engender excellent habits and in this way destroy the sins and vices of the soul (116). He clarifies the fact that to do good and to serve God it will be necessary for the soul's understanding not to make an error in what it knows. In recognizing the fact that it is not mistaken, the will may then begin to love what the intellect or understanding knows (117). This is in effect the second stage (degree, phase) of the spiritual journey because, once the soul knows who and what God really is, the individual contemplates God as He is, and in this way the will is moved through a burning love for God.

"Notable" VI discusses the power to act (work) that each individual possesses within the soul by using the highest instrument or spiritual function that it can possess: the will. This "Notable" contains a most important rule based on the premise of the freedom of the will (118-19). The will can be instrumental for attaining humility as well as for assisting each person in resembling Christ. The habits that each individual should acquire in order to better serve God are, according to Fray Alonso, love of God and of one's neighbor (even one's enemies), and the habit of practicing humility, patience, and abstinence for "Dios ama la humildad y paciencia" (121). In this way, by practicing the Christian virtues, the person will eradicate the deadly sins and vices from the soul. In "Notable" VII Fray Alonso aims at "la manera de plantar los buenos hábitos y desarraigar los malos con los sobredichos instrumentos", one of which is perfect charity (122).

There follows the "Segunda Parte Principal" of Fray Alonso's *Arte*. First, in this section he discusses "los ejercicios que el siervo de Dios sabe tener para reparo del ánima estragada" (ruined, ravaged, corrupted soul) (124). One of these exercises is meant to eradicate or undo all the evil of sin that may exist in the soul. Second, individuals must repair and then adorn the soul with good habits and the practice of the virtues that will allow them to better serve God (125). This second part is divided into chapters. The first, "De la Contrición", will assist the reader in eradicating the sins from the soul and to follow the pious example of Christ, because sin is a weight which will pull the soul downward. However, as all of the writers of spirituality teach, the person needs God's grace to accomplish the cleansing and repair of the soul, for sin will always lead to the loss of this needed grace, which can make this person one of the "vasallos del demonio" (126). Fray Alonso suggests that his readers should spend at least one month in the purgation of the soul if they seek to begin to serve God (127).

In order to practice humility, one must know oneself and despise one's sinfulness and lowliness (127). This will assist in the destruction of the bad habits of the soul. If one learns to despise oneself, then one will feel a certain compassion for oneself which will lead to learning to ultimately love oneself (128). Once the soul has been purged or emptied of self love, it can begin to be filled with God, "cuya bondad no vernos vacíos de nuestro amor y no hendirnos del suyo" (132). According to Fray Alonso, "nunca llegaremos a lo más alto de la caridad hasta que nos aborrezcamos" (134). He presents the reader in Chapter III with the necessary things that will adorn the soul, and these are the Christian virtues. In addition, the natural appetites must be in harmony and controlled by reason and by God's laws (134). This harmony in the soul, according to Fray Alonso, is nothing else but the abundance ("amontonamiento") or literally a piling up of the Christian virtues.[9] Through prayer the individual can beseech God's help to build up these habits of virtue and to keep in check the natural passions and appetites (134-35). Chapter IV is headed "De la oración", and once again Fray Alonso suggests that each person seek God's assistance, "para hermosear el alma con la compostura de las virtudes" (138). In a subsequent passage he presents the reader with images culled from nature that are very common in other religious writers including Osuna, Orozco and Teresa de Jesús. We read in Chapter IV:

> Acaesce estar dos leños juntos ardiendo, de los cuales uno está muy
> seco y encendido, y el otro no tanto; pero el grande encendimiento del
> uno hace al otro, que está verde, paresce que arde mucho, pero si los
> apartamos uno del otro, queda el no tan encendido casi sí blanco a
> arder. Bien así el amor que tenemos a Dios, como no está muy
> encendido pero juntado con el amor que a nosotros tenemos, paresce
> arder y que obramos grandes cosas por él; pero si apartamos el nuestro,
> luego se ve la flaqueza que de ese amor de Dios tenemos, porque casi
> no luce nada, antes paresce que quedamos resfriados. (139-40)

In chapter V titled "De algunas virtudes en común", Fray Alonso guides the reader in studying the virtues which exist in the book of life. This book is Christ, whom he considers to be the fountain of all wisdom both in this life and in the afterlife (141). Christ, for Fray Alonso, is likened to a gold mine that has been given by God to humanity so that everyone may consider and ponder Him as an example because Christ is always a model of the highest of virtues, for "en él están atesorados todos los tesoros de la divinidad" (142). In Christ are stored all of the divine treasures, which also include the virtues of humility and patience. The Franciscan teaches his readers to learn to practice humility from Christ Himself: "Pero, pues habemos de aprender esta humildad de nuestro Redentor paréceme que será menester poner delante nuestros ojos la su humildad" (143). He also admonishes readers to seek humility by knowing themselves, for this is the real origin of true humility in a person when compared to God's greatness, bounty, and goodness. He further suggests that each one "fabricar nuestra humildad a semejanza de nuestro Redentor" (144).

Chapter VII treats the vice identified as "vanagloria" (vainglory or conceit), which is opposed to humility and described as, "un placer o gozo que alguno toma de lo que no debe uno gozarse de los bienes que tiene." Put another way, this vice becomes "la alegría con que nos gloriamos de las mercedes que de Dios recibimos" (146). Fray Alonso seems to alternate the discussion of the virtues with those on the vices of the soul. In chapter VIII he treats patience which is the other virtue that Christ can teach each individual who reads the book (149). He reminds his reader that "con cuánta mansedumbre sufrió tantos corrimientos, persecuciones y amarguras y tormentos, con muerte tan dolorosa" (149). He adds that God's servant who is well-instructed in this *arte* of the Heavenly King's knighthood should also be prepared to ward off those same scourges and sufferings with the same patience (149-50).

Chapter IX deals with the natural passions of the soul which are joy, sadness, hope, and fear. If not kept at bay, these natural passions will severely damage the soul. They must be experienced in harmony and in the perspective of the soul's relation to God and to His creation. For example, sadness is normally felt when one loses something good because of a particular vice or sin. According to Fray Alonso, nothing else should sadden the soul as much as this loss. If the passions are kept in their proper perspective, or place if you will, Fray Alonso explains: "Aquel solo hará esto más cumplidamente que con más claridad conociere que todas las cosas son en él y para nosotros una nonada, salvo cuanto en sí mismos o de nosotros están enderezadas en Dios" (154). Fray Alonso makes the point that hope which is not a virtue is in fact passion: "ninguna cosa que esperamos debe hincar en nuestro corazón salvo Dios" (154).

In the "Tercera Parte Principal", Fray Alonso presents the reader with what one has to do in order to love God. In chapter I, "Del amor de Dios", charity is like a fire that God wants, and it will always burn in His altar, which is the soul (158). He once again includes love as a function of the will. He writes that love (*amor*) "es una obra o acto que la voluntad hace o produce, amando y queriendo fuertemente. . .con dulzor, que Dios sea quien es. . ." (160). He adds that humans have no higher end or destination than God, who is worthy of love simply because of who He is (161). The person must learn to love "el dulzor y sabor porque es cosa de Dios y le da aliento para más servir" (161). According to Fray Alonso, humble servants of God, "que tan preciso licor quiere recoger en su ánimo para glorificar con suavidad de gloria a su gran Dios", must exercise themselves many days in everything that he has written about above. In this he anticipates Francisco de Osuna in the use of the term *recogimiento*: ". . .y podíase uno tanto ejercitar en estos actos, aunque le fallase aquel dulzor que llaman devoción, que en todo lugar y en todo negocio amase muchas veces a Dios, sin buscar lugar secreto ni recogimiento nuevo como acaesce cada día que un amigo se goza de algún bien que nuevamente oye venido a otro su amigo" (171). In other words, in his use of the term *recogimiento* he wishes to point out that one can love and serve God anywhere; one does not have to find a secret or hidden place apart from life's responsibilities or one's place within the community.

Chapter II of this third part deals with the love that one must have for fellow human beings, and chapter IV finally treats the love that one has who chooses to follow the life and path of God's servant; that is, one who desires the good and avoids the bad (177).[10] It is important to keep in mind that we cannot consider Alonso de Madrid as a strict follower of the inner way of Recollection but more of a forerunner; however, his *Arte de servir a Dios* will guide his reader on how to love God and serve Him through the understanding of who God really is. Through the inner power of the soul's will the reader can be moved to this love and service, not only of God but also for one's fellow humans. It is an early work, but we do believe that it follows the inner path of seeking God by looking inside of oneself.

This brings us to what we believe to be the most important writer of this early spiritual literature of Recollection, Francisco de Osuna (1492-1540), born in the Andalusian town whose name he carries in his religious title. Osuna influenced later writers of Spanish spirituality, one of whom was none other than Teresa de Jesús, who herself considered him one of her spiritual masters. From the 1520 to 1560 Osuna was one of the most widely read of Spain's writers of spirituality. Educated at Alcalá, he was one of a group of religious reformers who would gather at the Castle of Don Diego López Pacheco, Marquis of Escalona, which also included the Erasmist Juan de Valdés as well as several reputed *alumbrados* (Illuminists).[11] Osuna is the author of the six volume *Abecedario espiritual*, the third of which is the most important to our study. In the *Tercer abecedario espiritual* (1527) Osuna defines and develops the inner path of Recollection as a means to reach God in this life. Osuna applies the format of the medieval spiritual alphabet books in his six *abecedarios*. In these works he presents a series of distichs corresponding to each letter of the alphabet. The introductory distich contains a religious thought which is followed by an extensive commentary which reminds us of the approach later taken by Juan de la Cruz in his poetry. The *Tercer abecedario espiritual* (Toledo, 1527) is made up of 23 *tratados*, with each one preceded by its introductory distich. Osuna himself explains in detail what he meant by *abecedario* or *alfabeto espiritual* in his *Primer abecedario*: "E quise los copiar por a, b, c, y en número ternario por imitar a Jeremías, y al sabio Salomón, y al rey David, los cuales solos en la Sagrada Escritura se hallan haber escrito por abecedario en cierta manera de metros que entonces usaba. . ." (Andrés M., *Teología esp.* 206). Andrés Martín writes that the system of the *abecedario* (alphabet book, primer) was common in the moral and exegetical dictionaries during the Middle Ages and as late as the fifteenth century. According to Andrés M., in the area of spirituality, it is Francisco de Osuna that popularized it during the sixteenth century. Juan de Valdés entitled one of his works *Alfabeto cristiano* (1538) (206-07).[12] Other important *abecedarios* for the spirituality of Recollection are the *Cuarto abecedario, Ley de amor* and the *Quinto abecedario*.

It is most interesting that Francisco de Osuna studied at the University of Alcalá de Henares, which was in fact the most important center of Spanish spirituality as well as of the reform movements at that time (1515-30). Osuna was also involved with the Franciscan reform movement and the Franciscan houses of retreat (*recolectorios*), where the practice of the inner way of Recollection was initiated in Spain. These houses were also called *casas de recogimiento*, which according to Andrés Martín in his introduction to the critical edition of the *Tercer abecedario espiritual*, "fueron los hogares más importantes de la espiritualidad española hasta que adquirieron pujanza los santos desiertos de los Carmelitas" (Osuna 9). They promoted a system of prayer and retirement to solitude that slowly evolved into the way of Recollection.[13] In fact, Osuna himself resided in the very important *Recolectorio de Nuestra Señora de la Salceda* from 1520 to 1523. Once again the Franciscans referred to these communities as *casas de oración* and *recolectorios*. These were predetermined convents in which monks lived a life of frugal austerity, silence, solitude and prayer; they not only worked and communed with nature but were as they expressed it "recogidos en Dios" (retired or recollected in prayer with God). These houses, as we have already stated, were the focal points for the Spanish reform in the latter half of the fifteenth and the first part of the sixteen centuries. The spiritual leaders of these houses insisted on personal prayer carried out in retirement (seclusion), as well as in the monks' participation in communal prayer. They also expected the members of their communities to fast, to keep total silence, and to practice Christian poverty, humility, and a rigorous solitude (Osuna 13). It was at La Salceda that Francisco de Osuna reached the heights as well as the depths of his spiritual life and formulated the inner way of the prayer of Recollection; it is also here that he composed several of his masterpieces of spirituality (Osuna 15).

In his introduction to the critical edition of the *Tercer abecedario espiritual*, Andrés Martín lists the various names by which the exercise of the inner way of

Recollection has been referred. Some of these are the following: "sufrimiento interior", "quieto corazón", "Jerusaleé del quieto corazón", "sábado interior", "vacación espiritual", "acallamiento del entendimiento", "camino de noche y de día", "aniquilamiento", "amor como vuelo", "no pensar nada", "silencio y asosegamiento del entendimiento", "desnudamiento de todo lo que no es Dios", "reposo", "suspensión de las potencias" (Osuna 31). Other words used to describe this type of spiritual prayer are "tinieblas" and "quietud", etc. (43).[14] It is interesting to note that the process of Recollection did not attempt to avoid vocal prayer, nor does it encourage avoiding public, liturgical practices. Cisneros, as well as Osuna, believed that the ideal form of theology would be the one that harmonized the speculative principles learned in the different faculties of Thomistic and Nominalistic studies with those of the ascetical and even mystical principles (Osuna 44).

It must not be forgotten that at the Dominican schools, Scholastic studies together with the interpretation of Thomas Aquinas's *Summa Theologica*, were also reformed and renewed. By not completely discarding speculative theology, the way of Recollection, meditation, contemplation, the practice of good works, love for God, and the longing for ultimate contemplation and union did not evolve into Illuminism, nor into an absolute Quietism in mainstream Spanish Catholicism. There were in effect extremist or fringe movements that were eradicated by the Spanish Inquisition, for it cannot be overlooked that mainstream Spanish spirituality also focused on ascetical practices, abnegation of self, the practice of the Christian and moral virtues, and the dominance of the personal will even when ecstatic union had been attained. In fact, when the intellect is in the state of repose or quietude, the will is inflamed by love for God and a desire for union. Personal effort and the involvement of the activities of the will are most important features of the theological system of spiritual Recollection in Spain. The inner way of Recollection never became a negation of exterior acts nor of the performing of good works; in effect, of personal responsibilities in the community. These external acts not only affirm the inner life of the soul, but are reflections of it.[15]

In our investigation of the *Tercer abecedario espiritual*, we shall be quoting from the Andrés Martín edition published in the series *Biblioteca de Autores Cristianos* (1972), and also from the *Tercer abecedario espirtual* which forms part of the three volume *Místicos franciscanos españoles*, also included in the same series, the latter edited by the Franciscan J. Bautista Gomis (1948). The difference between the two is that in the Gomis edition chapters are entitled "capítulos" rather than the original "tratados." The Gomis edition contains 22 of 23 "capítulos." We must confess ignorance as to how this came to be.

In "Tratado" I Osuna alludes to the pure spirit that one must possess in order to ultimately reach God; in addition, he suggests that the body and the soul must make the journey to God together (Osuna 129). He continues: "Esta sabiduría devota y muy dulce de que hablamos pone Dios en los corazones de los justos, que son vasos de oro con que El bebe nuestros buenos deseos" (134). Osuna defines wisdom ("sabiduría") as "gusto actual de Dios", for this wisdom (knowledge) of God brings sweetness to the human soul. In chapter V of "Tratado" I, he writes that there must be harmony within the individual's soul. In "Tratado" III Osuna demonstrates the condition of the soul which holds God within its innermost part. He adds that the soul must be still or quiet: "Pues que el Señor es Dios de las ciencias y quiere más que oren a El callando y en espíritu y verdad que no con palabras, mientras con mayor silencio le ruegan mas oye y mejor concede lo que demandan" (Osuna 184). God listens best when individuals pray without words, in silence. In "Tratado" IV Osuna teaches how the individuals must look into their own heart (soul) and empty it of all that is created: "desembarazar el corazón y vaciar todo lo criado" (195). In chapter II of "Tratado" IV, he suggests that one look into the soul as if one were entering into a castle wherein the three spiritual powers will be encountered: "Tres potencias tiene el ánima: la potencia racional y fuera de razón (intellect), la potencia irascible (memory), la potencia que desea (will). Osuna identifies and defines the process of "recogimiento" in chapter V. He leads the individual to withdraw into the soul: "Entra en el retraimiento de tu ánima, lanza todas las cosas dejando a Dios en él" (208). He reiterates that this knowledge, which is a "gusto dulce de las cosas celestiales", can be attained through experience and not just through study and speculation; further, it is best received "cuando esté más vacío el corazón de todas las otras cosas" (210). In "Tratado" VI, he discusses further the recollection of the soul and demonstrates how one can practice it and become proficient in its use. He recalls how Christ Himself would withdraw into the silence of the desert to pray and fast in order to "más secreta y espiritualmente orar en escondido a su

Padre celestial y nuestro" (233). He attempts to define this inner prayer of Recollection in the second chapter: "Teología mística (secret) que quiere decir escondida, porque en el secreto escondimiento del corazón la enseña el buen maestro Jesús" (235). Osuna also distinguishes between the two types of theology that were still viable in his lifetime; he identifies them as "especulativa o escudriñadora y la otra, escondida" (235). Mystical theology, according to Osuna, teaches one to love God instead of simply contemplating Him. Speculative theology belongs in the realm of the intellect, whereas mystical theology is called "voluntarista" because the will is inflamed in love for the Supreme Being (236). This second or secret theology is also affective: "La teología escondida de que hablamos, no se alcanza de esta manera tan bien como por afición piadosa y ejercicio en las virtudes morales que disponen y purgan el ánima" (236). The moral virtues are thus involved in the purgation of the soul. Osuna identifies the functions of the three phases of the spiritual ascent to reach God as "purgar", "alumbrar", and "perfeccionar."

"Tratado" VI continues with the identification and definition of "recogimiento": "Llámase también en la Escritura este ejercicio escondimiento, donde Dios se esconde en lo secreto del corazón del hombre" (239). God in effect hides in the most intimate or secret part of the soul. He adds: ". . .y a este escondimiento estando las puertas de los sentidos muy bien cerradas viene el Señor; y en este secreto lugar dice Dios la palabra escondida de su secreto, según dice Job" (241). Osuna uses other terms to further explain this spiritual process, one of which is "abstencia", not to be confused with abstinence, for it is more like abstaining from something such as abstaining from voting rather than abstention from food or drink. Other terms used by Osuna are "allegamiento", "encendimiento", "recibimiento", "redaño" (visceral, a biological term), "atraimiento", "prohijamiento" (adoption), "advenimiento", or the coming of God as Christ into the soul (241). It is an "alteza que levanta el ánima y amistad o abrazamiento del corazón devoto al de Cristo; ascensión espiritual en Cristo" (241). It is both a gathering in and a keeping of God hidden in the most intimate part of the soul. It is also a friendship with Christ where one ascends with Him in an embrace of the two hearts, Christ's and the individual's.

Osuna writes that the function of this spiritual process is "recoger y congregar lo disperso, y tanto lo recoge y allega que se llame él mismo recogimiento (243).

All the powers of the soul are gathered together into its most intimate part, and it is there that God will be encountered. Osuna reminds the reader that this type of spiritual exercise was practiced by the ancients, "que por recogerse mejor se retiraron a los ermitorios y lugares secretos por no se distraer entre la gente" (243). He calls it "recogimiento" first because it "recoge los hombres que lo usan haciéndolos de un corazón y amor, quitando de ellos toda diversión y discordia" (244). The Spanish word *recoger* implies not simply a withdrawal or retiring, but also a suspension and a collecting together, which also includes a reformation. It is interesting to note that the various meanings of the terms "recoger" and "recogimiento" include the different functions and results of this spiritual process.[16] "Recogido" may signify retired, secluded or contracted; "recogimiento", collection, assemblage, retreat, recollection, gathering, retirement, a collection or recollection of something. Osuna then defines in chapter iv of this same "Tratado", under the heading "De otras maneras de recogimiento", what this process can also accomplish: "recoge el mismo hombre a sí mismo" (244). Osuna continues with the explication of the term as a withdrawal into a secret or secluded place in order to pray and meditate. For the process is once again multifaceted; it is a physical withdrawal of the individual to a quiet and secret place, but at the same time it is a gathering in of the powers of the soul as well as a holding (possession) or a contemplation of God in this profoundest and most intimate part of the soul. It is a gathering in and a retirement (withdrawal): a place of solitude and silence (quietness). It involves a secret encounter in the soul, and the purging of this soul which will also bring it complete spiritual repose. It can also be seen as an ascent to God as well as God's descent into the soul.

Osuna continues: "lo que este ejercicio recoge es los sentidos del hombre a lo interior del corazón, donde está la gloria de la hija del rey, que es el ánima católica." Then he compares this soul with the sea-urchin: ". . .y así muy bien se puede comparar el hombre recogido al erizo, que todo se reduce a sí mismo y se retrae dentro en sí" (241). Osuna describes another important process in this prayer of Recollection, where the powers of the soul gather themselves in or recollect themselves to the highest point of the soul as ("apice" or "sindéresis"): "recoger las potencias del ánima a la sindéresis y muy alta parte de ella, donde la imagen de Dios está imprimida que se llama espíritu de los justos" (241). This is the essence of the spiritual exercises involved in the process of Recollection, wherein the three powers of the soul are recollected (ingathered) in the most intimate or highest point in the soul; it is in this very place where the individual may encounter God's image. He then explains the phenomenon which transpires in the soul which he labels the tenth manner of recollection: "la divina claridad como en vidriera o piedra cristalina, se infunde en el ánima, enviando delante como sol de rayos de su amor y gracia, que penetran en el corazón siendo en lo más alto del espíritu primero recibido" (247).

Osuna employs beautiful language in describing how this divine light, which he compares to a glass or crystal, is infused in the soul in forms of light rays and grace that penetrate the soul, and gather in the highest point. In this most intimate or highest part of the soul, which Osuna calls "sindéresis", the individual "junta y recoge a Dios con el ánima y el ánima con Dios y la participación de ella es en el mismo Señor, en el cual está recogida toda" (247). The soul participates in the life of God as it joins with Him. Osuna attempts to describe this phenomenon by comparing the contemplative with a soaring eagle: "El que sabe subir en alto por el vuelo de la contemplación y pone en las alturas el nido de su recogimiento no es justo que olvide a los que quedamos aquí debajo, sino que debemos movernos a volar" (19).

We read also in the Gomis edition of the *Tercer abecedario* how everyone can practice this y "arte del recogimiento" if one has learned the spiritual exercise well (20). Osuna explains his purpose for composing this book which is, "para dar a conocer a todos este ejercicio del recogimiento" (20). He adds a most cogent note: "Este ejercicio también es para casados. . . no pretendemos ser casados sino amigos de Dios, cosa que pueden ser los hombres y mujeres casados" (23). Married men and women can be taught the exercise of this art of Recollection. It is available for all to learn and use. According to Osuna, all persons can predispose themselves to receive this wondrous gift from God. He recommends the following: "A los que han recibido este don que lo comuniquen debidamente a todos los fieles cristianos que quieren dedicarse a este santo ejercicio" (25). He adds: "Muchas mujeres suben con El de Galilea a la espiritual Jerusalén, que es la oración pacífica y recogida y no solamente recibe a los que vienen sino que El los llama con sus inspiraciones para que lo reciban en la secreta morada del corazón" (27). He insists that married people have time to dedicate themselves to this type of prayer and contemplation (28). In fact, it is God who calls men and women to this supreme contemplation.

In "Tratado" X Osuna describes how the individual in devotion closes his mind to the senses, and the intellect is left "en tinieblas." He advises his readers to be recollected inside of their soul, and by cleansing the senses they cannot be distracted by any thoughts of vanity or mundane interests (82). Osuna describes Recollection as a narrow door through which only God can pass (84).[17] In addition, he emphasizes the inner nature of Recollection wherein he admonishes his readers to pay more attention to what is inside of each one. He refers to Richard of St. Victor's *Beniamin minor* or *De Praeparatione animi al contemplationem* 1:12, where the thirteenth century writer had taught one to enter into oneself, which is better than rising above oneself. According to Osuna's interpretation of Richard of St. Victor's writings both of these actions are involved in the way of Recollection: ". . .las dos son de esta vía del recogimiento. . .sin recogimiento no se puede hacer ni la una ni la otra. Que el hombre entre en sí mismo es el principio para subir sobre sí mismo" (118). In other words, the soul must be recollected into its essential part in order to be able to "subir en alto" (119). Osuna also teaches that the spiritual ascent or "subir sobre sí mismo" is a result of the recollecting or ingathering of the powers of the soul: "recoger el espíritu dentro" and "levantar el espíritu." The soul cannot be whole and entire if it is dispersed as a result of not keeping the senses under complete control. If the soul is not whole or entire, that is, if it is dispersed through the senses, it cannot gather into itself its three powers. In addition, the soul must also be in complete repose, and the body should be secluded or shut off from worldly affairs and preoccupations: "encerramiento espiritual" (121). Osuna here distinguishes between "espíritu", "alma" or "ánima." According to him, "el espíritu es lo más alto y el alma es la parte inferior" (122).

Osuna compares the grace that the soul receives from God in the prayer of Recollection to olive oil, bread, a river that flows out of the region of delights, wheat which nourishes a spiritual hunger, a column of fire that illuminates the dark night, a diamond which leads us to God, and pure water which cleanses the soul. He continues: "Es una semilla espiritual que arraiga secretamente en el alma y Dios da el crecimiento." It is also compared to wine that fills the soul with joy, and also likened to rain that fertilizes the soul so that it may give forth abundant fruit of good works (151). He also compares this grace to a ring by which the soul is united in a spiritual marriage to God and to a honeycomb through which God's divine sweetness comes to each individual. This same grace also has the function of illuminating the soul's intellect, just as the oil keeps the light burning in the tabernacle within God's temple (152-54).

And who is most deserving of this grace which is freely given? According to Osuna, it is the one who loves God. It is given to those who keep God and Christ constantly in their soul's memory: "Los que son devotos de la Sagrada Pasión del Señor la deben tener de continuo en la memoria, porque en esto se prueba su devoción y no hablar de esa devoción porque no hay duda de que el más devoto de ella la tiene más en la memoria, como cosa más amada" (170). Those who love God will keep Him present in their memory, and this can be done most efficaciously by meditating on the events of Christ's life, namely, the Passion in this particular instance. By keeping God in one's memory, love will be awakened, "porque las cosas que son de la divinidad mueven por sí mismas el amor y la devoción nuestra a Dios" (173). However, Osuna once again reminds the reader that the highest function of the memory is carried out within one's soul in the prayer of Recollection. Osuna considers the memory of God in recollection a spiritual resurrection:

> . . .ésta más alta memoria de Dios hace que actúen todas las cosas
> interiores y exteriores del hombre dándoles un obrar sencillo que se
> adecua bien al recogimiento, la cual (*memoria*) no es sino una
> representación de Dios en su desnudez ser. Si esta alta memoria de Dios
> en el recogimiento Dios se reviste en el hombre, y parece que de
> muerto hace vivo, y le aviva las entrañas y el corazón y los ojos . . .
> pues esta memoria es de solo Dios. (177)

This memory of God also involves the soul's intellect rather than the senses. He explains it in this way: ". . .pero la memoria tiene en sí la representación de la cosa sin pormenorizar en condiciones que la concreten" (177). Thus, God will not be held in the memory as a concrete entity but as a "ser no limitado de una bondad no medible, principio que no tiene comienzo, fin que no se acaba, plenitud en la que nada hay de vacío, fuerza invencible, saber que nada ignora. . ." (177). When this memory of God, or the recollection of God in the soul, fills the entire person, it allows him/her to cease to do all other things that do not pertain to God. Osuna reiterates: "Esta memoria debe estar dentro, en el alma, asentada en el corazón. Si hemos de tener memoria de Dios, ha de ser como de un amigo íntimo, que nos es más querido que el padre y el hermano" (181).

Osuna goes on to explain how the memory then serves the will, which is the power of the soul that more immediately serves and loves God. Osuna refers to the dark night of the soul as "nuestra luz en los deleites", where the soul will wait for God with its inner spiritual powers, and with the "memoria intelectual" (184). It is the moving of the will that makes one desire God in order to enjoy Him: "gustar de El" (197). This ultimate spiritual repose brings a "gusto espiritual" or spiritual delight or contentment to which Osuna dedicates "Tratado" or "Capítulo" XXI. In this section he writes about the two wings that the soul possesses so that it can make the ascent to God in solitude and the peace of inner recollection. These wings are the intellect and the will (201). He calls this flight "el reposo de la contemplación" (202), and refers to the person in this spiritual flight as "viador" or traveler in a mystical sense. The aim of this spiritual journey is to arrive at the "tranquilo puerto", which is the contemplation of God. God's potential for acting externally is limitless; hence, individuals' potential for reaching full understanding is never really complete, for they can always know and understand more. It is precisely this understanding of God that is needed to attain spiritual repose. According to Osuna, matter is the receptacle for all forms, and it can take all shapes and forms, although not all at once. This matter or power, which Osuna calls "materia" or "potencia", does not rest until it attains understanding (202-03). Yet, this knowledge and understanding has little to do with books and speculation.

Truly devoted persons must first find goodness and devout discipline before they can attain knowledge and understanding. This is the essence of this inner way of Recollection. Knowledge can never become an obstacle for true devotion (209). Osuna teaches that God instructs in many ways. However, it is in the soul's will that God's grace functions: "La casa del alma es el corazón, y no sólo a esta casa es Dios llevado sino a la cama, que es este recogimiento. En esta cama Dios descansa, porque dejó a oscuras la casa, cerrando las ventanas de los sentimientos y allí enseña Dios al alma por experiencia muchas cosas" (211). It is in the silence of the soul's bed or "cama" after the windows of sensory feelings have been closed and the dwelling is cloaked in darkness that God, who is also seeking rest, teaches the soul many spiritual things.

The understanding and knowledge of God and divine things inflame the soul with a desire for Him. It is all-consumed, and even falls ill, in order to be "traspasada de la llaga del amor" (pierced through with love's wound) (220). Spiritual consolation then becomes the fruit of exterior penance and strict ascetical practices. Osuna then goes on to describe the excellence of this "gusto espiritual": ". . .pero si ha gustado de las cosas de Dios es al revés, porque habiéndolas gustado está hambriento de saber y de gustar más, y se abren más los ojos del alma para ver, y el corazón para recibir más y se afila el conocimiento para conocer más. . ." (226). This tasting of God's spiritual delights and sweetness whets the appetite and sharpens the understanding to know more and to experience more (226). Osuna equates devotion with spiritual consolation, and adds that a good work done without devotion is dead (229). As he explains, this is so because in acting without devotion one is led to spiritual sterility and dryness.

This leads Osuna to the different manners of prayer, which he also designates as vocal and which he places in the first stage or phase of the "principiantes", who are initiates in the spiritual journey to God. He, as so many other writers of spirituality, proffers the example of the Lord's Prayer (Our Father) as the most perfect of all oral or vocal prayers (238).[18] The second form of prayer is practiced by those who have entered the second stage or phase of the inner spiritual way, that of the "proficientes": "La segunda manera de orar, es cuando dentro de nuestro corazón sin pronunciar por la boca vocalmente palabras, sólo nuestro corazón habla con el Señor, y dentro de nosotros le pedimos todo lo que necesitamos" (249). The third manner of praying Osuna calls mental or spiritual prayer, and in this prayer the highest (superior) part of the soul is raised with the affections to God, fortified by love. He describes vocal prayer as one of thought ("pensamiento"), silent prayer without words as one of the heart, and the mental prayer of Recollection as one of acts (deeds, works), which if sincere exceeds the other two of words and thoughts (258).

Osuna then makes an interesting statement when he teaches his readers how to prepare themselves physically for spiritual recollection.[19] He writes: ". . .he visto mercaderes de grandes fortunas y negocios que, viviendo sin pecado mortal, tomaron por cosa principal el recogimiento del alma" (324). He adds: ". . .el que está recogido tiene su corazón sosegado consigo mismo, haciendo como el caracol, y como la tortuga que anda muy recogida bajo su concha" (327). In "Tratado" XIX Osuna discusses the importance of humility, which the person needs to proceed in the spiritual journey to God. He writes: "La quietud se atribuye al recogimiento y la moderación a la humildad y entrambas las virtudes convienen al hombre del corazón, que es hombre espiritual y entrañable, que se esconde para hallar a Dios, que está dentro de nosotros. . ." (536). One must grow in humility in order to progress in this spiritual way. This humility will make every person eligible to proceed in the inner way of Recollection.

Another very important contributor to the development of the literature of the inner way of Recollection is Juan de Avila (1500-1569), who also influenced many other subsequent writers of Spanish spirituality, including Teresa de Jesús as well as the early Jesuits. Juan de Avila was a preacher who is also known as the Apostle of Andalucía. He was denounced and imprisoned in 1532 by the Inquisition for being suspected of Lutheranism; however, he was cleared in 1533. García de Diego in his edition of the *Epistolario espiritual* writes that Juan de Avila cannot be considered a mystic in the strictest sense, but he wrote in what this scholar describes as the initiation phase (xiv). He was a writer of devotional and meditative works whose motives was to offer advice to those who wish to practice devotional and ascetical rules which are part of the spiritual life of the soul. He also offered "particulares avisos" which promoted Church reform and the proper instruction of its youth (Avila xv). However, he was first and foremost a preacher. Luis Sala Balust in the prologue to Avila's complete works writes:

Creemos que en aquella gran corriente de renovación espiritual de nuestro Siglo de Oro que arrancando de la entraña del XV, cobra nuevo vigor con la reforma de

> Isabel y de Cisneros, rebulle en los círculos erasmistas e innovadores
> de Alcalá, se encauza en reformas como la del austero P. Hurtado, se
> enturbia en ciertos sectores iluministas, se remansa y aclara con la reno
> vación teológica que inicia en Salamanca el Mtro. Vitoria, se refuerza
> con las huestes de Ignacio, en la más exuberante floración mística que
> conoce la historia de la Iglesia. (Avila xix)

Juan de Avila's masterpiece *Audi, filia* is another major contribution to the spiritual renewal that Sala Balust identifies in his prologue. It is in effect a compendium of rules and advice for those who wish to serve God by advancing in the spiritual path to God. The title of this seminal work comes from the Psalm where King David writes: "Audi, filia et vide et inclina aurem tuam" (Psalm 44.11). The work was published at Alcalá in 1556.[20] Avila's popularity in his day was extraordinary, and Sala Balust writes that he would fill churches when he came to preach. The letters which he wrote to his friends and spiritual sons and daughters are collected in the *Epistolario espiritual*, written in the prisons of the Inquisition and published in 1547. It was not only Avila's spirituality that came under suspicion, but it is a fact that his father was of Jewish origin.

In his native Almodóvar del Campo, he lived a retired life of meditation and contemplation for about three years. At that time he practiced spiritual recollection, mental prayer as well as penitence. In addition, at the University of Alcalá de Henares he seems to have come into contact with the Erasmists (Avila 53-57). Avila advocated the reform of the Church and the education of secular priests that later influenced the incipient Society of Jesus. He was a director of a reform movement for priests that spearheaded a strengthening of an interior spirituality which included spiritual recollection, frequent confession and communion, a prayer which focused on Christ's passion, and the study of the New Testament, and most especially, of St. Paul (Avila 143). At a certain point in his career, Juan de Avila attempted to integrate his own *colegios* to those of the Jesuits.

Before we commence to study the *Audi, filia*, we will refer to a minor work by Avila called *Reglas del espíritu: Breve regla de vida cristiana* (Alcalá, 1556), which is in fact a primitive form of spiritual exercises (*exercitatorio*). Sala Balust informs us that it is included as an appendix in Luis de Granada's *Guía de pecadores*. Sala Balust writes that Juan de Avila sets aside appropriate parts of the day for prayer. One is in the morning, in order to better meditate on the mysteries of the Passion, and the other opportune time is at night in order to remember one's own mortality.

Avila presents the "Reglas muy provechosas para andar en el camino de Nuestro Señor." He writes in the sixth rule: "La sexta, busque algún rato o lugar desocupado cada día para que lea libros y piense en algún paso de la pasión de nuestro Señor Jesucristo, y en el artículo de su muerte" (Avila 1040). He adds that the best path to God is humble obedience. Juan de Avila then posits "diez documentos"; in the second one he writes: "El segundo sea que busque un lugar solo, donde cada mañana en levantándose, se recoja una hora o más" (1051). Once again he asks his readers to meditate on Christ's passion and the love which it implies. The "Nono documento" is in fact charity toward one's neighbor (1053).

It is worth noting that in a section called "Miscelánea breve", Avila composes a prologue to the Castilian translation of the *Imitación de Cristo* or the *Contemptus Mundi* published in Seville in 1536. We read: ". . .es bueno que sepas quién hizo este libro, no es Gerson como hasta aquí se intitulaba mas Fray Tomás de Kempis, Canónigo de San Agustín, el cual comienza así en el nombre de Jesucristo nuesto Señor" (1067). It is a fact that the *Imitatio Christi* had been attributed to Jean Gerson, but it is now universally acknowledged that Thomas à Kempis wrote it. In the section devoted to prayer, it is established that "el hablar con Dios ha de ser con gozo y amor" (1073). Through prayer one can directly communicate with God in a familiar way and at the same time obtain the favor of actually conversing with Him (1073). Juan de Avila presents the models for prayer as colloquies which will have an impact on the Ignatian exercises. We present one example:

> ¡Oh justísimo Juez! ¡Oh sumo aborrecedor de pecados y ¿Cómo habéis
> sufrido tantos años y tiempos cosa tan vil, tan ingrata y tan desleal
> delante de nuestros ojos? (1080) . . . ¿A dónde iré? ¿En qué hallaré
> remedio? ¿A quién descrubriré mi angustia y miseria? (1081) . . . ¡Oh
> hermosura incomparable! ¡Y cuánto estará mi corazón a vos solamente
> aficionado! ¿Cuándo, mi bien único mío, gustará mi ánima la
> dulcedumbre que gustan los que tal bien como vos poseen? ¿Cuándo
> veré yo mis deseos, mis pensamientos, mis cuidados, mis ansias y
> afectos, todos ocupados en solo vos? (1083). . . ¡Oh deleite tan sin falta
> y bajesa de todo lo que antes me parecía hermoso! ¡Oh dulcedumbre
> tan sin amargura! Júntame a vos con tanta firmeza, que nadie sea parte
> para de tal dulzura y de tales deleites desviarnme. . . vos sois la fuente
> de todo descanso. (1083).

Luis de Granada was a friend and disciple of Juan de Avila, who also wrote his biography called *Vida* and in this work details his apostolic mission, following his journey through dusty roads and inns in Andalucía. It is also an historical fact that Juan de Avila sent certain suggestions in the form of advice to the Council of Trent. These were called his *Advertencias al santo Concilio de Trento (Tercera convocatoria)* (Avila 1562). These are included in Avila's *Tratados de reforma*, and also feature the *Instrucción para el gobierno del reino, Advertencias necesarias para reyes*, and other treatises which promote reform.[21]

While Juan de Avila was in prison, he wrote the *Audi, filia* (1522-33). In an anecdote reminiscent of Cervantes's experience, Sala Balust writes: ". . .por un favor que de Dios tuvo estando preso en la Inquisición de Sevilla, tuvo la luz para escribir el *Audi, filia*: allí concibió el misterio de nuestra justificación e incorporación a Cristo a manera de un epitalamio místico entre la Iglesia—el alma —y el Rey divino" (Avila 53). Finally, the *Audi, filia* had an influence on Juan de Valdés's *Diálogo de la doctrina cristiana* (1529), Osuna's *Tercer abecedario*, and most probably Ignacio de Loyola's *Ejercicios espirituales*. Avila might have also influenced Bartolomé de Carranza's *Catecismo* and Luis de Granada's own book on prayer and meditation (Avila 202-05). Furthermore, the *Audi, filia* was created in the environment of reformation that produced *Lazarillo de Tormes*, as well as the phenomenon of the *Alumbrados* of Guadalajara.

In the *Prólogo* to the *Audi, filia*, Avila counsels his readers: "Porque muy poco aprovecha que suene la voz de la verdad divina en lo de fuera, si no hay orejas que la quieran oir en lo de dentro" (Avila 551). Avila distinguishes three languages, one of which is the language of the world that is not to be listened to because it is false (552). Earthly language will deceive individuals, and makes them order life "por el ciego norte del aplacamiento del mundo y engéndrasele un corazón deseoso de honra y de ser estimado de hombres. . ." (553). Avila proposes to offer remedies that will assist in despising all vain honors by keeping in mind and heart the great strength that Christ gives in order to conquer the desire for earthly honors (555). Avila discusses the "lumbre natural" that people possess that can lead them to do praiseworthy works, including the practice of virtue. Avila asks his readers to raise their eyes to Christ on the cross in order to increase the desire to despise all vanity. After having meditated on the sufferings of Christ on the cross, each Christian will feel like a lowly worm, but one which is filled with love. After having experienced this feeling of lowliness the person will be a follower of Christ, and hence be able to hear God's doctrines and truths (557). In chapter 4 Avila explains the difference between what Augustine defines as *amor uti* and *amor frui*. The honors and human esteem can be coveted not for themselves but for some final end.

In chapter 5 Avila shows how one should flee the attractions of the flesh which become one's perilous enemy. The flesh does battle using the many delights as its powerful armament. He advises arming oneself for the battle against the powers of the flesh: ". . .y quien quisiere salir vencedor de muchas y muy fuertes armas le conviene ir armado. Porque la preciosa joya de la castidad no se da a todos, mas a los que con muchos sudores de importunas oraciones y de santos trabajos la alcanzan de nuestro Señor" (563). In order to listen to God's truths and wisdom with the inner ear of the soul, the Christian must triumph over the flesh, and this involves "sudores" as well as prayers and "santos trabajos" (563). Through penitence, moderation, some form of fasting and treating the flesh with some amount of severity, "primeramente tratar con aspereza su carne, con apocarle la comida y el sueño, con dulzura de cama y de cilicios" (563). These are the ascetical exercises that will purge or cleanse the soul by subduing the flesh, and they belong to the first phase of the spiritual ascent to God. In this first phase individuals will also suffer temptations in order to prove that they belong to the "bando de Cristo" (565-68).

Once individuals have fortified the spirit and gained spiritual strength, they can begin to feel something of what will await them in paradise. They will come to experience God's limitless nature, His eternity, His gentleness, extreme simplicity and beauty, His inimitable nature and a good that is infinitely complete ("infinitamente completo"). Avila continues in chapter XXI: "Sobre todo entendimiento es tu ser, y también lo es tu dulcedumbre, la cual está guardada y escondida para los que le temen. . .es el mar de tu dulcedumbre tan sin medida que nadando y andando ellos embriagados y llenos de tu suavidad, queda tanto más que gozar de ella" (574). The unfettered soul is free to contemplate God's goodness and sweetness, as well as His boundless kindness.

In chapter 23 Avila reminds the reader that the way of perfection is indeed an arduous battle ("reñida batalla") against powerful enemies that are inside as well outside of each person (611). In chapter 26 Avila admonishes his readers to follow the way of the cross, practice obedience, be patient and have the strength of heart to struggle constantly against temptation (620). He adds that one's service to God is measured more by love than by the tenderness of devotion. He explains this love: "el cual no es devoción tierna, mas un libre ofrecimiento y propósito de nuestra voluntad para hacer lo que Dios y su Iglesia quieren que hagamos" (618). In chapter 29 Avila presents to his readers the arms that they must employ in order to fight the enemy as well as various temptations:

> Mas ¿qué son las armas con que se vence este enemigo para que vaya confundido de esta guerra como de la pasada? Estas son como dice San Pedro y San Pablo, la fe. Porque cuando un ánima, con el amor de Dios, que es vida de la fe, desprecia lo próspero y adverso del mundo y cree y confía en Dios al cual no ve, no hay por donde el demonio le entre. (625)

Persons will lose their faith if they do not practice charity, which is in turn the source of hope as well as of all the other Christian virtues (626). If one has faith, love, and hope, one will be able to fight the battles against temptations that God sends to His chosen ones ("los suyos") for their own good (628). He continues: "Porque no es señal de amigo verdadero acompañar en el descanso, mas está fijo con el amigo en el tiempo de la tribulación" (628).

In chapter 31 Avila presents his readers with what they should be able to hear concerning God. Each individual should be able to hear divine truth by means of faith, which is the beginning of all spiritual life (630). Avila describes this divine truth as a bright light which ". . . dícese morar en tinieblas, porque ningún ojo criado de hombre o ángel puede con su corazón alcanzar sus misterios y por eso para el tal ojo, tinieblas se llama la luz, no porque sea luz obscura, mas porque es luz que excede a todo entendimiento sobre toda manera" (635). This is a crucial element of the inner way of spiritual Recollection. The divine light is conceived as darkness or night not because it is a dark (obscure) light, but because it is a light that exceeds all understanding. It is believing something that cannot essentially be understood by reason alone. God is seen clearly with the inner eyes of the soul, and no human intellect can fully glimpse it (635). Individuals must abandon all earthly desires in order to follow and "caminar por el desierto de la vida espiritual y estrecho camino que lleva a la vida. . ." (646). Spiritual life is conceptualized as a desert and as a very narrow path which leads to a sharing in the life of God.

The person who follows this path and is able to hear God's truths will also receive various benefits as they enjoy being delivered by Christ Himself from any dangers that may beset the soul, as well as the attainment and possession of the spiritual benefits, or as Luke calls it as translated by Avila, "el reino de Dios dentro de vosotros está" (Luke 17.21; Avila 647). In addition to possessing God's kingdom within the soul, Christians will possess a sense of justice, peace, and the spiritual joy which accompanies the presence of the Holy Spirit. The love for justice and goodness, and the laws of virtue will be imprinted in the soul (643). Furthermore, Avila writes that love and faith will bring justification of the individual before God: "Claro habló aquí el Señor, si no quiere alguno cegarse en la luz y fe y amor por sus nombres, y entrambos se requieren para la justificación" (665).[22] In chapter 45 Avila reminds the reader that God ordered humans to save themselves by faith, and not by human reasoning (668). In addition, faith infused by God, illuminates the individual, and leads the soul to reach the knowledge of divine things once it has been cleansed or purged (678).

In chapter 50 Avila refers to the reform of the Church with these words: "No han faltado en nuestros tiempos personas que han tenido por cierto que ellos habían de reformar la Iglesia cristiana, y traerla a la perfección que a su principio tuvo" (687). He mentions that others have attempted shortcuts ("muy breve atajo") in order to more quickly reach God. We believe that here he is alluding to the *Alumbrados*:

> . . .y parecíales que dándose perfectamente a El, y dejándose en sus manos, eran tan tomados de Dios, y regidos por el Espíritu Santo que todo lo que a su corazón venía no era otra cosa sino lumbre e instinto de Dios. Y llegó a tanto este engaño que, si aqueste movimiento interior no les venía, no habían de moverse a hacer obra buena, por buena que fuese, y si les movía el corazón a hacer alguna obra, la habían de hacer, aunque fuese contra el mandamiento de Dios. (687)

Avila adds that this type of abandonment to God forgets one's obligation to act within the parameters of God's commandments. The laws of God must also be implanted in the soul, and those seeking the inner path to God cannot forget the obligation to themselves, to God, and to all fellow human beings.

In the following passage Avila presents a spiritual disposition that we believe could have inspired the anonymous poem "A Cristo crucificado", which appeared in the sixteenth century. Here is the passage taken from the *Audi, filia*:

> . . .y de aquí es que aunque no hobiese infierno que amenazase, ni paraíso que convidase, ni mandamiento que constriñere, obraría el justo por solo el amor de Dios lo que obra y por esta pobertad que tiene para con pecados y con trabajos, aborreciendo a los unos y amando a los otros, se llama libre y que al tal justo no le es puesta ley. (683-84)

The just person, or one who is justified in God's eyes, has the divine laws implanted in the soul and acts solely out of love for God, and not because of a just punishment or for some eternal reward. We present here the poem in its entirety so that we can clearly see a very similar manifestation of the spirituality which originated in the area of Guadalajara, Toledo, and other areas in central and southern Spain.[23]

> *No me mueve, mi Dios, para quererte*
> *el cielo que me tienes prometido;*
> *ni me mueve el infierno tan temido*
> *para dejar por eso de ofenderte.*
>
> *Tú me mueves, señor, muéveme verte*
> *clavado en una cruz y escarnecido,*
> *muéveme ver tu cuerpo tan herido,*
> *muéveme tus afrentas y tu muerte.*
>
> *Muéveme, en fin, tu amor, y en tal manera*
> *que aunque no hubiera cielo, yo te amara*
> *y aunque no hubiera infierno, te temiera.*
>
> *No tienes que me dar porque te quiera,*
> *pues aunque cuanto espero no esperara*
> *lo mismo que te quiero te quisiera.*

The poem follows Avila's passage closely. It reflects on Christ's humanity and on the meditation of His suffering during the Passion. It is in the form of an affective prayer (moved by love and a deep faith), where the inner meditation on the Passion moves the person's will to love Christ regardless of punishment or reward. It was a person who followed the spirituality contained in Avila's *Audi, filia,* if indeed it was not Avila himself, who composed this most powerful poem which is a masterpiece of the spirituality of Recollection.

In chapter 56 Avila recommends "recogimiento en la vista" in order to better see God with the eyes of the soul. However, before doing this the person must look into the soul and know him/herself. He adds: "Que debemos poner diligencia en el propio conocimiento y que conviene tener un lugar apartado—donde nos recoger un rato cada dia" (701). Avila prefaces the act of recollecting oneself to a secluded (retired) room (place) with knowledge of self. Knowing oneself is the vehicle by which the person can come to the knowledge of God. In knowing oneself one can learn the virtue of humility without which one cannot proceed to practice the other virtues necessary to commence and continue the spiritual journey to God (703). Humility will ward off arrogance, even the arrogance of the spiritually complacent. Avila quotes from Jerome who had advised a married woman in this way: "Busca un lugar conveniente para tu ánima, y algún tanto apartado del bullicio de la familia, al cual te vayas como quien se va a un puerto, huyendo de la gran tempestad de tus cuidados, y allí solamente haya lección de cosas divinas y oración continua y pensamientos de cosas del otro mundo" (704). The retired place or room is to be a refuge from the cares of everyday life, where the individual will read devotional literature, and practice prayer and meditate on divine things: "pensamientos de cosas del otro mundo" (704). Avila then informs his readers that they do not live for any other reason but principally "usar de la oración y recogimiento interior y exterior, debe buscar en su casa algún lugar escondido, y secreto, en el cual tenga sus libros devotos e imágenes devotas, diputado solamente para ver y gustar cuan suave es el Señor" (704). He recommends a secret and retired room in the house where the person can have access to devotional works and images that will be useful so that the person can see and taste God's kindness and goodness.

In chapter 59 Avila presents the spiritual exercises that will lead to self-knowledge as well as to how a person can take advantage of spiritual reading and prayer. He recommends retiring to this secret room at least twice each day (705). In the morning the person can meditate on Christ's passion and at night on the exercises that will lead to knowledge of self. Through the attainment of self-knowledge, Avila contends that the person will acquire the virtue of humility. He then asks the reader to consider two things when reflecting on sin: one is "el ser" (being) and the other "el buen ser" (the good being or being good). He claims that the "mal ser" is worse than "el no ser." Living in sin is worse than not existing at all (718). Persons in sin cannot begin the journey to God because they are weighted down by the flesh (lust), and thus are fettered and cannot attain contemplation of God when forced to look down, or as he explains it, "los corazones encorvados hacia la tierra." In short, the soul is weighted down and looks down to earth, and as a result is not free to look upward and begin the spiritual ascent to God (720-21).

In chapter 67 Avila describes the second or the illuminative phase of the mystical (inner, secret) way to God. It is the light that appears in the soul of individuals who come to have knowledge of God's greatness, which contrasts with the nothingness of the each person's unimportance: "y si el Señor es servido de os dar este conocimiento que deseáis, sentiréis que viene en vos una celestial lumbre y sentimiento en el ánima con que, quitadas unas gruesas tinieblas conoce y siente ningún bien ni ser ni fuerza en todo lo criado" (724). In order to come to this enlightenment there is no better way, according to Avila, than to meditate on the sufferings and death of Christ: "Esta es la nueva alegría predicada en la nueva Ley a todos los quebrantados de corazón, y les es dada una medicina muy más eficaz para su consuelo que sus llagas les pueden desconsolar así quien sintiere desmayo mirando sus culpas, alce sus ojos a Jesucristo, puesto en la cruz, y cobrará esfuerzo" (725-26). In order to proceed to God, individuals must feel penitence for sins committed. There is no better way to do this than to look upon the cross:

> Servirle ha también para esto, mirando una imagen del crucifijo o
> acordándose de El, pensar como él fue causa, por sus pecados, que el
> Señor padeciese tales tormentos, y métele bien de pies a cabeza,
> ponderando en cada pecado, pues las penas del Señor corresponden a
> nuestras culpas. (739)

Avila then divides the meditation of the Passion among the days of the week; on Monday, the agony and seizing of Christ in the garden; Tuesday, the accusations and judging of Christ before his judges, and the scourging at the pillar. Wednesday's meditations include the crowning of thorns; Thursday, the washing of the apostles' feet, and Friday, Christ going before Pilate and his sentencing to death as well as His crucifixion and death. Saturdays's meditations are on the descent from the cross and the burial, and Sunday's meditation is on the resurrection (739-40). Avila refers to the exercise of meditating on the "pasos" (scenes, events) of the life and death of Christ (741). He describes this meditation: ". . . representar a nuestra imaginación la figura corporal de nuestro Señor, o solamente pensar sin representación imaginaria con ojos corporales, para poderle mirar con los espirituales, que son de la fe, para ayudar al corazón piadoso a levantarse a las cosas espirituales" (741-42). All readers are asked to begin the spiritual journey by meditating on their sins, and then to lift their thoughts to "la sacra humanidad de Jesucristo nuestro Señor, para subir a la alteza de su divinidad" (740).[24] In what will later become an important ingredient in the Ignatian meditative process, Avila asks his readers to place the image of that particular scene of Christ's life before them as if they were there and then to meditate on it with the heart. He continues: "haced cuenta que la tienes allí cerquita de vos" (743). Avila even suggests that the reader not go in their thoughts all the way to Jerusalem where the scene occurs, "porque esto daña mucho la cabeza y seca la devoción, mas haced cuenta que lo tenéis allí presente y poned los ojos de vuestra ánima en los pies de El, o en el suelo cercano. . ." (743-44). He asks readers to place themselves directly before the scene as if they were there present. This is in fact the calling of the place to the mind which Ignacio de Loyola made a common practice in Catholic meditation.

He later refers to this "meditación sosegada", which takes place within the individual's heart: ". . .quitad aquella angustia del corazón y humillaos a Dios, con sosiego y simplicidad, pidiéndole gracia para pensar como El quiere. . . humillaos a El con un afecto sencillo y sabed que este negocio más es de corazón, pues, el amar es fin del pensar" (746). The end or goal of all meditation is indeed the movement of the will to love. Avila adds: ". . .y ya os he avisado que nuestra morada ha de ser en vuestro corazón donde como abeja solícita que dentro de su corcho hace la miel, habéis vos de enceraros" (746). From this meditation in repose into one's soul will come the divine light and spiritual sweetness ("dulcedumbre"). In the following chapters, Avila presents the "reglas para la oración", one of which is the imitation of Christ (749). He advocates austerity, severity, and mortification as well as the avoidance of fineries in dress, living conditions and food. Through the mortification of bodily and sensual passions will come "aquel dulcísimo sueño, que con sosiego en sus brazos se duerme, no es razón que se dé sino a los que primero han peleado y con trabajos vencidos a sí mismos" (754). Avila then proposes the important meditation of the benefits of God and of His creation. Once again this is to be carried out by way of Recollection, which will also lead individuals to love and this, as we have seen above, is the end of every meditation and law (765).

Finally, in accordance with this Spanish mode of spirituality, in chapter 95 Avila not only asks the reader to cultivate the knowledge of love for Christ, but also the inner way of Recollection in order to increase one's love for one's neighbors. Furthermore, in chapter 97 he makes reference to the members of the heavenly and earthly cities, and says that good people must coexist with the bad not only in a particular country or city, but in a household or a community of religious. He ends this discussion by establishing that Christians who do not practice charity belong to the earthly city instead of to the heavenly one. In addition, one must practice charity not only towards God but also towards one's fellow human beings (806).[25] In chapter 98 Avila pleads, "huir de la mala ciudad de los malos, que es el mundo" (809). Then, in chapter 99 he establishes premises that are crucial to the reform of Spanish practices, one of which is the vanity of the nobility of lineage, for the inheritance that being a Christian brings is much more important. He proclaims the unity of all humankind as children of God: "un hombre y una mujer hizo Dios en el principio del mundo de los cuales descendió la muchedumbre del género humano. . .Así el rico como el pobre, el libre y esclavo, son de linaje, y sin él no son hechos hijos de Dios. . .son igualmente vestidos con nobleza de honra celestial y divina" (813). This premise was to have lasting ramifications both within Spain, and most importantly, in America. In essence, God has created every soul, and it is Christ that beautifies the soul, not physical beauty, lineage or riches (813). This is one of the many legacies bequeathed to Western Christianity by the inner way of spiritual Recollection is Spain.

In this chapter we have investigated those writers who contributed to the development of the inner way of Recollection in its initial stages. These were the ones who first outlined the exercises of this particular mode of Spanish spirituality during the Renaissance. The following chapter deals with the full flowering of the spirituality of the inner way of Recollection established by writers such Pedro de Alcántara, Juan de los Angeles, and Bernardino de Laredo, and to a certain extent, Teresa's *Castillo interior o moradas* and the *Camino de perfección*, as well as Juan de la Cruz's *Noche oscura*. To reiterate, the writers whom we have investigated in this chapter established, defined, and laid the groundwork for the later flowering of the spirituality of Recollection. These lead us directly to the writings of Teresa de Jesús and Juan de la Cruz, whose works are in effect the culmination of this mode of spirituality, which is the mystical union of the soul with God. Recollection also led, however, to the passive spirituality of the *Alumbrados* or the Illuminists in Castile. These groups were harshly persecuted because in their abandonment to the Holy Spirit, they no longer felt the need for vocal prayer, the sacraments, and the clergy; their members did not even deem it necessary to attend mass or to practice the Christian virtues. They felt that their abandonment to God freed them from the constraints that other Catholics felt, including the fact that they were free from committing sin. They also went by the designation of *dejados*, and in the seventeenth century were called Quietists. The *Alumbrados* were centered around the cities of Toledo, Llerena, Guadalajara, Jaén, and Sevilla. Two important centers of this movement were the home of the Marquis of Villena at Escalona, as well as the palace of the Duques del Infantado in Guadalajara. Scholars believe that Illuminism became prevalent among some *conversos* (Márquez 67-68, 86). Well known *alumbrados* were Juan de Vergara, María de Santo Domingo, María de Cazalla, Isabel de la Cruz, together with Pedro Ruiz de Alcaraz. The latter of these was arrested on April 26, 1524 and condemned by the Inquisition after a lengthy trial. In 1525 an edict of the Inquisition of Toledo condemned all of the doctrines of the Illuminists (Márquez 20-22). Unfortunately, the charged atmosphere subsequent to 1525 led to the arrest of prominent figures of Spanish spirituality, such as Bishop Bartolomé de Carranza, as well as other people accused of being *alumbrados*. Between 1529 and 1539 most of the friends and sympathizers of the original *alumbrados* were arrested and tried by the Inquisition (Márquez 69). These *alumbrados* despised the external practices of the Catholic Church including devotional practices, vocal prayers and liturgical practices and ceremonies including the mass (Márquez 91).

Because of them, many who expounded on the inner way of Recollection were under suspicion by the inquisitorial authorities.

CHAPTER IV

The Full Flowering of the *Vía del Recogimiento* in Spain

> . . .*wisdom, knowledge, joy, he gives to*
> *the man who pleases him.*
> *(Eccl. I, 2.26-27)*
> *My dove, hiding in the clefts of*
> *the rock, in the coverts of the*
> *cliff, show me your face,*
> *let me hear your voice*
> *for your voice is sweet*
> *and your face is beautiful.*
> *(Song of Songs 2.14)*
> *How delicious is your love,*
> *more delicious than wine! (4.10)*
> *Honey and milk*
> *are under your tongue. (4.11)*
> *Breathe over my garden,*
> *to spread its sweet smell around.*
> *Let my beloved come into his garden*
> *let him taste its rarest fruit. (4.16)*

IN CHAPTER III WE STUDIED the initiators of the spiritual literature of Recollection, and those who paved the way and set the groundwork from which would flower a marvelous literary output that is indeed the glory of Spain. In this chapter we will study the works of Franciscan reformers such as Pedro de Alcántara, Francisco de Fuensalida, Bernardino de Laredo, Juan de los Angeles, and certain writings of the major Spanish mystics, Teresa de Jesús and Juan de la Cruz. As far as the latter two are concerned, we will only discuss works that fit within the parameters of the literature of Recollection; these are *Castillo interior*, *Camino de perfección*, and *Noche oscura*, which set the stage for mystical union which is the last phase of the *via mystica*. The works of Teresa and Juan de la Cruz are the fruition or the apogee of this inner way which leads to the contemplation and secret union with God within the deepest or highest part of the soul. The mysticism of Teresa and Juan de la Cruz is indeed the end product of this literature of spiritual Recollection. As we noted in the previous chapter, Recollection also produced a spin-off which was severely condemned by the Inquisition between 1520 and 1525; the members who followed this form of spirituality were called *alumbrados* and *dejados*. Another later offshoot of the spirituality of Recollection, Quietism, developed in the eighteenth century. It is important to understand that all of these manifestations of Spanish Renaissance spirituality—*recogimiento, oración vocal, oración mental, ejercicios espirituales, las tres vías, ascetismo, contemplación adquirida, contemplación infusa, meditación, lectura devota, transformación, unión deiforme*—are all part of the inner way of Recollection (*vía de recogimiento*). Yet, we have chosen to devote this last chapter to those writers who initiated and defined the movement.[1]

The first of these writers that we shall study is Fray Bernardino de Laredo (Seville, 1480-1540), a Franciscan who contributed to the inner way of Recollection with his important work *Subida del Monte Sión* (Seville, 1534). According to Juan Bautista Gomis in his "Introducción general" to Volume II of *Místicos franciscanos españoles*, "la introversión la hace psicológicamente" in that this spiritual looking inward becomes a psychological analysis of the soul, of its spiritual powers, of its desires and activities. Knowledge and experience take a secondary role with Bernardino de Laredo (3). According to Gomis the ascent to God, or the rising of the soul above itself, is accomplished in a Christological manner: "Cristo es el camino, la verdad y la vida, el origen, la subida y la cumbre de la espiritualidad" (13). In Bernardino's Christology, wisdom becomes more important than knowledge. He employs these terms to describe his spirituality: "sabiduría" is "ciencia sabrosa", "profundidad", "escondimiento de Dios en lo secreto del corazón del hombre", "abstinencia de todo amor humano", "unión entre Dios y el alma", "allegamiento a Dios", or union with God in a close friendship, "recibimiento", "consentimiento", "redaño", and "grosura", in reference to the weight of the body, "atraimiento", whereby the soul, being emptied or cleansed of all worldly creatures, attracts God who fills the soul, "enchimiento del corazón y pecho, prohijamiento", as the soul begins to enjoy the spiritual benefits of the Father, "advenimiento del Señor al ánima, ascensión espiritual con Cristo y cautividad", where Christ is held captive in the soul, "abrimiento del corazón devoto al de Cristo", "cielo tercero", to where the contemplatives are lifted, "recogimiento" ("recoge el mismo hombre a sí mismo haciéndole uno, íntegro y dueño de sí, refugio donde podemos retraernos"), a refuge from life's tempests, and from the wiles of the prince of darkness. Bernardino also describes the final "resurreción a vida espiritual" (Gomis II: 5-6). This is the terminology that Bernardino uses to express his own spiritual process and his inner ascent to God.

Bernardino was a medical doctor and personal physician to Don Juan III of Portugal. He wrote medical tracts such as *Metaphor medicinae* (1527) and *Modus facendi cum ordine medicandi* (1536). Apparently, he practiced medicine or was a male nurse for the Franciscan province of Los Angeles. His *Subida* demonstrates his training, wherein we read his incomparable descriptions of natural phenomena (Gomis II: 18). Bernardino had a direct influence on Teresa de Jesús, Juan de los Angeles, and even on Juan de la Cruz (Gomis II: 21). The *Subida del Monte Sión* was first published in Seville in 1534 with a revised edition published in the same city in 1538. There were subsequent editions published in Medina del Campo (1542), Valencia (1590), and in Alcalá (1617). It is divided into three parts. In Part I the author seeks the self-knowledge of the individual. Part II attempts to incite the reader to follow the steps taken by Christ and presents certain "reglas de la cruz" (Gomis II: 25-26). Part III calls the soul to "quietud de pura contemplación", which is the repose of pure contemplation brought about by God himself. He also presents a "Notable", wherein he describes his conception of Mount Sion: ". . .el monte Sión, ciudad del inmenso Rey, está al lado de aquilón. Distante está, apartado de las partes vacilables de esta tempestuosa vida." Mount Sion is placed above and beyond this tempestuous life, away from the cold north wind ("el aquilón"). The quiet and peaceful contemplation of God is placed above in a safe haven that, "está ladeado y muy alto" from the storms of life and the cold wind that blows in from the north. In Bernardino's work, we encounter a spiritual writer whose medical training allows him to interject details and concrete descriptions of natural phenomena in order to better explain the spiritual ones.[2]

From the mystical mountain the souls are positioned in watchtowers above the Christian virtues, from which they can "despeñar" or fling (hurl) the vices from the slope of the mountain (Bernardino, *Subida* 28). He invites the souls to rise above, "la natural tibieza, la flaca inclinación, de las roquedades, y suban al monte Sión" (Bernardino 29). In the "Libro primero", Bernardino sets forth the "reglas" for the first week which he subheads "De la aniquilación." It must be remembered that the etymological root of "aniquilación" is the Latin word *nihil* (nothing); the Spanish word used in this context means self-knowledge, because it is a result of meditating on one's own nothingness and insignificance when compared to God. On Monday, individuals ponder who they are; on Tuesday, from where they originate; Wednesday is devoted to the meditation on where one is at the present time. On Friday, his readers are asked to meditate on where they are going; Saturday is devoted to pondering what his readers will bring on the spiritual ascent, and, finally, Sunday is the day devoted to spiritual repose ("quietud") (29).

Bernardino's "Libro segundo" is devoted to the rules for the second week that deal with the mysteries in the life of Christ. On Monday, one is lead to meditate on Christ's passing from the Garden of Gethsemani to Caifas's house; Tuesday, from Caifas to the scourging at the pillar; Wednesday, from the scourging to the *Ecce homo* scene before Pilate; Thursday, from the fall on the way to Golgotha to Christ's being nailed to the cross; Friday, from the cross to the burial scene, and Sunday, from the scene at the sepulcher to the Resurrection (29). This second part is for the initiates, who are in the initial stages of the ascent to Mount Sion, which represents the quiet contemplation of God. In this part of the book Laredo describes the "sequedades", or spiritual dryness and sterility, and the purgation of the soul and the lack of devotion that accompanies the cleansing process. He also describes the pleasures of praying during this phase of the ascent (30). The "Reglas del Libro tercero" are devoted to the third week of the ascent to Mount Sion. The subheading for this "tercera semana" reads, "a quién corresponde el libro tercero, con quieta contemplación de lo puro intelectual" (30). Bernardino presents certain themes on which the individual may meditate for each day of the week. Monday's theme is "Donde hay caridad y amor está Dios"; Tuesday's is, "Engrandeced a Dios conmigo"; Wednesday, "En el principio crió Dios la tierra y el cielo"; Thursday's meditation is, "El ánima que a Dios se allega es un espíritu con El"; Friday's is, "Cristo padeció. Cómo se ha de sentir por quietud intelectual", in which we share in Christ's suffering through an intellectual repose; on Saturday, "Recibimos en medio de nuestro templo las misericordias vuestras"; Saturday's passage reads, "Ninguno conoce al Padre sino el Hijo" (30). It is evident that Bernardino is writing for his own community of monks, because he states that the exercise of "aniquilación" takes place between matins and prime. The meditation on Christ's mysteries takes place between prime and none. In addition, he devotes all of the "pasos" or scenes from Christ's passion to different canonical prayers.[3] True to Franciscan spirituality, he asks his readers to keep in mind all of God's creation: "Acuérdate que no hay más que un Creador, y aunque sea una yerbecita, o una flor, o una hormiga, le porná luego con Dios por particular noticia" (32).

Bernardino advises his readers to take part in devotional readings on Fridays that will represent "la dignidad de la cruz." He advocates meditation on the sharp pains ("agudos dolores") felt by the Virgin Mary at the foot of the cross. On Sundays, he asks his readers to read devotional literature pertaining to the Resurrection. He then features a "Presupuesto" I (Proposition I). In Proposition I Bernardino claims: "En la vía contemplativa, que quiere decir en el camino de la contemplación", one can "alcanzar de la divina clemencia más bienes y más riquezas" (32). He discusses mental prayer and how through it the soul may be, "mantenida y agraciada en la oración", and then he proposes how spiritual exercises can be further divided into the days of the week (33). "Presupuesto" II is composed of chapters that are written following in a strict sense the authority of Holy Scripture, and he guides the reader on how to read these chapters: ". . .con sosegada quietud y deseo aprovecharse leyere cualquiera de los capítulos de cualquier parte de este libro" (34). Bernardino adds in this summary of the book that God allows the person to feel certain "bienes" in contemplation in three ways; God grants certain people a "ciencia sabrosa no más que para sí solos, y éstos a solas negocian solos entre sí y su Dios" (34). However, to other individuals God offers his gift of contemplation with particular graces and delights (35). In "Presupuesto" III he warns the readers that they will find "cosas obscuras" in this book, and advises them not to be upset or afflicted. He suggests that they think long and quietly about these obscure sections: ". . .las tales obscuridades rumie él solo por sí en la mental oración, en el secreto escondido del alma dentro de sí misma, donde se suelen hablar en el libro de la vida que es Cristo" (30). The message will be communicated to the soul in its most hidden recesses by Christ in this inner or mental prayer. He adds that when Christ communicates this "ciencia sobrosa" to the soul, "entiende el ánima por experiencia el gusto de la divina conversación según puede ser posible en nuestra mortalidad." The soul experiences the delights of this divine conversation in the limited nature of this mortal existence. He urges his readers to continue to study this "oración escondida y mental" (36).

Bernardino opens the book proper with a "Prólogo responsorio." In the "Libro primero", chapter 1, he seeks to show his readers how they can "conocer su muy pobre estimación y la dignidad del ánima" (38). He suggests that our own presumption does not allow us to humbly know and understand God's generosity in creating us to be able to know ourselves and to be able to possess Him (40). Readers are encouraged to know themselves. Once this is done they will come to realize that they are imprisoned in such wretched material, from which the soul may be made to ascend to God since God created it for this very purpose; i.e., to rise above the material body. Bernardino, just as the other writers of affective spirituality, emphasizes the importance of love: "Sólo su amor hace al ánima racional hábil a gozar de las riquezas de Dios, para las cuales la crió; por esto le dió razón y capacidad en la cual le conociese, porque en conociéndolo no podría dejar de le amar" (41). The rational part of the soul has been given reason in order to be able to know God, and through this knowing, come to love Him (41). In chapter ii, "Que la vida de Cristo es cruz de Cristo", the reader learns that the way of the cross allows the individual to find glory in this desert. The glory of this life, according to Bernardino, is the contemplation of the life to come (42). The soul is exiled in this "muladar y en este valle abatida o abajada", but can later be lifted to contemplate God's riches. However, in order to reach the lofty heights of this mountain of contemplation, much effort is needed. Christ has left each one his experience on the cross to bring this to fruition. According to Bernardino, the cross of Christ consists in "menosprecio, dolor y pobreza, con humilde mansedumbre, y obediencia y caridad" (47). Christ's cross represents a spiritual lifestyle where one learns contempt for the things of this world, and learns to accept pain and poverty with humility, kindness, meekness, obedience and, most of all, charity. Bernardino declares: "Esta es nuestra cruz" (47). One must deny oneself and practice humility and this is accomplished through self-knowledge. In chapter iv, Bernardino teaches that without humility, "todo es nada" (47).

Bernardino establishes: ". . .el casado y el fraile hallará a Dios si lo busca con verdad." He asks everyone to recognize God in the smallest and unimportant creature: "no hay cosita por más mínima que sea, que no nos llame a ir a Dios y a nuestro conocimiento" (47). The smallest object of God's creation in nature can not only lead one to self-knowledge, but also to God. He adds that we are all part of creation, just as the ant, the lentil bean, the brick, and the tiniest blade of grass. In chapter 5, Bernardino presents the reader with a ladder of seventeen steps that the soul must ascend to reach temporal happiness (49). Some of these steps that involve the soul are what he calls, "conciencia apurada", or purified or cleansed conscience, which is a way of referring to the soul that is not preoccupied with temporal things; another step is the imitation of Christ (49). In chapter viii, Laredo writes that in order to enter through the door of the cross, or take up the cross, one must love. He describes this desire to find ways to love God:

> . . .y el medio para poder haber esto ("love for God") es quietísima
> oración, en la cual, y no sin ella, se sabe a qué sabe la conversación de
> Cristo, por la cual conversación entra el ánima a la divina presencia y
> permanece en quietud con su amantísimo Dios. (56)

The end of quiet contemplation is this perpetual possession of God. He describes this quiet contemplation of the recollected soul:

> . . .parece que el ánima recogida está delante de Dios y tanto más
> delante de él cuanto más recogida en sí está, y si siempre en sí está
> recogida, siempre está en presencia de su dulcísimo Dios por particular
> noticia. (57)

The more recollected the soul is, the more it will be in the presence of God through a particular "noticia", or special knowledge or knowing of God.

In the meditation of the first day of this first week, the readers are led to know themselves by pondering what they are, which is dirt (dust, *humus*) and this makes them wretched or vile ("harto astrosa") beings. In chapter xxii, the second day, exercitants are asked to consider the fact that they receive their being from God. Hence, Bernardino demonstrates how they go from the consideration of exterior things and pass on to interior ones, which is in effect what the soul will see inside of itself in spiritual recollection (63). Bernardino adds: "De manera que de las cosas que ha recibido este cuerpo pasemos a recogernos en las íntimas del ánima, y será pasar de las exteriores a las interiores, porque de aquestos de dentro suba el ánima a la parte superior", which is to contemplate God, "que es gozarse en su inmenso Señor Dios. . . sola a solas . . ." (64). One does not only look inside of one's soul when one is recollected, but rises to the highest part of the soul where one will enjoy the contemplation of God.[4] In chapter xiv, when individuals ask where they are, the answer is to be found in Thursday's meditation on the miseries of the exile which is life in this world where the soul is seen as being imprisoned in the body (68). Individuals are compared to exiled citizens of the heavenly city: "Pues yo soy el ciudadano desterrado en esta miserable isla de la presencia de mi rey y gran señor de la compañía de los justos que me esperan hasta que mi Dios me vuelva allá libre de aquesta custodia o de aqueste muladar de mi miserable cuerpo. La cárcel, esta carne, ya sentenciada a muerte" (69). He establishes the difference between the body and the soul, the latter of which has been created in God's image in that it is pure substance with distinct spiritual powers (70). He explains the soul's pure substance: ". . .esta substancia esencial a imagen de su Criador cuando se considera vivificador el ánima racional, llámase *ánima* y cuando vuelva a su Dios, llámase *espíritu* y cuando se quieta y reposa en él en pura y quietísima contemplación entonces se llama *mens*" (70). He also refers to the soul as "ánima animosa" and "ánimo" when it functions "esforzada fuertemente con rigurosa afición" (70). In chapter xxv, in Friday's exercise, the meditation reflects the end of sensual delights and the death of the physical body. Then, when the question is posed about where one will end up, the response is to the "tierra cenagosa", the muddy (mired) earth which is the end of riches and pleasures (71-72). The body returns to the dust from whence it was created (80). Thus, the reader will come to recognize the brevity of life and the fragile insignificance of the body.

Through this prayer of Recollection, God nourishes the soul in what Bernardino describes as an inner desert. One looks inward and goes inside of the soul, "desierta de las criaturas, y sin querer de ellas más de lo que dejar no puede" (88). He describes, "el escondido encerramiento del ánima en sí misma; pues dentro en sí tiene a su Dios" (88). As one begins the journey, Bernardino describes the provisions that the soul must take with it on the ascent to the mountain of contemplation. He refers to horses, bridles, reins, spurs, for these are the virtues that the soul must possess. The bridles are meant to silence so that one may not speak words that are not the truth; these will also assist one in keeping silence when unnecessary words are not appropriate. Chapter xx contains the material for the second Tuesday; Bernardino describes how one must pull in the reins of this, "desenfrenada bestia", or the unbridled beast which gives rein to the passions and physical desires. The reins that will bridle this beast are love and charity, and God is in fact charity: "y aqueste querer [con] que Dios vivo quiere amarse, porque es causa su bondad, siente que el ánima en quieta contemplación, que es la caridad de Dios en Dios es encendido fuego vivo" (91-92). Bernardino links this love for God with that of love for one's neighbor:

> . . .así que cuando el que posee a Dios ve al prójimo atribulado que
> aquella tribulación siente en sí y así se le compadece como si realmente
> lo poseyere sólo él. . .y el amor de Cristo y la caridad de Cristo hacen
> que aquello sienta el hombre en sí mismo. (92)

Those who possess God must also love their neighbors and feel compassion for their tribulations. Then, Bernardino offers this discussion on the controversial subject of predestination:

> . . .y tiene predestinados a la salvación eterna dende antes que criase el
> mundo a aquellos que él escogió y quiso que salvos fuesen, sabiendo su
> sabiduría infinita cuantos se habían de salvar y por cuáles buenas obras.
> (94)

God has predestined some to be saved from before the time that they were created. He adds: "Todos los que se salvan son escogidos de Dios, y todos los condenados son reprobados de Cristo y son desechados de Él" (94). This is a clear case of belief in the predestination of God's elect. It must be kept in mind that Bernardino's work is pre-Council of Trent and the Church's stance against the doctrine of predestination had not as of yet been formulated. He even goes on to write that God chooses whom He wishes and that He infuses in that person's soul the Christian virtues that please Him (95). He compares human beings to glasses into which God pours graces and virtues. He explains:

> Todas las ánimas cría en igual perfición cuanto al puro ser del ánima
> dejado aparte el aumento de las gracias que en los vasos que le place en

las ánimas que él quiere, cuando quiere y cómo quiere aumenta cuantos
bienes a él le place querer. (95)

In chapter xii, Thursday of the second week, Bernardino discusses "recogimiento
interior y exterior de la oración" (101). There are two parts or "corazones"
involved in Recollection: "interior recogimiento" and "concierto en lo exterior",
which implies the harmony of the body's parts and subjugation and obedience.
The harmonious function of the body not only involves subjection and obedience,
but spiritual poverty and contempt for worldly things, as well as charity and
humility (101). He adds that one's chair "silla" is "la reposada oración" and that
"la cabeza del ánima" is the "espíritu de la suave devoción que en su reposo se
llama "mens" (101).

In order to begin the ascent to God, one's life must be ordered ("vida
ordenada") and then the soul can be elevated ("ánima elelvada"). He describes the
process of Recollection once again here: "la ánima en la oración mental elevada
debe tener continuo recogimiento [que] es estar siempre el ánima dentro de sí"
(102). He discusses the process further as "estar fuera de toda criatura", "estar en
el Criador" and "estar el ánima encerrada en libertad recogida." Then, in his
discussion on prayer he makes the statement that, "no hay oración sin corazón
limpio", and also discusses the illumination of the soul when he writes that "la luz
de la eterna claridad que las ánimas reciben de Dios para conoscer a Dios" (102).
One cannot know God if the soul is not illuminated by Him. He continues with
the statement that the seat of our Christian knighthood is "reposada oración" and
the stirrups ("estribos") are patience and humility (106).[5] The ascent is perceived
by Bernardino as a type of knighthood, and Christ is the spiritual Captain. The
spurs for the soul which has set out on the ascent to God are filial love and fear of
God (109). The "caminantes" (journeymen or women) are guided by justice to
reach their destination, which is God.

The Second Part of the *Subida* deals with the mysteries of Christ's humanity.
In chapter i, Fray Bernardino presents the way in which one will contemplate the
profound mystery of the Incarnation as a fundamental element of the Christian
faith. He describes with beautiful images this mystery:

Del escondimiento oculto del secreto inacesible de esta inmensa y
coetánea Majestad nasce ab aeterno una fuente de agua viva la cual sale

del paraíso y siempre está dentro en ella en sí se es paraíso y riega el
huerto de todas las plantaciones. Establesce en tres ríos de eterna
divinidad. . .infinita potencia. . .sabiduría infinita. . .un todo en bondad
inmensa. (150)

According to him, this fountain of life has no beginning and this "piélago" has no
end (151). Christ is visualized as a living fountain with three rivers that flow into
an endless sea; the three rivers can also be perceived as the three persons of the
Trinity which is made up of a most simple substance. The soul in quiet repose
may drink of this fountain: ". . .con quieta simplicidad llega a beber a la fuente de
la fe, la esperanza, y caridad que Dios inmenso le dio gozarse sobre los ríos. .
.deja allí la fe, la esperanza y caridad" (153). The soul may enter into this "golfo
infinito" and "piélago de inmensidad", which is God (153).

This "contemplación alta" commences in the purest unity and passes on to the
immense perfection of the Trinity where the infinite sea is the immensity of God's
boundlessness, the river is Christ's sacred humanity, and the fountain is the source
of grace, which was once housed in the Virgin Mary's womb where God's word
was enclosed.[6] Chapter iii discusses the efficacy of the words of Christ's mother
and the perfect work that is Christ's Incarnation, when the "inaccessible Trinidad"
worked within Mary's womb and the Word became incarnate.[7] However, the
triune substance is never separated (162). Bernardino explains further that the
image of the fountain represents the divinity of Christ, and the river His humanity.
What astounds the imagination of the writer is how the immensity of God can be
made to fit and be poured into a tiny particle and enclosed in Mary's womb.[8] In
chapter viii, Bernardino explains how God's essence is in all of creation: "la
esencia divina da esencia a todo y todo ser criado es temporal, no es esencia
substancial, porque ha de perder su substancia" (169). He continues explaining
that God's most perfect essence exists within each person and it is in all of his
creation: "está Dios en sus criaturas por potencia, por presencia y por esencia"
(169). He continues: "Porque en este obscuro desierto las ánimas a su Dios
aficionadas luce en ellas en medio de estas tinieblas, la divina claridad con que su
Dios la alumbra" (170). God illuminates the human soul in the darkness of this
life. However, Bernardino goes on to explain that God's potential ("potencia")
exists in each blade of grass and in each flower: ". . .y en todo lo demás está la

divina potencia de Dios y la sabiduría de Dios, y la bondad de Dios y la esencia de Dios." God animates all of His creation; however, He enlightens the human soul.

The soul in contemplation, according to Bernardino, "se engolfa en Dios que no se sabe nombrar a sí misma sino que toda esté en Dios." In other words, the human soul looses itself in God's endless sea (178). He ends chapter xii with a discussion of the mystery of Christ's Nativity, and goes on in Chapter xiii to discuss the meditation on the Passion before a crucifix (201). Bernardino here recalls the mental prayer of St. Francis: "Oh alto y glorioso Dios. Alumbra las tinieblas de mi corazón y dame fe derecha, esperanza cierta y caridad perfecta, y conocimiento de Ti, Señor, así que yo haga el tu santo y verdadero mandamiento. Amén" (201). In chapter xiv, he demonstrates how one can meditate on our own wretched state, as well as the humanity of Christ and, "la quietud intelectual", which he describes as "contemplación quieta de las altezas de Dios incomprensible" (202). He offers five terms which are part of this spiritual ladder to Christian perfection; these are "lición" (devotional and meditative reading), "oración" (prayer), "meditación", "contemplación", and "espiritualidad", which is spiritual perfection or sharing in the life of God. He adds: "se entiende en esta escala que en tanto que el ánima en su contemplación, cuanto quiera que sea quieta, no se alza a la comunicación de las cosas intelectuales incorpóreas o sin cuerpo que no puedan ser habidas con sentidos corporales" (205). This contemplation must be achieved without the aid of bodily senses. The next few chapters deal with the agonies and suffering of Christ during the Passion. As a result of his previous medical training, Bernardino offers his readers a physiological description and analysis of the agony in the Garden of Gethsemani in chapter xxvii (206). He describes the event with an analysis of Christ's sweat and blood shed during the agony. Chapter 28 and 29 meditate on different passages that recount the Passion (215-33). These include meditations on the nailing to the cross, the suffering and pains suffered by Christ's mother at the foot of the cross. He also depicts the manner in which the reader should meditate on and adore the cross. In chapter xxxiii, he posits for meditation the three days which Christ spent after his death (237). He then presents the meditations on his death, the figures at the foot of the cross, Christ in the arms of his mother, the resurrected Christ, the scenes at the sepulcher and Christ in limbo (237). Chapter 35 includes a meditation on the joy that is the triumph of the Resurrection (243).

He discusses the glories of the blessed, the final resurrection and what he calls "las fábricas del paraíso" and "los tesoros de Dios" (243).

Chapter xxxvi deals with this "vista intellectual" which the soul experiences. He states that this intellectual vision (sight), "penetra la pared y los cielos y el infierno y en todas partes ve a Dios si tiene buenos antojos sin los cuales no le es posible ver bien" (249). He calls these "antojos de la vista intelectual", or the eyeglasses of the intellectual vision and the desires of one's free will. He adds that when the soul is freed of the body while it is in the exile of this life, it is lifted to God's presence: "goza a Dios y tiene y contempla a Dios cara a cara en aqueste gozar. . . es la gloria que los ángeles poseen" (252).[9] Bernardino then discusses this "centro sin circumferencia." He describes the center of an orange: "En una naranja es el centro el punto que es más el medio de ella de manera que, si las partes por medio y le pusiéredes un compás que dé vuelta igual, el punto que el compás torna en medio de la más interior parte de ella es el centro. . ." (255). God's immense incomprehensibility is the most perfect center, and no one has seen Him as He really is. Bernardino's conclusion is that if we are to know and contemplate God in this life, we must not do it with the human intellect, but with only the will which desires to enjoy God in contemplation (256). He then goes on to describe the soul's center: "El centro en nuestro hombre es el más oculto secreto y el más abscondido encerramiento de las entrañas del ánima racional" (257). Bernardino then begins to interpret the first words of the "Our Father" (*Pater Noster*). According to him, the just pray not only for the coming of God's kingdom on earth, but also for the blessedness of the life to come when they shall recuperate their bodies, and they will be perfected in glory (260). In Chapter xlii Bernardino discusses different spiritual treasures, which in fact are the virtues, the infinite treasure which is God who is the beginning and end of all (266). According to Bernardino, the virtues which enrich each individual's soul are: poverty of spirit, humility, obedience, a clean heart, charity and compassion for one's neighbor (266).

In Chapter xliv, Bernardino offers us a vivid and most beautiful description of how the soul is illuminated to come to know spiritual and incorporeal things. The subtitle for Chapter 46 reads: "Que pone la fábrica de la ciudad de Dios por tales comparaciones, que alzan el entendimiento y alegran el corazón." The beauties of the celestial city raise one's understanding and gladden the heart (270). He continues:

> . . .y procure de cercarle todo de un fino cristal, que piedra clara y preciosa. . .tome el entendimiento un campo de igual llaneza y de toda graciosura, y tal que puesta el ánima en medio de él, pueda verle del todo en todas partes en muy cuadrada igualdad. . .y en cada uno de los paños o piezas de aquel cuadrado, se han de levantar tres torres labradas en preciosa pedrería digo de gemmas preciosas con que aquesta cerca torreada haga cercada ciudad, y que sea *civitas sancta*, Jerusalén celestial cuyos muros está escrito que son de piedras preciosas. (268)

In Bernardino's "cuadro" or mental picture, there are four pieces of cloth and three towers. From each tower there should hang four golden shields. In the middle of this square, one should be able to see a small Paschal candle. This candle is meant to represent Christ's body and the wick represents the soul. By means of this candle's light, the soul's intellect is illuminated so that it may rise to the Trinity. The precious stones and glass in the celestial city all reflect the luminous light of the candle, for each stone shares and participates in the light of the other stones (271).[10] This is a beautiful image of the celestial city with its towers, castles and fortresses all pictured in the soul of the person in contemplation. This is what one will see in this "contemplación quieta." It is interesting to note that the Virgin Mary represents the door which leads to God. Christ is the candle through which one is illuminated in the celestial city, but Mary symbolizes the door by which one enters therein.

Finally, it is in the Third Part of the *Subida* that the soul is called to withdraw into itself in order to arrive at this silent or quiet contemplation. Bernardino tells his readers that they are laborers and the land to be cultivated and tilled is the physical body (298). Winter is the period of toil and work: "Los fríos os muestran las sequedades y falta de devoción; las lágrimas ya está dicho que son las lluvias, el revolver de la tierra es vuestra aniquilación en la quietud y la alegría de nuestro espíritu cogeréis en este tercero libro lo que en el primero y segundo sembrar en lágrimas" (298-99). This Third Book is in effect compared to a type of spiritual harvest where the quiet sterility of winter, the rains which are one's tears, and the toils of tilling the land, bring an abundant harvest for the soul. It is in chapter 1 that Bernardino outlines the three stages of the inner, secret or mystical way to reach God. The first part of the Third Book is in fact the Purgative Way, the second is the Illuminative, and in the third part, the soul will rise to the Unitive Way, which is "la unión o juntamiento del ánima con Dios", and this is brought about "por atadura de amor", which is a bond of love (299). He describes his work *Subida* as the gradual ascent of the soul by means of purging it and also through its being enlightened. This third and last stage is described once again as the soul having ascended to the top of the mountain of quiet contemplation, which Bernardino describes as the "cumbre del monte Sión" where union takes place (300). Bernardino claims that this contemplation is an act of the highest perfection, which is why it is called mental prayer and is associated with Sion translated as "atalaya" (watchtower).

In chapter xv of this section, Bernardino refers to Richard of St. Victor's *De arca mystica* where this Medieval writer of spirituality defines speculation and contemplation. It is interesting that the word speculation is derived from the Latin *speculum* (mirror) for it is a looking into the mirror, which is the creature through which one can see God; whereas in contemplation the soul is lifted to God by love. The person in contemplation meditates on God directly without any "envolvimiento o nublado u obscuridad. . .absoluta, pura y momentáneamente se quiete el ánima en Dios por puro y desnudo amor" (303). According to Bernardino, God's fire will be found in Zion, "porque las ánimas contemplativas lo poseen en esta vida." The love for God will situate each soul in the celestial city, which is the heavenly Jerusalem (304). God's fire inflames the soul in love, and as a consequence, it will fly to him burning with love in order to find spiritual repose. He explains this phenomenon further: ". . .y el mismo espíritu que ha volado, cuando se reposa en quieta contemplación, llámase mente y de aguí viene que la contemplación quietísima y reposada, y muy pura llámase oración mental que quiere decir oración de sola el ánima en su pura substancia esencial, ajena de sus potencias inferiores" (305). In other words, in mental prayer the soul contemplates God in its purest essence, having freed itself of its inferior powers. Bernardino describes this prayer of Recollection in this manner: "el ánima encerrada en su quietud, no entendiendo en lo que contempla está empleada en sólo amor, no sabe entender en aquel su esencial encerramiento otra cosa sino amor" (306). He refers to "recogimiento" as "esencial encerramiento", or a retreat enclosing the essential elements of the soul).[11]

Bernardino in chapter vii teaches one how to seek Christian perfection as well how to recollect the soul: "Quédanos de aquí visto que mucha perfección del contemplativo está en el más estrecho encerramiento del ánima dentro en sí misma" (321). The soul has reached the final or third period of spirituality, which is in effect Christian perfection. In chapter viii he describes, "cuán grandes bienes están en el sosiego del ánima en silencio de potencias"; i.e., the repose (tranquillity, peacefulness) of the soul and the silence of the soul's powers (322). In the third or perfective phase of the spiritual journey to God, individuals find themselves raised to the top ("cumbre") of the spiritual mountain, and once there it may rest in hidden (secret) silence ("escondido"). Alone on the top of the mountain of contemplation, the soul is completely tranquil and at peace fully prepared to enjoy the vision of God (or Christ) in intimate solitude and secret silence or repose. This silence is not the silence of words, but the silencing of the intellect together with the stillness or quietness of the will (323). This knowledge is secret, that is, it is a secret knowing (science) that God infuses into the soul that encloses itself in this spiritual stillness.[12] Bernardino explains this secret knowledge of divine contemplation: ". . .el ánima por divino enseñamiento es alzada súbitamente a se ayuntar por amor, por vía de sola afectiva, a su amantísimo Dios sin que intervenga medio de algún pensamiento ni de natural razón" (325). The soul's only power or function in this secret knowing is situated in the will or desire for God, who is the one fully operating in this spiritual process. It is love that lifts the soul to unite with God.[13]

Bernardino then describes the "sabiduría" to which he had previously made reference: "La sabiduría de que hablamos es un conocimiento muy alto de Dios el cual es conocido por modo de no saber, según el ayuntamiento de la voluntad siendo apartada de todas las cosas criadas" (329). He refers to it as "aquesta sabiduría ascondida", which raises (lifts) the will to God without the mediation of the intellect or without the use of natural reason (329). In Chapter xxii Bernardino refers to "los dos ojos del ánima", and explains divine reason as well as the expression "afectiva", which involves the role of the affections and, most especially, that of love. This mental prayer of Recollection is an ascent of the soul by means of the affections: love, hope, desire. The soul's will is moved by love alone, and the eyes of the soul are in fact the will and the intellect (330-31). Through the intellect or understanding, the soul sees as through a mirror and also sees God through all of his creation (speculation). The second eye with which the soul sees God is the will, and through it the soul can see God without seeing any creatures, for the will contemplates God directly. Bernardino here explains a term that is very important to the inner spirituality of Recollection, and this is "sindéresis" or "sintéresis", which he defines as "atención viva, entera y levantada al soberano bien, por largo uso acostumbrada" (331). Others describe this as the highest or essential part or function of the soul.

In chapter xxvii, Bernardino also refers to this "ciencia" as "sabiduría sabrosa." The soul inflamed in love rests in God as it relies on nothing that concerns its own efforts. It is rendered thus solely by God's goodness; through this goodness the soul is led through the "vía de aspiración", or the path or way of the strong desire (love) for an ultimate achievement, which is union with God. The "sueño de las potencias" (silence of the soul's powers) awakens the soul to begin the flight or spiritual journey powered by pure love (346). This process of unitive love is compared to the work of the bees and the flowers. Bernardino writes:

> . . .teniendo el entendimiento hallada la verdad, vuelve luego a su
> colmena, esto es, a se recoger en la substancia del ánima. En aqueste su
> recogimiento entiende sin ruido lo que cogió y aquello que
> comprehendiendo entiende, tómalo la voluntad, y así como en un panal,
> lo coge y lo sella y en la memoria lo guarda. (351)

In chapter xxii, he demonstrates how the soul's powers are recollected and the soul is lifted up to God (357).

The soul is always being described with a dual function in the process of recollecting itself. One is "recogerse dentro de sí mismo." Another is recollecting its powers beyond or above (outside) of itself, which is "recogerese fuera de sí" (357). Sometimes the soul is recollected in order to contemplate God in its most profound essence or center, or it rises above itself to find God: "el ánima haga ir fuera de sí misma para buscar a su Dios muy cierto es que está nuestro Dios dentro de vuestra ánima y que para buscarlo conviene entraros dentro de vos" (357). Whether the powers of the soul are gathered in or gathered up, the point is that this takes place within individuals' souls. This is the crucial element of this inner spirituality to reach God. This process also is compared to the action of turtles and sea-urchins:

> Un erizo, o una tortuga, o galápago son animales que se encierran dentro en sí, y cuando están encerrados obran guardando su vida en muy callada quietud, y nadie los ve en lo interior. (359)

This is equivalent to the "ánima recogida y que ha hecho reflexión de sus potencias a sí misma" (359). In chapter xxiv, Bernardino describes God's gifts which true contemplation brings to the soul. These are an interior (inner) peace and tranquillity, for the soul pays no attention to anything that is not God. Other spiritual gifts received through contemplation are wisdom, intelligence, and knowledge ("sapiencia", "inteligencia", and "ciencia") (363). These are received in an aura of delightful enjoyment so that the soul may place its attention in quiet recollection to "los toques de amor", or strokes of love (364). He distinguishes between ordinary contemplation and pure contemplation, in which the soul feels or knows pure, unitive love. Each person's soul knows this love, not through acquired grace ("gracia adquirida o adquisitiva"), but through infused grace ("gracia infundida") (366). In addition to this, Bernardino in chapter xxvi presents four types of love: "amor operativo", "amor desnudo", "amor esencial" and "amor unitivo."[14] This fourth or unitive love is part of the third or unitive phase and it belongs to those who are perfected in the Christian life.

Bernardino goes on to describe the phenomenon of this unitive love which, "hace juntamento del que ama y del que es amado" (369). He describes this union of love as "atacamiento de gracia" or union of grace: "el ánima que desea infundirse y transformarse en el abismo y infinto amor increado es menester ser trasmudada en amor, y que este amor vaya al centro donde salió, a su Dios" (369). The soul is fused with or is engulfed in the infinite sea which is God: "quiere decir que el amado así se pierde de sí, que no queda nada de él por la infinidad del amor en quien hace su infusión" (370). In the last few chapters, Bernardino describes this mental prayer and pure contemplation, where the individual does not think anything at intervals but does at times pray aloud. However, mental prayer is superior to vocal prayer, as we have seen in other writers of this form of spirituality. He explains: "porque en aquesta quietud está más pronta la atención mediante la cual alcanza el ánima orando las cosas que pide con toda la humildad a nuestro benigno Dios" (375). It is a more simple and pure form of prayer as well as more "trascendente." Finally, perfect or pure contemplation is accompanied by the virtues of piety, charity, and love as well as humility in the memory of Christ (ch. 30-33).

Bernardino devotes the next few chapters to the importance of frequent communion and closes his work with a series of "versos del amor." For example, "Verso" I reads: "El que con amor trabaja / holgando gana ventaja" (410), "Verso" II, "Si quiere siempre holgar, nunca deje de amar" (410), "Verso" III reads: "El gusto del vero amor / en todo tome sabor" (411). He reminds readers that one of the names that the Pseudo-Dionysius uses to refer to God is indeed love. We end this discussion of Bernardino de Laredo with a quote from "Verso" IX: "El amor, si mucho dura / él sólo en sí se asegura" (415). Love is like a gentle lamb whose rest is only in God: "Es como un cordero manso, y en Dios sólo es su descanso" (417).[15] This love lifts the soul to unite with God which is its ultimate repose ("descanso"), for it is like a wounded dear seeking solace. Bernardino concludes that contemplation never reaches its perfection until it "cuadra en sosegada quietud", which is that it rests in peaceful repose or peaceful calm (427).

The next writer of the inner way of Recollection is not very well known. However, he wrote a spiritual tract called *Breve summa llamada sosiego y descano del ánima*, which presents an early and brief outline of the spirituality of Recollection. His name is Francisco de Fuensalida, and this treatise was published in 1541 at Alcalá de Henares, an important center of the Spanish reform movement.[16] In the prologue to the 1947 edition, the editor writes about Fuensalida's role in the reform of Spanish pedagogy, and about his humanism within the Erasmian school of thought (Fuensalida vi-vii). Fuensalida was also a teacher of Latin in Avila. This brief treatise is not an educational tract, but a treatise that belongs within the category of religious asceticism (ix). Fuensalida's purpose for writing it was also to bring some order to people's conduct with novel precepts and norms, which were set forth by a layperson instead of a religious. Fuensalida shows the reader that true Christian perfection and supreme wisdom consist in looking within oneself, which is in fact the way of Recollection. Although the book is an ascetical treatise, it is important to note that in Fuensalida we have a layperson who is attempting a reform from a lay perspective. He aims to demonstrate the way individuals can reform themselves by looking inward in spiritual recollection: "morar dentro de sí y recogerse consigo mismo" (ix). It is in this inward looking that individuals may ultimately reach a state of spiritual contentment and inner peace ("aquietamiento interior") (ix).

This is how the editor of the religious tract describes Fuensalida's process:

> . . .a este estado se llega, según el maestro abulense, por todo un largo proceso que comienza en el recogimiento del ánimo, que ordena la vida, hácela real y no fingida, afronta sin miedo sus adversidades y dolores, conténtase con lo que posee, no se deja deslumbrar en los tiempos de la prosperidad; da reglas seguras para combatir la tristeza y melancolía, rehuye la vanagloria, y tras de enfrentarse por último con la muerte se abraza con aquellos dos bienes supremos de la vida por todo varón que se sienta fuerte y superior a los demás; la soledad y la pobreza. (ix-x)

Here the inner path of Recollection is advocated for the reform and perfection of each individual; this Christian perfection is solidified by poverty and solitude. The prologue informs us that one of the most important influences on Fuensalida is Seneca's stoicism, which involves the renunciation of all of the vanities of the world which can also be attained through the contemplation of nature (x).

This prologue also alludes to social solidarity, which the author terms a modern idea. This "solidaridad social" unites all in the society so that it may benefit the common good, which will also have the effect of transforming the lives of everyone into servants of this common good. The editor adds: "Este librillo es como un código de buen vivir como arte de filosofía moral y estoica para que el hombre pueda caminar seguro y sereno por esa larga y triste peregrinación, que es su existencia" (x). The book is in essence a code of good conduct, which employs the process of Recollection for the advancement of the common good. In the dedications of the book we read: "Al muy Illustre y muy Magnífico Marqués de las Navas, y señor de la Casa de Villa Franca. Su servidor y capellán, Francisco de Fuensalida, profesor de latín en la muy noble ciudad de Avila" (7). In this dedication he presents to the Marqués de las Navas the idea that one of the things that is necessary for a happy life on earth is the attainment of peace and the security of the soul. He calls his short work a "libro manual" that offers advice in an agreeable and as he calls it sweet manner (8).

He opens his first chapter with a discussion of "recogimiento del ánima." This chapter contains the following heading: "Tracta del recogimiento del ánimo, como principal fundamento" (8). It is fascinating to note that the fundamental premise of learning how to "buen vivir" in society is the recollection of the soul. He also explains: "Como la fuente de nuestro ser y obrar sea el ánimo ante todas las cosas debes procurar que él en sí tenga sosiego, esté tan libre de comunes opiniones y vulgares y tan desencadenado de las cosas" (9). In this passage Fuensalida refers to the soul which must unfetter itself of all things in order to achieve true peace. He adds that the appetites must be subjected to reason, for it must be reined in and recollected constantly. He subsequently promotes the meditation on death and life's brevity and the vanity of all created things (10). He then advises that one must conquer the appetites in order to have control over the passions. Fuensalida dedicated chapter ii to how one must carry on in life as well as in one' affairs. Everyone must learn to examine oneself in one's profession and business as well as in one's station in life. Individuals must ask themselves why they have chosen a certain profession or station in life. In addition, the teacher encourages everyone to know themselves.

In chapter iii, he emphasizes that one's life must have a certain order to it. It must have certainty, security and peace, for it is important to him that one not change one's purpose and station periodically. One's life must have a clear direction with few deviations: ". . .hombres mudables y que siempre querrán nueva manera de vivir. . .todo les da enojo, el servir, el mandar, tener mujer, los hijos . . . "(13). These people live an unhappy and unsettled way of life. Fuensalida claims that each person's business and work should have a definite end or goal. In chapter iv, he presents the order that each one must follow in life. One should accustom oneself to different manners of living one's life; for example, alternating solitude and conversation with others, work and the necessity for honest recreation (15). Each individual must learn how to live by imitating nature. Fuensalida teaches that nature places before each one of us two qualities. Rational beings use their reason and this is common to each person; the other is particular to each individual because some persons are sad, others are serious and again others are recollected ("recogidos"). In chapter vi, he admonishes each person to practice the virtues of prudence and patience when faced with life's trials and adversities (20). He asks his readers to imitate God's patience and humility and adds that life must be perceived as service: "En fin, toda la vida si miras es un servicio y por eso cada uno debe darse buena manera en su estado y procurar tener contento en él, y lo malo que hay con el desimularlo, y recoger y aprovecharse del bien. . ."(21). He advises his readers to be happy in their station in life, and to find a way to serve within the social and religious parameters (22). In fact, chapter vii opens with this heading: "Que debemos vivir contentos en el estado que tenemos" (24). This is part of the "conocimiento de sí mismo" where individuals come to know themselves.

Chapter viii treats the subject of what his readers must do in times of prosperity, which can be fraught with danger for the well-being of the soul (29). He writes that in times of prosperity each one should act with justice, liberality and meekness (30). In chapter ix he then proceeds to discuss how one must act in times of adversity. He writes that only the body is subject to the wiles of fortune: ". . .y las partes nuestras que pertenecen a la virtud ninguna cosa puede vencer sin nuestro mandamiento o consentimiento" (33). Fortune can make individuals poor or it can exhaust them and even place them in a certain locality, position, job or station in life; however, it should not diminish each person's virtues neither should it make one weak, mean, envious, etc. It should not affect the virtues which the soul possesses. He adds:

> . . .y desta manera fueron los trabajos de los justos, los cuales por
> ásperos que fuesen, pero por la bondad de Dios estaban tan
> acompañados de consolaciones y humilde paciencia que era mayor al
> deleite y consolación que con ellas recebían que la pesadumbre y fatiga
> que les daban. (35)

Fuensalida concludes that virtue will bring more peace to the soul than riches. He also claims that one of the riches that the good person possesses is of supreme value, and this in fact is the inner path of Recollection:

> el cual entre otros bienes que tiene, tiene uno que es mucho mayor, osar
> morar dentro de sí y recogerse consigo mismo, porque la virtud en
> cualquier estado es el premio de sí misma. . .el virtuoso en sus

adversidades tiene más descanso y contentamiento que el vicioso en su prosperidad, fatigado y acosado de la mala conciencia. (35)

He promotes the act of "desembarazar el ánimo" (disengage the soul) allowing it to enjoy or delight in spiritual things and to come to the knowledge of God (36).

In chapter xii ("De la muerte") he discusses death as he tries to teach his readers to live as if they possess nothing including life itself. Life is seen as something which is on loan to each one and it can be easily lost or taken away at any given moment. In chapter xiv, Fuensalida writes about the vices which afflict the soul of the good person. Life's afflictions, according to him, have inspired many to seek solitude and peace in the desert, where they have also found joy in this peacefulness. Fuensalida discusses the virtues of patience in adversity (ch. xv), the types of people that one should select for conversation (ch. xvi), and then goes on to discuss arrogance and vanity (ch. xvii). He closes his work with another pitch for Recollection: "En todas maneras es gran medio estar el hombre recogido así en obras como en pensamiento, porque cuando viniere tempestad de fortuna mejor te hallará cogidas las velas" (57-58). Although Fuensalida mentions spiritual Recollection, this is purely a physical separation from the trials and afflictions of life in order to become more virtuous. It is a more practical Recollection meant for a lay readership. Fuensalida does not describe the gathering-in of the soul's spiritual powers nor the contemplation of God in unitive love, even though he does write that individuals can better come to know God and spiritual things by withdrawing into themselves. It is Recollection for the layperson which can be used as a tool to fight life's trails, as well as ward off the vices of the soul. What is interesting is that Francisco de Fuensalida, a lay school teacher, composes a guidebook to assist in the way one conducts one's life and to attempt to reform society from within beginning with the individual.

Pedro de Alcántara (1499-1562) is the next writer of spirituality which we shall study, and he is also one of the earlier and most important contributors to the literature of Recollection with his important work called *Tratado de oración y meditación* (1557-58). This treatise should not be confused with Luis de Granada's work which has a similar title. Pedro de Alcántara also belonged to the Franciscan Order and formed part of the reform of that order. Alcántara was not only a religious writer and reformer, but he was also a great preacher who lived an exemplary life. He was educated at Salamanca and became involved with the reform of the Franciscan Order in Castile and also in Extremadura. He ultimately retired to live in a solitary place in the mountains near Arábida, where he established what he referred to as a "custodia", which was a group of friars under the direction of a "custos" (guardian). These "custodias" were inhabited by very austere, contemplative Franciscans who practiced the spirituality of Recollection as their particular lifestyle. In 1556 Alcántara withdrew to complete his contemplative retirement ("recogimiento") to a place near Badajoz, where he wrote the above mentioned spiritual treatise. It is a devotional tract dedicated to the exercise of inner prayer and meditation; in fact, it is a guide to an inner spiritual life which was inspired by Osuna's *Tercer abecedario espiritual*. We shall discuss in the remainder of this chapter the portions of the tract which deal directly with Recollection, the spiritual processes of mental prayer, meditation and contemplation, which are other manifestations of this special mode of spirituality.[17] Moreover, Alcántara is also known for being Teresa de Jesus's spiritual mentor.

We have opted to use Dominic Devas's 1949 translation of the *Tratado de oración* into English, which seems to be the more recent one. Devas informs us that Pedro was born in Alcántara where his father was governor, and that he studied at the university of Salamanca. For thirteen years Alcántara was engaged in an active apostolic life and was involved in a good deal of preaching (Alcántara, *Treatise* i). He also occupied himself in the work of reform and in Pedroso he build his ideal convent based on the strictest poverty.[18]

In the dedication composed for Rodrigo de Chaves we read: "This cheap and slender volume will be accessible even to the poor who cannot buy more expensive books and, being written clearly, will profit the simple who are not rich in understanding" (xiii). In Part I, ch. i Alcántara describes the fruit that one may draw from what he calls spiritual exercises in the path of virtues to attain one's end. He quotes from Paul's Epistle to the Romans vii, 22.23, where it says, "I am delighted with the Law of God, according to the inward man." He adds that in order to assist in fighting the evil inclination of the heart, and the difficulty and disinclination to do what is right, one needs devotion: "Devotion", as St. Thomas says (II a IIae, q. 82.a.I) is nothing else than a certain promptitude and facility in well-doing, which banishes from our soul all difficulty and heaviness and makes us prompt and ready to undertake all that is good. It is a spiritual nourishment, a refreshment, a dew from heaven, a breath wafted to us from the Holy Spirit, a supernatural affection" (Alcántara, *Treatise* 4). He goes on to describe devotion as something which regulates, strengthens and transforms the heart of individuals and gives them a "new taste and keenness for sensual things" (4). By means of contemplation and meditation on divine things, there is engendered an affection and sentiment in the soul's will, which Alcántara calls devotion. According to him, this urges the individual to do good.

In chapter ii, Alcántara divides the subject matter of meditation into groups following the Creed. There are two sets of meditations for each day of the week on these essential mysteries of the faith outlined in the Apostles' Creed: one is to be carried out in the morning, and the second in the evening. He also refers to "two repasts", or spiritual nourishment to be derived from meditation on the Passion, Death and Resurrection, as well as on the other mysteries represented in that public prayer (8). He advises individuals to recollect themselves twice per day in order to more effectively meditate on these mysteries (9). Alcántara then presents the first series of meditations for each day of the week; on Monday, the meditation is on sin and knowledge of self. Alcántara writes that "this is the way to win humility, the mother of all virtues" (9). He asks his readers to reflect on the Ten Commandments, on the seven deadly sins, on the five senses, and on how these have been used or misused. In relation to sin, he posits the following questions: "against whom? In what way? and Why?" He then asks individuals to meditate on their own nothingness and to consider themselves in the lowest esteem (12-13).

Tuesday's meditation includes a reflection on the miseries of this life and the vanity of the glories attained in this life. In addition, he includes a meditation on the brevity and uncertainty of this life with all of its frailties and changes of fortune. On Wednesday, he guides the individual on the meditation on death and on Thursday, the Final Judgment, fear of God and hatred for sin (15-25). Friday's meditation describes the pains of hell: "This dreadful abode gives rise to two principal kinds of pain: that which is called the pain of sense, and also the pain of loss" (30). He also focuses on the eternity of suffering (33). On Saturday, he advises individuals to meditate on heaven and the glory of the blessed, so that they may be moved to feel contempt for this world. He describes the excellence of the place, the bliss, the vision of God, the body in its glory, and the complete gathering together of every good thing (34). On this same meditation for Sunday, the individual is taught to meditate on the benefits of God, which are the creation, conservation, redemption, vocation, and all personal and hidden favors which include the powers of the soul (35-39).

Alcántara adds on Sunday's meditation that individuals should learn to better appreciate what they owe Christ for all that he has suffered. He asks them to consider four principal points that are part of the mystery of the Passion. Once again, he does this in the form of questions with their answers: "Who suffers and what does he suffer?, the greatest torments and dishonor. For whom does he suffer, and why?, because of his love and mercy" (40). In chapter iv, he presents his readers with seven meditations on the Passion, and the specific method to be employed. The seven meditations include the Passion, Death, Resurrection and Ascension of Christ (44). He then describes this meditation using a method that predates the Ignatian composition of place:

> It is fitting, moreover, in all these mysteries, to consider Christ as
> present before our eyes, and ourselves as there with him in his
> sufferings and not merely to think of the history of the Passion as a
> whole, but all the circumstances of it. . . (46)

The next week's meditation includes seven meditations on the Passion: Monday, the washing of the feet and the institution of the Eucharist; Tuesday, the Prayer in the Garden, the Arrest and the Events before Annas. He takes readers on to Friday where they are guided in the meditation on the Crucifixion and on the Seven words (72-73).[19] Saturday's meditation is on the piercing with the lance, the descent from the cross, and, finally, the Ascension (73).

Alcántara then goes on to describe the six parts that comprise the exercise of prayer; one is the reading of devotional literature, where the intellect and the will are applied. After these passages, readers will find the meditation on what has just been read (88-89). Alcántara describes what he calls intellectual meditation which employs the understanding, and imaginative meditation which involves the bringing to the imagination of the scenes from the life of Christ. He writes: "When the meditation is imaginative we must figure each detail as it actually exists, or actually happens and must consider it as taking place in the very spot where we are and in our presence" (90). He adds that this meditation must take place within the soul where the love for God is born as a result of this meditation. Alcántara also offers the reader special prayers for the love of God, one of which reads as follows:

> Oh, thou art all my hope and all my glory, my refuge, my whole joy. O best beloved of all: spouse emblossomed honest and sweet. O Sweetness of my heart, life of my soul, joyous resting place of my spirit! O day of eternity, beautiful and bright, my innermost light serene, flowering paradise of my heart; . . .Make ready, O my God, more ready Lord, a pleasant dwelling place within me for thyself? (98)

Well within the mainstream of this inner and affective manifestation of spirituality, Alcántara offers a certain amount of guidance for the successful completion of this exercise. The second of these "consejos" reads:

> That one should strive to avoid in this holy exercise an excessive use of the speculative intellect endeavoring to treat the matter in hand with the affections and sentiments of the will rather than with speculative reasonings of the intellect. (104)

Also in consonance with other developers of the inner way of Recollection, Alcántara counsels the complete cancellation of the function of the understanding in order to entrust this operation to the will.

In the sixth "consejo", Alcántara advises that anything less than an hour and a half or two hours is a short amount of time to assign to this spiritual exercise (108-10). In his eighth counsel, which he considers the most important, he concludes: "one should endeavor in this holy exercise to mingle meditation with contemplation, making of the one a ladder whereby to mount to the others" (112). In this chapter, we are concerned with the development of the art of Recollection foremost as the way and means to exercise oneself spiritually, meditate, contemplate and form a unitive bond with God. In the section on the fruit of meditation through which one comes to a familiarity with God's attributes, and also to the knowledge of the divine essence through faith Alcántara adds: "Let him busy himself in the very centre of his soul, where is the image of God and therein he will come to know his attributes, and to taste of his divine sweetness" (115-17).

Part II of his treatise deals with the art of devotion, which makes "a man ready for every good work" (121). In Chapter ii of Part II, he presents to the reader five aids for securing devotion, one of which reads: "The contemplative soul should be as one deaf, blind and dumb for the less he dissipates his energies abroad the more will he be recollected within himself" (126). In the inner way of Recollection, it is known that the soul's spiritual powers are concentrated or recollected in the essence of the soul, and thus are not dissipated in the corporeal part of the person. He adds that one should be inclined toward a solitary life (126). He invites the person to "enter more into himself, and to occupy himself alone with God." While alone, individuals should make a practice of reading spiritual and devotional books from which they may cull the material for meditation. He also advises austerity and bodily abstinence, "a poor table, a hard bed, hair-shirt, and discipline" (127). Most importantly, he counsels the practice of works of mercy. In chapter iii, he presents the various hindrances which will impede devotion, which are venial and mortal sins (129). Other things that will prevent the partaking of God's sweetness and the development of a good conscience and spiritual joy are what he calls the pleasures of worldly consolations including the delicacy and over-abundance of food and drink, in addition to intellectual curiosity. Chapter iv presents the temptations and the ways to combat against them as well as the lack of spiritual consolation. Alcántara once again offers readers advice on how to ward off temptations and guides them on how to examine their consciences. He reminds the reader not to make too much of these temptations because sin involves consent (135). Some of the temptations mentioned include importunate thoughts, blasphemy, infidelity, an excessive tendency to sleep, diffidence and presumption, an immoderate desire to study and to gain secular knowledge. Alcántara posits in chapter v certain counsels necessary for those who give themselves to prayer, which he calls an intercourse with God.

This intercourse with God will bring each person a wonderful sweetness that surpasses all others (142). He adds that the purpose of spiritual reading is to secure God's favor and to experience his kindness (143). Alcántara counsels that visions, revelations, and ecstasies in this prayer may be dangerous if not founded in the virtue of humility. He then presents a brief instruction meant for those who are just beginning to serve God. He determines that this interior life can only be maintained by means of spiritual exercises. He then posits three things that should be practiced by one who wishes to advance in the spiritual life in a relatively short time. The first is austerity and mortification of the flesh accompanied by temperance, discipline, fasting. and the guidance of a spiritual director.[20] The second thing is for the person to be intent upon the interior mortification of self by exercising interior and exterior virtue, and the third is to be increasingly intent upon prayer (161-62). The main purpose of these practices is the reformation of a person in soul, mind, and body (163). They lead to the life of a perfect Christian in prayer and in work, as part of the contemplative life and the active life (165). The aim of Alcántara's treatise on prayer and meditation is the reform of individuals' souls, minds, and bodies, so that they may lead a life of Christian perfection, which will be manifest in private prayer and public works. These meditative practices will also enhance the attainment of interior and exterior virtues, which assist the person in meeting all responsibilities to family, neighbor, community, and the society at large.

Before we discuss another Franciscan, Juan de los Angeles who is the culmination of the literature of Recollection, we shall deal here with the two most important Spanish mystics since one of them was a disciple of Pedro de Alcántara. It is necessary that we place Teresa de Jesús and Juan de la Cruz in their proper perspective within the inner path of Recollection, for they have also contributed to the literature of Recollection. In the introduction to Kieran Kavanaugh's and Otilio Rodriguez's translation of *The Collected Works of St. Theresa of Avila*, Vol. 2, we read about the suspicion that this inner way of Recollection aroused in the Spanish Church:

> The Spanish people in general were officially taught to follow the "level" and "safe" paths of both the ascetical life and vocal prayer and to shun the extraordinary ways of mysticism, especially its accessory phenomena of locutions, visions, and revelations. (Kavanaugh 10)

It is important to keep in mind that the Illuminists and Erasmists also practiced mental prayer while shunning ascetical practices and disciplinary exercises, together with vocal prayers. Many theologians including the Dominican Melchor Cano feared that the practice of mental prayer would plant the seeds of Protestantism in the very center of Spain.[21] As her predecessors had done, Teresa de Jesús defends mental prayer, but at the same time emphasizes the importance of vocal prayer. Both are part of the process which leads to perfect contemplation and ultimate union.[22]

Teresa de Jesús contributed to the Spanish reform by organizing the reformation of the female convents of the Carmelite Order. The hermits of antiquity who spent their days in solitude and contemplation on Mount Carmel were one of her inspirations (Kavanaugh 26). The rule for the Carmelite mendicants was approved in 1247 and was meant to "emphasize the practice of solitude through enclosure and withdrawal from the world. . ." (26). Kavanaugh and Rodríguez inform us in their introduction to the *Way of Perfection* that this work is a practical book of advice and counsel destined to initiate the Carmelite nun into the life of prayer (28). It is crucial that the individual have peace in order to lead a life of prayer. Also, the person must learn to love her neighbor and practice humility for the "happy result of detachment is inner freedom, freedom from worry about bodily comfort, honor, and wealth" (36). Teresa's method of prayer involves discursive meditation and the prayer of Recollection, where as we have already seen in so many cases, "the soul collects its faculties together and enters within itself to be with its God" (32). However, it is important to note that in all of the writers who outline and promote the prayer of Recollection, and Teresa is one of these, it is always accompanied by vocal prayer (33). Kavanaugh adds: "At times during the prayer, the soul will feel a passive quieting and be drawn gradually to a greater silence", which is called the prayer of quietness or silence. Finally, in what is called the prayer of union, all the faculties of the soul come to rest in inner silence (34).[23]

In chapter iv of the *Camino de perfección*, Teresa presents her rule on prayer wherein she counsels her nuns on the importance of the ascetical practices: ". . . que es lo más importante, no se dejaran de complir los ayunos y disciplinas y silencio que manda la Orden, porque ya sabéis que para ser la oración verdadera se ha de ayudar con esto, que regalo y oración no se compadece."[24] She subsequently adds: "Amemos las virtudes y lo bueno interior y siempre con estudio tráiganos cuidado de apartarnos de hacer caso de esto exterior" (Teresa 664). In chapter viii, Teresa discusses how one must "desasirse de lo criado interior y exteriormente" (684). She begins to explain to her sisters in chapter xvi what mental prayer is without forgetting the practice of the virtues (714-15). She writes: "Digo que no vendrá el Rey de la gloria a nuestra alma—digo a estar unido con ella—si no nos esforzamos a ganar las virtudes grandes" (715). She continues by explaining that humility is the "ejercico principal de oración" (719). She adds that God does not lead everyone in the path to spiritual perfection (720). This implies that everyone that enters into this mental prayer cannot reach contemplation. Teresa distinguishes between "oración mental" and other forms of prayer such as "oración vocal", "lección" and "coloquios con Dios" (724). Those who cannot perform mental prayer can take part in other forms of prayer common to Recollection.

Teresa reiterates the crucial place that humility has in mental prayer as well as in the active life.: "así, los contemplativos han de llevar levantada la bandera de la humildad y sufrir cuantos golpes les dieren sin dar ninguno, porque su oficio es padecer como Cristo, llevar en alto la cruz, no la dejar de las manos por peligros en que se vean, ni que vean en él flaqueza en padecer, para eso le dan tan honroso oficio" (725). Teresa refers to "tantos libros escritos y tan buenos y de personas tales. . .tenéis libros tales adonde van por días de la semana repartidos los misterios de la vida del Señor y de su Pasión y meditaciones del juicio e infierno y nuestra nonada. . . "(728). In effect, she is referring to the devotional books such as Luis de Granada's *Libro de la oración y meditación* and Pedro de Alcántara's *Tratados de la oración y contemplación*, which had already been recommended to the nuns of her convents in *Constituciones* 1:13. She adds: "Quien pudiere y tuviere ya costumbre de llevar este modo de oración, no hay que decir que por tan buen camino el Señor le sacara a puerto de luz, y todos los que puedieren ir por él llevaran descanso y seguridad porque, atado el entendimiento vase con descanso" (728). Once again, we can see how the intellect ties the soul down and, encumbered by it, cannot rise peacefully to its end which is God. Teresa offers this advice to her nuns:

> No os espantéis, hijas, de las muchas cosas que es menester mirar para
> comenzar este viaje divino que es camino real para el cielo. Gánase
> yendo por el gran tesoro; no es mucho que cueste mucho a nuestro
> parecer. Tiempo vendrá que se entienda cuán nonada es todo para tal
> precio. Ahora, tornando a los que quieren ir por él y no parar hasta el
> fin, que es llegar a beber de esta agua de vida. (741)

She opens the process by advocating certain vocal prayers, and these are the *Pater Noster* and the *Ave Maria*: "Siempre es gran bien fundar nuestra oración sobre oraciones dichas de tal boca como la del Señor" (742). She adds: "Siempre yo he sido aficionada y me han recogido más las palabras de los Evangelios que libros muy concertados" (743). She promotes established prayers such as the Our Father and the spiritual reading of the Gospels. She reaffirms that oral and mental prayers are important in the religious life of her community: "Yo no hablo ahora en que sea mental o vocal para todos; para vosotras digo que lo uno y lo otro habéis menester, éste es el oficio de los religiosos" (744). In chapter xxii, she relates what mental prayer is: "Sabed, hijas, que no está la falta para ser o no ser oración mental en tener cerrada la boca; si hablando estoy enteramente entendiendo y viendo que hablo con Dios con más advertencia que en las palabras que digo, junto esta oración mental y vocal" (746). In other words, one can combine vocal and mental prayer into one and perform them at the same time. She admonishes her nuns: "No me estéis hablando con Dios y pensando en otras cosas, que esto hace no entender qué cosa es oración mental" (751).

Teresa writes that mental prayer involves "recogimiento" and what she refers to as "atar los entendimientos." One must recollect oneself in body and soul and at the same time cease the functioning of the intellect which are integral parts of mental prayer (754). She brings together "oración mental" and "contemplación", and also explains how many people actually fear this type of prayer, or feel that they cannot carry it out successfully. She adds that vocal prayers such as the *Credo* and the *Pater Noster* vary the process of mental prayer, because they give the individual a bit of respite from the purely meditative part. It is important to note that Teresa at all times, as do almost all of the writers of the spirituality of Recollection, stresses the importance of vocal prayer as well as mental prayer. She demonstrates how mental prayer should be carried out: "Lo que podemos hacer nosotros es procurar estar a solas para que entendamos con quién estamos y lo que nos responde el Señor a nuestras peticiones" (757). Teresa insists that mental prayer is focused on thinking about and understanding what we are saying and with whom we are mentally conversing (759). In mental prayer, "Su Majestad es el que todo lo hace. . ." (759). In short, mental prayer is God working within us.

Teresa describes "el modo para recoger el pensamiento. . ." (760). She also reminds her community that for years she was not able to silence her mind (intellect): "sosegar el pensamiento" (761). She adds: "No os pido ahora que pienses en El, ni que saques muchos conceptos ni que hagáis grandes y delicadas consideraciones" (761). She does not ask her nuns to reflect intellectually; she asks them to contemplate God with the eyes of the soul (761). She demonstrates how they can do this:

> Si estáis alegre, miradle resucitado, que sólo imaginar cómo salió del sepulcro os alegrará. Mas,¡con qué claridad y con qué hermosura, con qué majestad, qué victorioso, qué alegre! Como quien tan bien salió de la batalla adonde ha ganado un tan gran reino, que todo le quiere para vos, y a Sí con él. Pues, ¿es mucho que a quien tanto os da volváis una vez los ojos a mirarle? Si estáis con trabajos o tristes, miradle camino del Huerto, ¡qué aflicción tan grande llevaba en mi alma, pues con ser el mismo sufrimiento la dice y se queja de ella. ¡O miradle atado a la columna lleno de dolores, todas sus carnes hechas a pedazos por lo mucho que os ama; (762)

Teresa's mental prayer and meditation are not as systematic as Alcántara's or Gómez de Cisneros's, since they are more involved with the moods and mental state of her nuns. If they are happy, then can then meditate on and contemplate Christ in his resurrection. If they are troubled or sad, they can contemplate Christ in his agony in the Garden of Gethsemani.

She continues her instruction on mental prayer and contemplation: "Lo que podéis hacer para ayuda de esto, procurad traer una imagen o retrato de este Señor que sea a vuestro gusto, no para hablar muchas veces con El, que El os dará que le decir. Como habláis con otras personas, ¿por qué os han más de faltar palabras para hablar con Dios?" (764). Chapter xviii is important because of the fact that Teresa explains what the prayer of Recollection is. She reaffirms the fact that indeed God is everywhere, as she reminds her nuns that Augustine found God within himself (770).[25] She also refers to the fact that the unrecollected soul's powers are dispersed ("entendimiento derramado"). The soul's functions (powers) cannot be dispersed in this spiritual process, but must be recollected together or gathered in. She adds that one does not have to put on wings to go in search of God, "sino ponerse en soledad y mirarle dentro de sí y no extrañarse de tan buen huésped, sino con gran humildad hablarle como a Padre, pedirle como a Padre, contarle sus trabajos, pedirle remedio, para ellos. . ." (770). She continues: ". . . este modo de rezar. . . .Llámase recogimiento porque recoge el alma todas las potencias y se entra dentro de sí con su Dios, y viene con más brevedad a enseñarle su divino Maestro y a darla oración de quietud, que de ninguna otra manera" (771). She adds that the soul, ". . .allí metida consigo misma puede pensar en la Pasión, y representar allí al Hijo, y ofrecerle al Padre y no cansar el entendimiento andándole buscando en el Monte de Calvario, y al Huerto y a la Columna" (771). The intellect is quiet (stilled) and subjugated as the soul enters into itself, finds God there, and contemplates the mysteries of Christ's passion and death.

Teresa even refers to the soul as "cielo pequeño", or as a piece of heaven. The goal of this spiritual journey is to ultimately drink of the waters gushing forth from the fountain of life (771). The soul is like a ship which is free of land and in the open sea. By recollecting the senses into one point, the person is freed from them as the ship from the land. She also visualizes this entering into one's soul as going into a strong castle so that it can find protection from the enemies that assail it: "Un retirarse los sentidos de estas cosas exteriores y darles de tal manera de mano que sin entenderse, se le cierran los ojos por no verlos, y porque más se despierte la vista a los del alma" (772). Teresa also compares this inner prayer to the action of the bees when they enter their hives: ". . .que se vienen las abejas a la colmena y se entran en ella para librar la miel. . ." (772). Teresa also offers the metaphor of the soul as a rich palace: "Pues hagamos cuenta que dentro de nosotras está un palacio de grandísima riqueza todo su edificio de oro y piedras preciosas, en fin, como para tu señor y que sois vos parte para que este edificio sea tal, como a la verdad es así—que no hay edificio de tanta hermosura como un alma limpia y llena de virtudes, y mientras mayores, más resplandecen las piedras" (773). The King sits in his precious throne in this inner palace, which is in fact the essence or the very center of the soul (774).

In chapter xxix, she presents the reader with the ways to successfully accomplish this inner prayer of Recollection:

> Vase ganando esto de muchas maneras, como está escrito en algunos
> libros, que nos hemos de desocupar de todo para llegarnos
> interiormente a Dios y aun en las mismas ocupaciones retirarnos a
> nosotros mismos. Aunque sea por un momento solo, aquel acuerdo de

que tengo compañía dentro de mí, es gran provecho. En fin, irnos
acostumbrando a gustar de que no es menester dar voces para hablarle,
porque Su Majestad se dará a sentir cómo está allí. (778)

One of the books to which Teresa refers is *Tercer abecedario espiritual*, where
she had come into contact with the section on the "oración de recogimiento"
called "oración de quietud" in her own *Libro de la vida*, chapter iv, section vii.
She explains what she has learned from Alcantara's book:

> Procurando lo más que podrá traer a Jesucristo, nuestro Bien y Señor
> dentro de mí presente, y ésta era mi manera de oración: si pensaba en
> algún paso, le representaba en lo interior, aunque lo más gustaba en leer
> buenos libros, que era toda mi recreación, porque no me dio Dios
> talento de discurrir con el entendimiento ni de aprovecharme con la
> imaginación—que la tengo tan torpe que aun para pensar y representar
> en mí, como lo procuraba, traer la humanidad del Señor nunca
> acababa.[26]

In Chapter xxxi of the *Camino de perfección*, Teresa explains the art of this
"oración de quietud" where all of the soul's powers or functions are at rest: ". . .
todas las potencias se sosiegan." She also explains that at this point in the prayer
of Recollection, with the powers of the soul gathered in and in complete repose,
the soul feels that it is now before God and soon "llegará a éstas hecha una misma
cosa con El por unión" (784). In this mystical, hidden, secret, or inner union, the
soul becomes one with God, who is now present therein sharing in the divine life.
The person through this union, "siéntese deleite en el cuerpo, y grande
satisfacción en el alma." Individuals feel a profound joy being so close to the
fountain of life that they feel spiritually satiated (785). Teresa describes the will as
God's captive ("cautiva"), and if the will feels any pain, it is in the fact that it
must once again be free from God's unitive power (786-88). She also describes
what the soul experiences in this prayer of quietude, silence, or stillness
comparing it to that of a baby breast-feeding: "Está el alma como un niño que aun
mama, cuando está a los pechos de su madre, y ella sin que él paladee, échale la
leche en la boca por regalarle" (789). Subsequent chapters in the *Camino* are
devoted to commentaries on different sentences of the Our Father. For example,
chapter xxxii deals with the words, "Fiat voluntas tua sicut in coelo et in terra"

(Let Thy will be done on earth as it is in heaven) (793-99). Chapter xxxiii reflects on the words, "Panem nostrum quotidianum da nobis hodie" (Give us this day our daily bread) (799-83). Chapter xxxvi treats the words, "Dimitte nobis debita nostra" (Forgive us our debts) (815-23), and chapter xxxvii deals with the spiritual excellence of the prayer in itself (823-26). She explains in chapter xxx that we need to ask God to grant us what we ask of Him with words that also beseech him not to lead us into temptation, and finally, that each one be delivered from every evil (826-32).

Teresa's other masterpiece is *Castillo interior o Las moradas* (1588), an image which she had introduced in the *Camino de perfección*. It is in fact in the fourth section or "cuarta morada" that she develops the process of the prayer of Recollection to which she had previously referred in her *Vida* and in the *Camino*. In the first "morada", Teresa follows the pattern established by her predecessors in the art of meditation and self-knowledge to prepare the soul for subsequent "moradas":

> Por la mayor parte tienen estas devociones las almas de las moradas
> pasadas, porque van casi continuo con obra de entendimiento
> empleadas en discurrir con el entendimiento y en meditación. (Teresa
> 908)

In chapter ii, Teresa discusses spiritual delights or "gustos de Dios", which she calls the "oración de quietud." She describes two fountains with troughs that are filled to the brim with water. Teresa compares these fountains with those of the spirit or spiritual fountains. These two troughs fill up with water in two manners; one is filled up with water by means of pipes that bring it from a long distance; the other is filled up by a spring that originates on the very spot (914): ". . .y el otro está hecho en el mismo nacimiento del agua y vase hinchendo sin ningún ruido, y si es manantial caudaloso como éste de que hablamos despúes de henchido este pilón procede un gran arroyo" . . . (914). Teresa writes that the water which flows through the conduits or pipes to fill the fountain is like the spiritual joys derived from meditation. However, the other fountain, where the water springs from the very source, which is God himself, produces peace, silence, and sweetness in the innermost part of the soul. She continues: "vase revertiendo este agua por todas moradas y potencias hasta llegar al cuerpo, que por esto dije que comienza de Dios y acaba con nosotros;" (915).

The soul, according to Teresa, is expanded and raised up at the same time ("ensanchamiento"). The celestial waters of this spring produce this in the most profound recesses of the individual's soul, and produce delights and joys that cannot be described by the intellect. In addition, the soul distinguishes a heavenly fragrance: "entiende una fragancia, digamos ahora, como si en aquel hondón interior estuviese un brasero adonde se echasen olorosos perfumes" (916). In chapter iii of the "cuarta morada", Teresa deals once again with the "oración de recogimiento." She writes:

> Dicen que el alma "se entra dentro de sí" y otras veces que "sube sobre sí." Por este lenguaje no sabré yo adorar nada, que esto tengo malo, que por el que yo lo sé decir pienso que me habéis de entender y quizá será sólo para mí. Hagamos cuenta que estos sentimientos y potencias, que ya he dicho que son la gente de este castillo, que es lo que he tomado para saber decir algo, que se han ido afuera y andan con gente extraña enemiga del bien de este castillo días y años; . . .Visto ya el gran Rey, que está en la morada de este castillo su buena voluntad, por su gran misericordia quererlos tornar a él y, como buen pastor, con un silbo tan suave que aun casi ellos mismos no le entienden haré que conozcan su voz y que no anden tan perdidos sino que se tornen a su morada y tiene tanta fuerza este silbo del pastor que desamparan las cosas exteriores en que estaban enajenados y métense en el castillo. (Teresa 919-20)

God is both king and shepherd who leads one to enter into this castle with his whistle ("silbo"). Teresa teaches that one does not listen to this spiritual whistle with the ear: ". . .mas siéntese notablemente un encogimiento suave (a gentle contraction, ingathering) a lo interior como verá quien pasa por ella, que yo no lo sé aclarar mejor" (920). She alludes at this point to the famous images of the turtle and to that of the sea-urchin. She reminds her readers that these animals, "se retiran hacia sí" when they wish; this, however, does not occur in this inner prayer, because it happens when God wishes to extend this favor or grace to the individual (920-21).

Teresa reiterates that the prayer of Recollection is granted by God as a special favor to a few persons. Here, she refers to the "hacinamiento" or accumulation of God's graces. In this prayer of Recollection, Teresa reminds the reader that the intellect is at rest and does not think, but the will desires to act ("quiere hacer"). She adds here: "cuando por sus secretos caminos parece que entendemos que nos oye, entonces es bien callar, pues nos ha dejado estar cerca de él, y no será malo procurar no obrar con el entendimiento si podemos, digo" (922). One leaves the soul in God's hands, and allows him to operate in it: ". . sino dejarse el alma en las manos de Dios, haga lo que quisiera de ella, con el mayor descuido de su provecho que pudiere y mayor resignación a la voluntad de Dios" (922). When God wishes that the functions of the soul cease operating, he gives the soul the light of knowledge above the one that one may attain on one's own (923). Individuals use their thoughts and understanding to become cognizant of the fact that God is immediately before them and thus come to the understanding of who He is (923). The inner prayer of Recollection precedes the delights and spiritual joys of knowing and sharing in God's life. It is the stage which precedes the ascent to and the uniting with God in love. During the prayer of Recollection, Teresa advises her readers never to abandon meditation and at the same time learn how to silence the intellect as the will takes over: "La voluntad le tiene tan grande en su Dios, que la da gran pesadumbre su bullicio, y así no ha menester hacer caso de él, que la hará perder mucho de lo que goza, sino dejarle y dejarse a sí en los brazos del amor, que su Majestad la enseñará lo que ha de hacer en aquel puntos" (924).[27] In "Moradas quintas", Teresa commences to treat how the soul is united to God in this inner prayer.

Teresa reminds the reader that very few are chosen to enter into the door of this particular "aposento" or room of the interior castle. All Carmelites are called to prayer, meditation, and even contemplation. Teresa describes the soul as asleep to the things of this world, "porque parece está el alma como adormecida, que ni bien parece está dormida, ni se siente despierta" (929-30). She describes this sleep as, "una muerte sabrosa, un arrancamiento del alma de todas las operaciones que puede tener estando en el cuerpo. . . " (930). The expression "arrancamiento de las operaciones" suggests the extirpation, destruction or silencing of its spiritual powers or functions (operations). She adds that no thing, no memory, no intellectual functions can impede this spiritual favor. God's true wisdom is imparted to the soul which contemplates and knows God yet does not see, hear or think at this time. The soul in experiencing this true knowledge of God, "ni ve, ni oye, ni entiende en el tiempo que está así que siempre es breve y aun harto más breve le parece a ella de lo que debe ser fijo Dios a sí mimso en lo interior de aquel alma. . . " (933). The soul is in God, and God is in the soul. This union with God is in essence not a vision, according to Teresa, but a certainty, a fact which remains in the soul that has experienced it (934). God is present in the soul which she compares to a wine-cellar. Teresa at this point quotes from the Song of Solomon, where the Bride goes in search of here beloved.[28] In her description of this union, Teresa alludes to the silkworm and to the butterfly in flight:

> Pues veamos qué se hace este gusano que es para lo que he dicho todo
> lo demás, que cuando está en esta oración, bien muerto está al mundo,
> sale una mariposa blanca, ¡Oh grandeza de Dios, y cual sale un alma de
> aquí de haber estado un poquito metida en la grandeza de Dios, y tan
> junta con él que, a mí parecer, nunca llega a media hora. Yo os digo de
> verdad que la misma alma no se conoce a sí, porque mirad: a diferencia
> que hay de un gusano feo una mariposa blanca, que la misma hay acá.
> ("Moradas quintas" ch. ii)

The soul becomes a white butterfly in flight after having united with and experienced God as He really is in a spiritual process that does not exceed a period of half-hour. In chapter iii, Teresa shows how this unitive act involves love for one's neighbor: "Que no, hermanas, no; obras quiere el Señor, y que si ves una enferma a quien puedes dar algún alivio, no se te dé nada de perder esa devoción y te compadezcas de ella; y si tiene algún dolor te duela a ti" (949). Union with God is the highest gift, but it lasts a short time; it does not take away one's responsibility to other humans. The few that are chosen by God to take part in this culminating act of the inner way of Recollection, meditation and contemplation, are not exempt from doing good works on behalf of other members of the community.

Although Teresa's disciple, Juan de la Cruz, partakes more than his mentor does of speculative theology, he also drinks from the inspirational waters of the inner way of Recollection. As is the case with Teresa, since volumes have been written about him and his work, our purpose here is to place his major works within the historical context of this particular manifestation of Golden Age spirituality. In his *Subida del Monte Carmelo*, he describes the "noche oscura por la cual pasa el alma para llegar a la divina ley de la unión perfecta del amor de Dios" (Juan de la Cruz 187).[29] His images of the dark night of the soul, the spiritual espousal, unitive love, the flame of spiritual desire, the transformation of the soul into God as it participates in the divine life, all fit very well within this spiritual tradition in Spain. In this same prologue, Juan de la Cruz informs his readers that the "noche oscura" does not depend on the science of theology and on experience; however, these he admits will be of assistance in the successful completion of this spiritual process. He also places emphasis on the individual who allow God to lead in the spiritual ascent to attain Christian perfection, which to him is symbolized by Mount Carmel. In Book I, Juan de la Cruz teaches his readers that for them to reach the state of perfection, they must pass through two types of nights, one of which is the cleansing or purgation of the sensual appetites and vices of the soul. He explains that he calls these dark nights because the soul progresses in darkness as if it were night. He explains these two dark nights the first of which involves the purgation of the sensitive part of the soul, and the second, the spiritual part of the same (192-93). The first of these dark nights is pertinent to the initiates ("principiantes") up to the point where God commences to place the soul in the state of contemplation. The second dark night pertains to those who are proficient in this spiritual journey. This begins at the point when God begins to prepare the soul for subsequent union (193).

In one of his *Cánticos espirituales*, Juan de la Cruz writes that his house is already at peace or quiet, which means that his soul is in repose and at peace because it has been cleansed or purged of sensual appetites, and everything that involves exterior or material things. Once the soul is at peace, it can ascend to the other stages of the inner path to God. He adds that individuals must make this journey assisted by the power of faith, which is also a type of night as far as the intellectual function of the soul is concerned (194). In the other type of night involved, God effects a dark night in the soul which must exist in the body. This night involves the silencing of the senses, faith, and God Himself. In chapter iii, Juan explains that this faith involves the privation of light in the fact that it does not make use of the light of natural reason, but resides in the mortification of the appetites and of the bodily senses (197-98). The soul is at this time deprived of the "gusto del apetitio en todas las cosas", and he continues that this is like the soul's remaining "a oscuras y sin nada" (196). He then reflects on the nothingness of the human being when compared to God. This always will lead the person to self-knowledge, which in turn leads to a sincere humility: "De manera que todas las criaturas en esta manera nada son y las aficiones de ellas menos que nada podemos decir que son, pues son impedimento y privación de la transformación en Dios" (200). Affection for the things of this world is always a stumbling block in the ascent that leads to the transformation of the soul into God. According to Juan de la Cruz, the appetites "entibian y enflaquecen" the soul so that it cannot proceed in the practice of the Christian virtues (227).

Juan de la Cruz, as do the followers of this inner path of Recollection, describes how the soul is dispersed if dragged down by the appetites, both bodily and spiritually: ". . .y por tanto, está claro que, si el apetito de la voluntad se derrama en otra cosa fuera de la virtud, ha de quedar más flaco para la virtud y así el alma que tiene la voluntad repartida en menudencias es como el agua que, teniendo por donde se derramar hacia bajo, no crece para arriba y así no es de provecho" (222). Juan focuses on the dispersing of the will instead of the other two functions of the soul. He then adds: "así el alma no recogida en un solo apetito de Dios pierde el calor y vigor en la virtud" (223). Furthermore, Juan de la Cruz offers two ways of entering into this dark night; one is active and the other is passive: "Activa es lo que el alma puede hacer y hace de su parte para entrar en ella. Pasiva es en que el alma no hace nada, sino Dios la obra en ella, y ella se ha como paciente" (232).

The active phase of this dark night, as in the case of the other writers of this inner way, involves the imitation of Christ. In order to best imitate Christ, Juan de la Cruz establishes that "cualquier gusto que se le ofrece a los sentidos como no sea puramente para honra y gloria de Dios, renúncielo y quédese vacío de él por amor de Jesucristo, el cual en esta vida no tuvo otro gusto, ni le quiso, que hacer la voluntad de su Padre, lo cual llamaba él su comida y manjar" (John 4.45; Juan de la Cruz 233). In this dark night of the journey to God, Juan teaches that individuals must mortify and pacify the four natural passions: "gozo", "esperanza", "temor" and "dolor." In this part, he presents the reader with the famous poem which so beautifully describes this mortification and pacification of the passions meant to inspire the reader to desire nothing ("nada").[30]

In the "Libro Segundo", he describes the way in which individuals can begin the spiritual ascent that culminates in transforming or deforming union. Once the soul is at peace with the appetites and the passions are mortified, the individual prepares to enter "esta oscuridad interior, que es la desnudez espiritual de todas las cosas, así sensuales como espirituales, sólo estribando en pura fe y sabiendo por ella a Dios" (239). He presents the terms "escala" (ladder) and "secreta" in the second stanza of the poem, wherein he describes the secret or inner ascent to God: "A escuras y en celada / estando mi casa sosegada" (239). This spiritual ladder of faith will lead the individual to penetrate "hasta lo profundo de Dios" (240). The intellect, enlightened by God, will then lead the soul in the darkness. In chapter v of the second book, Juan presents his readers with a description of the union of the soul with God. He informs them that God dwells in everyone's soul. In this union, as we have seen in the other Spanish writers, the individual's soul preserves its being and spiritual identity: "está conservando el ser que tienen" (251). He adds: ". . .y así, cuando hablamos de unión del alma con Dios, no hablamos de esta sustancial, que siempre está hecha, sino de la unión y transformación del alma con Dios, que no está siempre hecha, sino sólo cuando viene a haber semejanza de amor" (251). This union he terms "unión de semejanza", because the soul shares in the life of God through a similarity of love. God communicates his supernatural life to the soul, and it is communicated through love and grace (252). In other words, the soul is similar to God in purity without any admixture of imperfections and this transformation takes place through participation ("transformación participante"): ". . .y el alma más parece Dios que alma, y aun es Dios por participación, aunque es verdad que su ser naturalmente tan distinto se le tiene del de Dios como antes aunque está transformada, como también la vidriera le tiene distinto del rayo, estando de él clarificada" (254). The glass is penetrated and illumined by the sun's rays as the soul participates in God's divine life and light. At the end of chapter viii, Juan makes reference to the Pseudo-Dionysius in his attempt to define the contemplation of God: ". . .y de aquí es que la contemplación por la cual el entendimiento tiene más alta noticia de Dios llaman *Teología Mística*, que quiere decir sabiduría de Dios secreta; porque es secreta al mimso entendimiento que la recibe" (268).

In chapter xiii, Juan de la Cruz describes how the individual will leave meditation and prayer and enter into the state of contemplation. He describes here the inner prayer of Recollection: ". . .y más cierta es si el alma gusta de estarse a solas con atención amorosa a Dios, sin particular consideración, en paz interior y quietud y descanso y sin actos y ejercicios de las potencias, memoria, entendimiento y voluntad" (285). He emphasizes the inner nature of this contemplation: "y de esta manera va Dios llevando al alma de grado en grado hasta lo más interior" (307). In chapter 29, Juan cautions the reader on such phenomena as revelations, visions, and locutions that a person in contemplation can experience. The contemplation of and discourse with God must engender humility, charity, mortification, silence and holy simplicity, and not false visions of what God may have said. . . (371). According to Juan, the Holy Spirit is the one who illuminates the intellect of the "recogido": ". . .digo que el Espíritu Santo alumbra al entendimiento recogido, y que le alumbra al modo de su recogimiento y que el entendimiento no puede hallar otro mayor recogimiento que en fe y así no le alumbrará el Espíritu Santo en otra cosa más que en fe, . . . " (371). The gifts of the Holy Spirit are communicated to the soul through charity.

The dark night of the will involves good works. In the dark night of each of the soul's powers, each of the three theological virtues are involved. A person can purge the intellect by having it grounded on faith; memory is cleansed through hope, and the will is purged through charity: ". . .si no purgásemos también la voluntad acerca de la tercera virtud, que es la caridad, por la cual las obras hechas en fe son vivas y tienen gran valor, y sin ellas no valen nada, pues, como dice Santiago, sin obras de caridad, la fe es muerta" (414). When the will is aligned with God's, union will then occur (415). It is the part of the soul that Juan calls "espíritu" which is perfected. He calls the spirit "la porción superior del alma que tiene respecto y comunicaciones con Dios. . ."(443). It is in fact this part of the soul which assumes all of God's attributes for it perfects itself through God's spiritual gifts (443). Having been purified, the spirit can enjoy God's goods and spiritual gifts which bring spiritual joy to the will. In chapter xl of the Third Book, Juan de la Cruz proceeds to show how the soul can advance by leading the person to "recogimiento interior": "prosigue encaminando el espíritu al recogimiento interior acerca de lo dicho" (477). He stresses that although a church or oratory is a proper place for prayer, and that a sacred image can effectively increase devotion, the inner recollection of the soul takes place in a living temple: ". . . orar en el templo vivo, que es el recogimiento interior del alma." Statues, churches and temples are examples of "lugar decente y dedicado para oración"; however, the prayer of Recollection takes place in one's soul, a living temple (477).

In *Noche oscura de la subida al Monte Carmelo*, Juan de la Cruz focuses on mortification of the imperfections common to the initiates or "principiantes" in this spiritual process. He opens chapter i with these words:

> En esta noche oscura comienzan a entrar las almas cuando Dios las va sociando del estado de principiantes que es de los que meditan en el camino espiritual y los comienza a poner en el de los aprovechantes que es ya el de contemplativos para que estando por aquí lleguen al estado de los perfectos, que es el de divina unión del alma con Dios. (517)

In the spiritual journey to God, meditation and prayer are part of the first phase which includes the "principiantes." Once they have purged the soul of its vices, they move into the second phase or the contemplative stage of the "aprovechantes", the proficient or advanced. Once these are illuminated by contemplating God as He really is, the person enters the final stage of Christian perfection, which as we have already seen, is union with and the sharing in the divine life. The spiritual functions of the soul are involved in each one of the stages. Memory, intellect and will are each assisted by the theological virtues of faith, hope, and charity. Some of the imperfections which must be purged are outlined in subsequent chapters: for example, arrogance ("soberbia"), spiritual avarice ("avaricia espiritual"), spiritual and physical lust ("lujuria"), anger ("ira"), physical and spiritual gluttony ("gula"), envy ("envidia"), and sloth ("acidia").[31]

In Chapter viii, he refers to "noche" as "contemplación." He adds that this "noche" is "sensitiva" and "espiritual": "Y así, la una noche o purgación será sensitiva con que se purga y desnuda el alma según el espíritu, aproximándole y dirigiéndole para la unión con Dios" (537). The "noche sensitiva" purges the senses and the "noche espiritual" in the second phase of the journey purges the soul, thus preparing it for union. The "noche sensitiva" or the purgation of the senses belongs to the "principiantes", and the "noche espiritual" with all of its "sequedades" (loss of pleasure for anything) is common to the phase of the "aprovechadas" or "aprovechantes" (538-40). These "sequedades" (spiritual dryness or sterility) are common in the second stage, where the spirit is being cleansed of spiritual vices:

> La primera, si así como no halla gusto ni consuelo en las cosas de Dios,
> tampoco lo halla en algunas cosas criadas. . .y en esto se conoce
> probablemente que esta sequedad y sinsabor no proviene ni de recados
> ni de imperfecciones nuevamente cometidos; (540)

God Himself is the origin of this spiritual sterility, lack of spiritual solace and consolation, as well as a "sinsabor" (disgust) with everything spiritual or natural. This phenomenon is discussed by most followers of this inner way of Recollection. Another cause is that both the body and the soul have become accustomed to pleasures, delights, and once purged of these, the soul is left empty and dry (541-42). Having accomplished the sensitive as well as the spiritual purgation of the soul, individuals may enter the second phase of the journey to God, which are the illuminative and contemplative stages.

At the end of Chapter x, Juan defines contemplation: ". . .porque contemplación no es otra cosa que infusión secreta, pacífica y amorosa de Dios, que si le dan lugar, inflama al alma en espíritu de amor, según ella lo da a entender en el verso siguiente, `con ansias en amores inflamada'" (547). Once the sensual appetites have been purged, the soul will also have to be purged of the spiritual vices, and thus is dry and completely empty ("seca y vacía"). Then, God will illuminate the soul in this darkness, "hacia tu luz en las tinieblas" (Isaiah 58.10; Juan de la Cruz 547). God's light will consequently shine in this darkness and this is the only thing that that soul will see at this point. The intellect is also unencumbered and free in order to not only be able to see God, but to ascend to Him; upon seeing Him the soul will gaze upon God's truth as it really is (554). In the darkness of the soul's night, once purged, the intellect is illuminated and can see God as He really is. It is at this point, as we have seen with other writers of the spirituality of Recollection, that the soul acquires the Christian virtues and imitates Christ. Moreover, as the other Spanish writers, this infused contemplation takes place in secret and in the innermost recesses of the soul. Juan writes: "esta noche oscura es una influencia de Dios en el alma que la purga de su ignorancia e imperfecciones habituales, naturales y espirituales, que llaman los contemplativos contemplación infusa o mística teológica en que de secreto enseña Dios al alma y la instruye en perfección de amo. . . (572-73). The soul does nothing and knows nothing as God instructs it by infusing this secret contemplation of His true essence. This is a light which illuminates the intellect, and moves the will to desire union. In chapter xi Juan writes: "Siéntese aquí el espíritu apasionado en amor mucho, porque esta inflamación espiritual hace pasión de amor, que por cuanto este amor es infuso, es más pasivo que activo, y así engendra en el alma pasión fuerte de amor" (599). He continues: "Va teniendo ya este amor algo de unión con Dios, y así participa algo de sus propiedades, las cuales son más acciones de Dios que de la misma alma, las cuales se sujetan en ella pasivamente, aunque el alma lo que aquí hace es dar [el] consentimiento" (599-600). The soul is passive as it participates in God's life, but it does consent and accept it, albeit passively.

This infused contemplation, according to Juan, is secret; it is also a stairway to God ("secreta escala"). This spiritual ascent or stairway is also an infused knowledge of love ("ciencia de amor"): ". . .por qué aquí se llama escala es porque la contemplación es ciencia de amor, la cual, como habemos dicho, es noticia infusa de Dios amorosa, que juntamente va ilustrando y enamorando al alma hasta subirla de grado [en grado] hasta Dios . . . (627). Infused contemplation is a science of love because through this secret knowledge, God instructs, illuminates, and enamors the soul with this burning love. It begins to ascend gradually by degrees, or in a gradual progression until it reaches God in unitive love, which unites and joins the soul to God (627).[32] Finally, it is in *Cántico espiritual* that the love between the soul and its spouse, Christ, is fully developed. The editor of the critical edition of Juan de la Cruz's *Obras completas* explains: "A lo largo de sus cuarenta canciones, narra y canta una larga historia de amor entre dos enamorados, esposa y esposo. . .Se trata de la unión de amor entre Dios y el hombre llevado hasta las más íntimas posibilidades de la gracia" (665). This work describes the experiences Juan felt in his mystical union. We shall conclude here our discussion of Juan de la Cruz because our purpose has been to demonstrate how his works, albeit more speculative because of a certain influence from Thomas Aquinas and other Scholastics, are part of the spiritual process that is known as the spirituality of Recollection. He, as does his mentor, Teresa de Jesús, devotes many pages to the discussion of the inner way of Recollection which is part of the process that leads eventually to mystical union. Mystical union is the actual culmination of the inner way of Recollection.[33]

The last writer with whom we shall deal in this chapter is Juan de los Angeles (Franciscan, 1536-1609). He also contributed to the literature of Recollection with his *Diálogos de la conquista del espiritual y secreto reino de Dios* (1595), and with its second part called *Manual de vida perfecta* (1608).[34] Juan de los Angeles has been referred to as "la culminación de siglos espirituales" (Gomis III: 461). Juan B. Gomis, in his introduction to the third volume of *Místicos franciscanos* writes:

> En la ciencia mística española fray Luis de León significa el saber teológico, San Juan de la Cruz, la psicología sobrenatural; Santa Teresa la experiencia plena de los misterios que Dios obra en las almas de generoso espíritu y fray Juan de los Angeles, la filosofía de amor, la suma y compendio de sus predecesores. . .la sabiduría mística. (461)

This philosophy of love is peculiar to the members of the Franciscan Order.[35] Juan de los Angeles contributed important works to the Spanish spirituality of the Golden Age dealing with divine love, mental prayer, and contemplation. These are *Vergel espiritual del ánima religiosa*, *Lucha espiritual y amorosa*, and *Triunfos del amor de Dios*. Fray Juan follows both Teresa de Jesús and Juan de la Cruz in chronological order, and he is influenced by both of these masters, in addition to other earlier writers such as Bernardino de Laredo. For a long time it was believed that he was born in La Corchuela (Oropesa). However, we have learned more about his life in an article entitled "Epítome de la vida de fray Juan de los Angeles", written by don Julián García Sánchez of the Cofradía Internacional de Investigadores. The article states that Juan de los Angeles entered the Franciscan Order in the province of San José: "Su prestigio de orador sagrado, su fama de hombre de letras y director de almas transcendían las fronteras de su Instituto. . ." (4). He was named Provincial of his order and was confessor to the Descalzas Reales in Madrid. He was also spiritual director to Doña Margarita de la Cruz, the daughter of Emperor Maximilian II and of Doña María de Austria, Felipe II's sister. García Sánchez presents enough evidence in his article to support the fact that Juan was born in the small town of Lagartera in the province of Toledo, instead of La Corchuela (6-7). García Sánchez discovered a baptismal certificate that gives his birthplace as Lagartera.

We shall begin to discuss the first part of his treatise *Diálogos de la Conquista del espiritual y secreto reino de Dios*, subtitled *que según el Santo Evangelio está dentro de nostros mismos* (1595). Suggesting Humanistic influence, this work is composed as a dialogue between a master and his disciple. In the "Prólogo al lector", Fray Juan establishes the fact that these dialogues are a "tratado de oración y contemplación", and in the "Diálogo Primero", he sets out to discuss the inner life and center of the soul and the kingdom of God which exists therein (Juan de los Angeles 35). He claims that if one is good in the innermost part of the soul, that this will be reflected in one's good works. If individuals are just and upright within their souls, they will also be just and upright in the way that they live (41). The master tells his disciple: "Lo que te doy por respuesta es que hasta que halles dentro de ti ese centro o íntimo no habrás sabido qué cosa es vida interior o esencial" (41). He informs his student that his primary intention is to inspire a fondness for delving into himself, and to inspire in him a fondness for a life that is essentially good (42). The master quotes from Luke 17, where the evangelist writes that the kingdom of God is within each individual. Fray Juan refers to the German theologian Tauler, and presents terms that identify this center or most intimate part of the soul; these are, "centro", "íntimo", "ápice de espíritu", "mente", "summo", and "hondón" (42).

Fray Juan adds: "Aquí mana una fuente de agua viva que da saltos para la vida eterna" (43). He had also compared this most intimate part of the soul with the grove or garden of the Creator, which in Spanish is the "soto del Criador" (42). As do the other writers of the spirituality of Recollection, Fray Juan identifies the sensual or animal appetites that cause the affections to seek exterior or material things (44). He also mentions "afecto racional o apetito de razón." He views the rational life of the spirit as imperfect and defective because it lacks an ingredient that goes beyond human reason. He claims that outside of God there can be nothing that will satisfy the rational soul. Fray Juan goes on to discuss divine life, wherein the cognitive powers of the soul receive a certain natural illumination from God, which allows it to receive a gentle, pleasant, and pure love which inclines the soul toward the Supreme Good. He discusses three types of humans; "primer hombre", "segundo hombre", and, "tercer hombre." The "primer hombre" is the sensual person, the "segundo hombre" is the rational person. This second type of individual weighs what is good and what is bad according to free will. The "tercer hombre" or the third person is called "suprema simple inteligencia o mente" and he/she is "es fuerza cognitiva del ánima, que recibe inmediatamente cierta lumbre natural de Dios" (44). The soul of this third type of person is lifted by this pure love and is literally engulfed (swallowed up) by God, or "tragado de Dios", and transformed into Him. In the participation of the divine life, the soul contemplates God and unites with Him by means of "desnudo amor." Once joined to God, the soul enjoys and delights in His sweetness: "le goza y gusta cuánta sea su dulcedumbre." (44).

Fray Juan associates this knowledge ("sabiduría") with "el gusto dulce de las cosas celestiales", which are best received by the soul when it is most empty and least preoccupied (46). The soul is void of all images and things that are not God once the powers and images of the memory have been purged. Emptied of all that is not God, the three powers of the soul are then concentrated (gathered in, recollected) to the center of the soul where God is present and, in fact, dwells (47). The student questions his master on the words "vivo y no vivo", which is the Biblical image of the fact that one loves, and yet does not live because Christ lives in one. He informs his student that "nuestro Padre fray Pedro de Alcántara se recogía con solas estas palabras" (50). He reminds his readers that it is in these words that Christ lives in the soul, "está la suma de toda la mística teología y que es fuente de vida perfecta y camino certísimo para la perfecta unión con Dios" (50). The second "Diálogo" deals with the actual conquest of God's kingdom which, as we already know, is inside of ourselves. He also discusses true penitence and the expulsion ("destierro") of our sins and vices, which in effect are part of the first phase of this inner journey to God and to a life of Christian perfection. He refers his disciple to Augustine's *Confessions*, Book I, where the Church Father relates the difficulties of the initial stages of his conversion because it was so difficult for him to ascend the spiritual ladder to reach perfection.[36] Augustine describes huge, painted lions that appeared to him which were about to devour him; according to Fray Juan, these lions exist in the imagination of cowards who are afraid to make the spiritual journey (51). He also refers to "cobardía en el servicio de Dios", and adds that the Kingdom of God is seized by valiant and courageous souls. These are the ones who actually take possession of God's Kingdom ("apoderarse") and who come to enjoy it.

It seems that Fray Juan compares the soul in this spiritual ascent to God to a soldier's military campaign. He refers to a "chapitel redondo" (round head of a pillar), as well as to a crown that is given to a soldier that has fought valiantly. In this battle to conquer the Kingdom of God, there are also gradations that the soldier must ascend, and these are the virtues. However, there are lions on both sides of the path which represent any function or deed that is extraneous to the Christian virtues: in other words, the worldly vices as well as sins (51). At this point the disciple becomes aware that the lions are waging war against him. The master informs him that he alone must suffer the wounds and blows to fend them off. He adds that this conquest is also over the vices of the soul, and the object is to expel all sin from the soul through the ascetical practices that accompany true penance. The master also admonishes his pupil the following: ". . .pelear con doce enemigos que defienden la entrada deste divino Reino como doce fieros jayanes" (52). He must fight off the twelve giant enemies that defend the entrance into God's Kingdom. Furthermore, the master declares that the disciple cannot have true penance if it is not accompanied by love; one cannot be converted to a new spiritual life without this love (52). Love involves ascetical practices as well as good works: "el ayuno, la limosna, la oración, el cilicio, el remiendo, el pie descalzo y lo demás que tiene apariencia de santidad y justicia" (60).

In the third "Diálogo", Fray Juan treats the four doors or entrances into God's Kingdom, which are humility, abnegation of the will, tribulation suffered with patience, and the death of Christ.[37] He stresses the point that humility is the most important recourse that individuals have at their disposal to enter into the Kingdom. The master states: "No es mayor el que más ayuna, ni el que más se agota, ni el que más limosna da, ni el que tiene más letras, ni el que más alta contemplación alcanza, sino el que más se humilla" (62). All of the alms-giving, penitence, fasting, learning, and contemplation is worthless if one does not practice humility. One of the ways in which individuals can look within their soul is to gaze devotedly at the Cross: "Conserva, pues, esta imagen preciosa de Cristo viva en tu memoria en todo tiempo, lugar y negocio, así en la prosperidad como en la adversidad" (57). The disciple here is asked to keep this image of Christ's cross in his memory at all times. He then counsels solitude and recollection: "La soledad, el recogimiento, el silencio, y la vigilantísima observancia del corazón, y la alienación a la habla o inspiración divina, es la base y el fundamento de la vida espiritual" (58). "Recogimiento" for Fray Juan, at least in this passage, is a physical retiring into a secluded or private place. In order to be able to hear God's words and be inspired, one must have humility and purity of heart, which according to Juan are "virtudes voladoras", which free the soul to take flight and ascend to God. This is also why solitude, silence, and physical isolation are crucial (64).

An important part of the initial stages of the spiritual journey to God is knowledge of self and self-abnegation. The disciple responds: "Al fin habemos de confesar todos que el principio de la verdad es la disciplina y conocimiento de sí mismo" (70). Self-discipline, self-knowledge, self-abnegation and humility are constantly interrelated in this initial stage. Fray Juan adds: "ninguna cosa te puede suceder mejor que ser corregido, despreciado y tenido en poco" (70). He then enters into a discussion of the way of life which he calls, illuminative, "que hace a los hombres sabios de sabiduría verdádera" (71). He then adds in typical Franciscan fashion that in every little blade of grass, in every small bird, ant, elephant, in fact, in all of creation, the wise person can contemplate God in essence and power, as Creator and Preserver of everything and everyone (71). He ends the dialogue by having the master declare that, "este negamiento propio y desamparo de ti mismo es el camino real para Dios, y la senda derecha aunque dificultosa, para la cumbre de la perfección evangélica" (74). The illumination of the individual's soul frees it from the vices so that the person may become wise in the knowledge of God, who can be contemplated not only in the very center of the soul, but in all of creation.

The fourth "Diálogo" deals with the fourth door into the Kingdom of God which is tribulation. Tribulation and spiritual affliction cause the purification of the soul (76). Fray Juan refers here to the tribulation of the just (77). He adds that ascetical mortification and self-discipline keep carnal concupiscence and spiritual vices at bay. The disciple then alludes to the depravity of the present times as he deplores the loss of the ancient virtues, to which the master responds the following:

> Verdad es que el mundo está ya en lo último y allegado a la decrépita, porque aun en materia de virtud se hallan en él cien mil novedades y disparates nunca vistos, y así me persuado que los Santos de la fama, los generales y capitanes del pueblo cristiano, y que la gente que ahora se hace para el cielo es de a pie gente menuda, gente afeminada . . .que ni un papirote saben sufrir por Dios. (79)

The master then adds that people are attracted "ya de solos los hábitos y ceremonias de virtuosos, estando muy lejos de nuestros corazones y sin virtud" (80). People cling to the outward manifestations of the faith, and do not reflect the virtues in their hearts where they should also keep Christ present. He purports that true penitence, mortification, self-abnegation, discipline, and other purely ascetical practices predispose the person to be able to receive the supernatural benefits. The body as the temple of God must be purged; however, the soul is God's dwelling-place, and because of this, it is crucial that it remain completely cleansed of everything that represents an affection or attraction for worldly things (80-82).

Juan de los Angeles, as did Juan de la Cruz and other followers of this spirituality, describes the condition wherein God holds back all consolation and solace from the soul which is in search for Him. He describes in much the same way as the others: "sequedad", and "desamparo" (helplessness). It is here that Fray Juan alludes to the *Alumbrados* of Extremadura. He refers to their actions as "gula espiritual o demasía de las cosas del espíritu", for these people, "se arrobaban y sentían gustos tan excesivos que se enflaquecían y deleitaban y les faltaban las fuerzas corporales y quedaban muchas veces yertos, y los miembros intratables y helados, y ellos sin ningún sentido" (Juan de los Angeles 83). Fray Juan then returns to his discussion of tribulation and spiritual affliction, where he explains that helplessness and spiritual desconsolateness help to test and to purge the soul. He adds:

> . . .multiplicándose las tribulaciones y trabajos espirituales y corporales es sublimada y levantada sobre sí y sobre todas las cosas criadas y se le muestra y aun se le entrega el Reino de Dios, que es la quietud y paz espiritual de que comienza a gozar dentro de sí en esta vida. (84)

The soul is sublimated and lifted up to God through tribulations, sufferings and spiritual afflictions.

In the fifth "Diálogo", Fray Juan writes about the fifth door into God's Kingdom which is the Passion of Christ. The master explains that the memory of Christ's Passion is a shortcut ("atajo") to Christian perfection and other spiritual benefits (85). If the soul is engaged in contemplation of the passion, there can be no place for carnal concupiscence (86). Fray Juan posits seven "circunstancias" (details, particulars) involved in the contemplation of Christ's Passion: the person who suffers (Christ), His qualities, His greatness, the cause that moved Him to undertake this sacrifice, the manner in which He dies, the injuries that He suffers, and the fruit of His death, which is the opening of the seven seals (89). The sixth "Diálogo" discusses the sufferings of Francis of Assisi and the tribulation undergone by other saints. The seventh "Diálogo" treats the seven enemies that guard the entrance into God's Kingdom. Once again, he refers to them as "jayanes" (giants) reminding us of Don Quijote's own battle against the giants in his own mind. Some examples of these enemies of the soul, which have the power to extinguish devotion and the aspiration to reach God are: "amor de alabanza:, "pertinacia de propia voluntad", "negligencia", "escrupulosidad", "solicitud temporal", "acidia o tedio en la virtud", "gula espiritual", and "especulación." In order to battle these spiritual enemies, Fray Juan advises that individuals arm themselves with faith and Sacred Scripture, which are "las armas de nuestra milicia" (111-12). The virtues will counteract these enemies. In addition, he gives the example of how obedience will crush one's own stubbornness and obstinacy as well as excessive scrupulousness, which in fact does not foster love, for there is a type of spiritual gluttony and a certain arrogance in the exaggeration of ascetical practices and spiritual exercises (117).

Fray Juan presents in the eighth "Diálogo" the spiritual exercises which contemplatives, who have discovered and already conquered God's Kingdom in their souls, must practice. The master informs his disciple that, "toda la armonía de los espirituales ejercicios y todas las riquezas del hombre interior están en cuatro puntos":

> . . .en subir con libertad por hacimiento de gracias a la Majestad de
> Dios. En descender por humildad y abnegación de la voluntad propia,
> debajo de su propia mano. En salir virtuosamente a todos los hombres
> con amor general y caridad bien ordenada. En entrar uniformemente a
> sí mismo por olvido de todas las cosas a los brazos y unión del Esposo.
> (112)

Four verbs exemplify this spirituality when the person is immersed in contemplation. The individual rises ("subir") to God by an abundant accumulation ("hacimiento") of God's graces. The person also descends ("bajar", "descender") through complete humility and abnegation of self. Further, the individual goes out ("salir") to perform good works of charity on behalf of fellow humans; finally, the person enters into the innermost center of the soul, where union with God takes place. Fray Juan presents four "vías" for his spiritual journey, instead of the traditional three: "purgativa", "iluminativa", "amativa", and "unitiva" (121). These four are more accurate because in the illuminative stage the soul receives the light from God and comes to know Him through the power of its intellect. This in effect is what moves the will to love and desire God with a burning love, which is usually compared to a flame ("llama"). To reiterate, this love is expressed in the will and it is what moves the soul to seek transforming union, wherein the soul shares in God's life and thus brings about the culmination of the path to Christian perfection.[38] Fray Juan summarizes his spiritual exercises in this way: "Digo, pues, que unas veces se ha de subir, otras bajar, unas salir afuera y otras entrar dentro de sí" (125). He adds that all of the conditions necessary for perfect prayer and union with God can be found in this brief axiom: "Asentarse ha el solitario y callará, y levantarse ha sobre sí. Lo primero es asentarse, lo segundo, soledad, lo tercero silencio, lo cuarto, elevación y rapto." This summarizes Fray Juan's spiritual journey to God (125).

The Disciple then asks his master to distinguish between "pensar" ("cogitación"), "meditar" ("meditación"), and "contemplar" ("contemplación"). The master answers that is a vain thought, it is vain and lacking in spiritual fruit because it focuses its attention on the things of this world. He has this to say about meditation:

> La meditación es pensamiento próvido y deseo sabio del ánima que
> busca alguna verdad en que no poco se fatiga y congoja aunque el
> aprovechamiento es mucho, porque se enciende en ella el fuego de la
> caridad, que es el fin de toda meditación. (126)

He establishes that contemplation and meditation at a certain stage of the spiritual journey are the same, because both consider (ponder) celestial things that are propitious for the soul. However, they differ in the fact that meditation takes more effort and may cause one to tire, but contemplation is done with pleasure and its effects are sweetness and spiritual delights without grief, sorrow or displeasure (126). He adds:

> Los que se ocupan en la meditación reciben gran provecho della:
> hácense sabios, enciéndense en el amor de Dios, crecen en la devoción,
> en la humildad y menosprecio del mundo, y finalmente en todo género
> de virtudes; y lo que es más, llegan a lo sabroso y gustoso de la
> contemplación, mediante la cual oración la criatura es unida con su
> criador y sabrosamente le gusta. (126)

The individual ends up united to God and actually tasting and enjoying the divine sweetness. However, only persons who practice humility can achieve and attain this state for they must learn to be oblivious to themselves and to all that is not God in this life.[39]

The master also discusses silence in the act of contemplation: "Cuando todas las cosas callen en el hombre y duermen y sólo el espíritu puro vela y está atento a Dios" (127). This is not in reality the dark night of the senses, which Juan de la Cruz describes so effectively, but it is the silence that follows union with God and rapture (ecstasy). He adds: "A este silencio sigue el rapto que por otro nombre llaman los Santos muerte de beso, porque se hace mediante el contacto suavísimo de Dios con nuestra ánima en la parte superior" (127). This rapture is a contact between the highest or most essential part of the soul and God, which Fray Juan describes with the image of the "muerte de beso" or death by a kiss. He compares this phenomenon with the case of the sick person who needs to sleep; in order to sleep well the house must be completely silent and all the doors and windows must be closed (128). This spiritual sleep is also described as a gulf where the oars of the intellect and reason cause more damage than good to the soul: "luego que comienzan a remar, se acaba aquel gusto sabrosísimo y de gran deleite que siente el alma engolfado en Dios" (128). He advises his student not to waste his time defining, distinguishing and constructing syllogisms and long discourses in the attempt to try to define these spiritual phenomena, and to discover who and what God is and where He dwells (129). He posits the rhetorical question, "¿Por qué has tú de querer comprender al que es incomprensible y medir con la vara corta de tu juicio al que es inmenso, y estando en el destierro saber como los que le gozan en la patria" (129).

Finally, in the ninth "Diálogo", Fray Juan shows how the soul should aspire to reach God, and at the same time enter into itself so that the person can achieve self-knowledge. Through this process the individual may come to the knowledge of "lo alto de Dios" and "la nada de los hombres" (129). He also mentions the wonders of Christian charity, and the joys and delights of what he calls "la santa ociosidad" or holy otium. He adds that the same love which calls one to God's sweetness in his embrace will also see to it that one does not forget one's fellow human beings. The love of God, and union with Him should inspire individuals to go outside of themselves to love all humans, since all are created in God's image. Fray Juan then begins to discuss the different activities that are involved in the journey to God; these are "lección" ("busca", searches), "meditacón" ("halla", finds), "oración" ("pide", asks), and "contemplación" ("goza", enjoys). He describes the contemplative life as "vida de espíritu", "vida interior", "vida esencial", "vida religiosa y de gusto grande" (137). The contemplative life results in what Fray Juan calls the "hombre espiritual." The tenth "Diálogo" goes on to describe "la uniformidad de las introversiones o entradas del alma a su íntimo o centro", which is in fact the Kingdom of God; he also discusses "recogimiento" here. He calls these "introversiones vueltas a dentro" of the soul as "entradas" or "encierramiento" into the center or most intimate part of the soul so that the soul could be alone with its God. He describes the person who accomplishes that as the "hombre interior" (143). In a reference to Ruysbroeck he writes: "La vida y ejercicio de los varones recogiods (dice Rusbrochio) es recogerse a Dios dentro de sí mismos, y salir a fuera de sí mismos" (145). Once again, it is important for us to note that the spirituality of Recollection involved a gathering in of the soul's powers or functions to its very center, or to the essential point where God is present; in addition, individuals are taught to go outside of themselves to do good works for their fellow human beings. This is, in our opinion, the beauty of this particular manifestation of Spanish spirituality, for it at all times maintains the importance of our responsibilities to other members of the community whether it be in a house, a convent, a monastery, or an entire community or society; indeed, it emphasizes the links that each individual has to people in the entire world, for each one shares the breath of the divine life. Fray Juan explains: ". . .extroversión o salida fuera es una displicencia que de sí mismos tienen y desestimación y aniquilación propia" (143). He goes on: "Las salidas andan acompañadas de la razón, y fúndanse en caridad, en piadosos ejercicios, buenas costumbres, en obras santas, y de virtud" (148). Alluding to Osuna, he writes about the degrees and gradations of this "recogimiento." The first "grado" involves mortification which silences the soul; in the second grade of Recollection, each person's intellect keeps watch over him/her, and the third grade is where "el ánima está dentro de su cuerpo como en una caja muy cerrada, y allí se goza consigo misma con algún calor espiritual" (144).

This brings to a close our study which deals with the works that establish the spirituality of Recollection in Spain and the writers who describe and outline this spiritual process of looking inward into the center of the soul where one encounters God, comes to know Him, and is moved to desire union in order to share in the divine life. It is a spirituality that, as we have seen, has born wondrous fruit not only in Spain, but outside of it. The spirituality of Recollection involves a complicated process which is perceived as a spiritual journey that begins by this looking inward and culminates in the union with God and in the attainment of Christian perfection. It also involves a number of spiritual exercises that include vocal prayer, devotional reading, meditation, ascetical practices and self-discipline, the practice of the Christian virtues, mental prayer, the imitation of Christ and of his mother, pure contemplation, a burning love for God, union and rapture, and ultimately, Christian perfection, which in turn inspires the person to lead a life of profound spirituality that includes both the love of God as well as that of one's neighbors. It begins with the renovation and spiritual renewal of the "hombre interior", which allows the person to become an "hombre espiritual", and beginning with the individual person, goes on to renew and reform the Church, politics, and the society at large.

EPILOGUE

IT HAS BEEN OUR ATTEMPT in this study to offer a rather thorough outline and explanation of the inner way of spiritual Recollection as developed in Spain at the end of the fifteenth century and throughout the sixteenth. It is interesting to note that the spiritual process of Recollection to a great extent was a phenomenon that originated in certain areas of Castile or central Spain. It is almost as if this dry, somewhat harsh and rocky terrain was well adapted to a looking inward into the innermost areas of the human soul, a divesting of the self of all that is material, and therein, to not only encounter God, but share in the life of the Divine Essence. In addition to having originated in the dry hills and mountains of central Spain, there are certain features that are unique to the inner way of Recollection. One is that it developed in Franciscan houses of retreat, where monks followed a primitive form of Christianity largely inspired by the life and experiences of Francis of Assisi. It later was expanded through the reform of religious communities, and the creation of theological schools at universities.

These religious men and women devoted large segments of the day to devotional reading, silent prayer and inner meditation, and contemplation. Several, such as Pedro de Alcántara, and Francisco de Osuna, described, outlined and named the process Recollection. Throughout the text we have opted to capitalize the term *Recogimiento* and Recollection, since we have tried to identify the process of Recollection as more than a withdrawal into a cell or monastic garden to be alone and away from others in the community. Recollection does involve this physical withdrawal to and solitude in a private room, cell, or chapel; however, it also includes a series of ascetical exercises, devotional readings, inner or mental prayer, spiritual exercises, and the practice of the Christian virtues.

These ascetical practices and exercises, as well as mental prayer and devotional readings, will lead to the gathering in of all three of the souls powers or functions (memory, intellect, will) into the very center or the highest point of the soul. By withdrawing and gathering in both the spiritual and physical functions of the soul, the exercitants will be unencumbered and thus free to make the spiritual ascent to God, or to encounter God within this most profound part of the soul.

Some writers describe this experience as the soul's being transformed into God, or the sharing in the divine life of God. The crucial point in this spiritual process is that, whether it is described as an ascent to God, or a withdrawal and in-gathering into the deepest point in the soul, individuals encounter God within their souls. The person is thus transformed and achieves Christian perfection as a result of the encounter. Another important point is that the experience is not a passive abandonment to God, but an active sharing in the divine life, where the soul is transformed into God and becomes as these writers describe, "deiforme." The soul partakes of the Divine Essence, but is not engulfed or dissolved into the Divine Essence. When one compares the Spanish terms *recogimiento-recoger* with the English recollection-to recollect, we find differences. In English recollection simply means to call to mind or to remember, as a recollection of something or someone. However, the past participle recollected does include this additional meaning: "characterized or given to contemplation". The Spanish words *recogimiento, recogido, recoger* include a wider range of meanings that involve certain aspects of the spirituality of Recollection. *Recogimiento* is defined in this way: "Acción y efecto de recoger o recogerse" (*Dic. leng. esp* 1235). *Recogido* is defined: "Que tiene recogimiento y vive retirado del trato y comunicación de las gentes" (1235). The reflexive form *recogerse* does suggest a spiritual process: "Apartarse o abstraerse el espíritu de todo lo terreno que le pueda impedir la meditación o contemplación" (1235). The feature which is missing from the dictionaries of both languages is one of the main ingredients of the spirituality of Recollection, and it is the gathering-in of all of the soul's functions to the deepest or highest part of the soul. The person's body is thus not weighted down by an interest in or affection for material things, and is free to make the ascent or withdrawal into the soul depending on who is describing the process. Unification or transformation can take place only after an arduous series of exercises, meditations, and an infused contemplation, which inspire love in the will, which is what pushes the soul toward union.

As we stated above, the inner way of Recollection had its origins in the Franciscan retreat houses. This means that it is a product of a religious tradition that goes back to certain Biblical sources like the Songs of Solomon and St. Paul, as well as Augustine, and the Pseudo-Dionysius. As part of the Platonic-Augustinian and Franciscan tradition, God is sought through the affections rather than exclusively through speculative theology. The tradition is reinforced beyond Francis through Bonaventure, Bernard, the Victorines, together with the German mystics. In addition to the above, its purely affective and mystical elements are kept in check by means of certain Dominican and Carmelite writers who are imbued with Thomistic speculative theology. All of these spiritual currents converge in central Spain and guided, or kept in check by the Inquisition, as well as the monarchy, produced a flowering of religious literature that has rarely been witnessed in one particular period of one country.

There were approximately 3,000 religious treatises produced in Spain during the sixteenth and seventeenth centuries. Our intention was to highlight the inner way of Recollection that started with the humble origins within the Franciscan reform movement and culminated with the great Spanish mystics: Teresa de Jesús and Juan de la Cruz. This literature of religious Recollection also spawned radical movements such as the *Alumbrados*, *Dejados*, and the *Quietistas*, all of which were severely condemned by the Inquisition. There were many other writers of this religious literature, such as Bishop Bartolomé de Carranza, Luis de Granada and Juan de la Cruz himself, who were persecuted by the Inquisitorial authorities. Inner devotional practices, inner prayer and meditation, and secret contemplation have always had the potential of eschewing the outward manifestations of the Catholic religion. Recollection, as we have attempted to demonstrate, is a long and arduous process that leads to union but needs a spiritual guide or director. However, individuals must never lose sight of their responsibility to the other human beings in the community. Reform begins from within but fans out to the community and the nation as a whole.

Chapter I
Endnotes

1. Henri S. Marrou. *St. Augustine and His Influence through the Ages*. Trans. Patrick H. Scott. London: Longmans, n.d. The *Confessions* was translated into Castilian in 1554. It is in fact a spiritual autobiography as well as a spiritual and psychological self-analysis. The German Hispanist Ludwig Pfandl comments on this book's influence in Spain, and most especially, on Santa Teresa de Jesús (*Historia de la literatura nacional española de la edad de oro*. Trans. Jorge Rubió Balaguer. Madrid: n.p., 1933, p. 6). The *Confessions* trace a man's conversion from a life of sin to one which is lived in God's grace and in the delight for spiritual things. Augustine states that he had previously longed after the material objects of this life; in other words, he had longed for things which would not be able to lead him toward God (*Confessions* IV: xi, 79). In a crucial passage of Book VI he describes how he entered into his own soul: "I entered and with the eyes of my soul I saw above the same eyes of my soul above my mind, the unchangeable Light" (VI: x, 149). In Book IX Augustine discusses the sin of vanity and in Book X he explains the function of memory (X: ii, 227-30). He writes about the effects of sin and the desire for lowly things (II: v, 24-25). He also writes about the vices of arrogance, ambition, the cruelty of the powerful, sloth, lasciviousness and the conditions which will lead the individual downward and not upward toward God (26-27).

2. In Morón Arroyo's book *La mística española*, I we read from an excerpt of the Pseudo-Dionysius's *De la jerarquía eclesiástica*, chapter iii: "Porque la beatitud divina, para hablar en lenguaje humano, carece de toda desemejanza

y es la plenitud de la luz sempiterna, perfecta que no carece de perfección alguna que purifica: esta misma sagrada purificación, iluminación y perfeccionamiento están sobre toda purificación y sobre toda iluminación" (80-81). Here the Areopagite outlines the three ways—*vías*—of the mystical process (Madrid: Ed. Alcalá, 1971).

3. Houston writes in his introduction to Bernard's works that Medieval monastic learning wanted to "taste God" more than to talk about Him. Individuals such as Bernard were not preoccupied with the theological equivalents of a Ph.D. in academia (xxxii). In Bernard's theory of love, it is the gift of love that orients the soul to God (xxxi). He adds that Bernard's treatise *On Free Will and Grace* is fundamental to the philosophy of love. To love God with disinterested love, a person must be free (xxxi). Bernard obviously draws much from Augustine since the exercise of love lies in the will. In other words, love enlightens reason and reason instructs love (xxxi). Houston makes the valid point that spiritual renewal in Bernard's time as well as in our own must include a new reverence for love, the reality of the love of God, and the practical demonstration of God's love in our personal relationships. The dimension of the heart according to Houston needs to be reinstated as more fundamental than the clearness of our brains (xxxvii).

4. In his study *Los grandes maestros de la vida espiritual* A. Royo Marín quotes from the Spanish translation of Bernard's commentary on the name of Mary: "Y el nombre de la virgen era María (Lc: 1, 27). Díganos algo acerca de este nombre, que significa Estrella del mar, y se adapta a la Virgen Madre con la mayor propiedad. Se compara a María oportunísimamente a la estrella, porque así como la estrella despide el rayo de su luz sin corrupción de sí misma así sin lesión suya, dio a luz la Virgen a su Hijo (122). In a sermon delivered on Christmas Eve Bernard refers to Mary's role as universal mediator. We here quote from Royo Marín's study: "Contemplad, pues, más altamente con cuanto afecto de devoción quiso fuese honrada María por nosotros aquel Señor que puso en ella toda la plenitud del bien para que, consiguientemente, si en nosotros hay algo de esperanza, algo de gracia, algo de salud, conozcamos que redunda de aquella que subió rebosando en delicias (*Sermón 3 en la vigilia de Navidad*, no. 10) (Royo Marín, 173).

5. Copleston adds in his discussion on Bonaventure: "God is not known by means of a likeness drawn from sense but rather by the soul's reflection on itself. It is made in the image of God and oriented towards God in desire and will. In this sense the idea of God is innate. . .The knowledge of the virtues too must be innate in the sense that it is not desired from sense-perception" (II: 285). He adds: "There is present in the soul a natural light by which it can recognize truth and rectitude and there is present also an affection or inclination of the will: charity" (286).

6. In the *Triple Way* Bonaventure describes the process of contemplation: "We desire to love the Spouse perfectly; we realize that the Beloved cannot be perceived through the sense, since He is neither seen nor heard, smelled, tasted or touched. He is not perceptible, yet He is a delight. He cannot be seen through senses, He is unimaginable, but He is all delight. He cannot be conceived through the intellect. He is beyond demonstration, definition, opinion, estimation, or investigation. He is inconceivable, but He is all delight" (Vinck, *Triple Way*, 71).

7. Bonaventure teaches that according to the original plan of nature humanity was created to enjoy the rest and peace of mystical contemplation. Unfortunately, humans turned away from this path with their fall which brought about ignorance of mind and the unruly passion of the flesh. In the contemplative model set forth by Bonaventure, the individual may achieve contemplation through prayer by which he/she receives grace through a reformation of one's manner of loving meditation for knowledge or enlightenment and contemplation, wherein the soul arrives at elevating wisdom (Bonaventure 34). In the *Triple Way* in chapter iii "On Contemplation" Bonaventure teaches how true wisdom is attained: "We attain true wisdom in its fullness through contemplation, our spirit enters the heavenly Jerusalem, eternal possession of supreme peace, the clear vision of supreme truth, the full enjoyment of supreme goodness or love" (Vinck, *Triple Way*, 77).

8. In the lecture given by Manuel de Castro and others at the Fundación Universitaria Español we read: "El descubrimiento del arte de imprimir revolucionó las disciplinas docentes y promovió de modo insospechado la interioridad. La multiplicación de libros espirituales a precio accesible, sacó

la espiritualidad de los conventos donde estaba celada y encubierta y posiblitó la meditación del coro conventual" (115).

9. Sanchís Alventosa writes on their designs to be the reformers of those Germanic lands affected by what he terms, "el aseglarmiento de las altas potestades eclesiásticas" (21). He adds: "No quieren que consista la vida cristiana en grandes pompas y solemnidades sino en vivir quieta y sosegadamente en lo íntimo del alma" (15). They followed the teaching that declared that the reign of God was within each individual. As in Spain, this quietude (complete repose) of the soul led to the establishment of groups that resembled the *alumbrados* in the sixteenth century, such as the Waldensians and the Poor Ones of Lyon (15).

10. In chapter vi of the *Directorio* Herp capsulizes his ascetico-mystical process which involved both the active as well as the contemplative life with these words: "Algunos, al convertirse eligen obedecer a Dios, a la Santa Iglesia y a sus superiores, se ejercitan en las virtudes, buenas costumbres, fiel observancia de los estatutos y ordenanzas, buscando en todo honrar a Dios y no a sí mesmos. Creen que la máxima perfección consiste en los ejercicios propios de la vida activa: oraciones vocales, meditación de los propios pecados, de la muerte, del juicio. Sólo la vida contemplativa amortigua todas las pasiones naturales, es decir, el desorden de la alegría, tristeza, complacencia, vanagloria, impaciencia, esperanzas vanas, excesivas. . .Se privan a sí mismos de la paz y del conocimiento del hombre interior, porque no andan bien recogidos ni están unidos plenamente a Dios. Sólo entonces descubrirán los íntimos, ocultos y amables caminos del Señor" (Herp 282-83). In the third "Tratado" of the *Directorio de contemplativos* we may read Herp's words in Spanish translation regarding the mystical way as he refers to the Pseudo-Dionysius: ". . .es una sabiduría recóndita, comunicada por Dios directamente al hombre en lo más hondo de su alma. . .Esta ciencia se inscribe en el corazón por iluminación divina como energía celestial proyectada sobre el alma. Cualquier persona por simple e iletrada que fuere, con tal que frecuente las virtudes y prácticas piadosas podrá recibirla inmediatamente de Dios, mediante amorosos afectos y elevaciones hacia El (Cap. xxii, 320).

11. Sanchís Alventosa describes Ruysbroeck's ascetical and mystical process: "La persona que ha llegado a la divina unión, allí se pierde en aquel abismo con fin de las divinas tinieblas. La Naturaleza divina es en contraposición con la Divina Esencia, Dios actuando, Dios en cuanto es principio de operaciones" (76). He adds subsequently: "El principio de la vida sobrenatural es como todo progreso en el camino del alma, tiene su origen en un misterioso toque divino en la ápice del espíritu" (78).

12. Ruysbroeck describes the richness of this inner devotion as a spiritual inebriation. He adds: "This is the richest life in manner of physical sensation that any man can attain upon this earth" (102). He makes here his analogy with the bee employing a beautiful metaphor: "The heart that is plundered as the bee robs the flower, and into which Christ the everlasting Sun does shine. He causes to swell and bloom and flower, and all its inward powers with joy and sweetness" (103-04).

13. See San Juan de la Cruz, *Noche oscura*, cf. T.S. Eliot's *Wasteland*.

14. In his introduction to the Spanish translation of the *Imitatio* Francisco Montes de Oca discusses Gerard de Groote, the founder of the Brothers of the Common Life, and the foremost developer of the *devotio moderna*. Montes de Oca writes: ". . .de Groote atacaba los vicios y abusos pero supo respetar a la Iglesia y a sus pastores y la absoluta ortodoxia de la *Devotio moderna*" (Kempis xiii). He describes this movement of renewal as "una reacción contra la espiritualidad especulativa" (ix). He adds: "Retorno a la puramente afectiva empírica, sin arte ni sistema. Propone dar al alma consejos apropiados a sus necesidades más bien que escritas, los misterios de la unión mística. . .el humilde conocimiento de ti mismo es más cierto camino para Dios que escrudiñar la profundidad de la ciencia. . ." (x). Montes de Oca ascertains that the *Devotio moderna* was a calling to conversion, moderation and the imitation of Christ in his life; from his passion and death to a life of charity and humility (xxi). It is Christocentric, its path is freedom, and the end of the imitation of Christ's life is union and conformity with God in contemplation.

Chapter II
Endnotes

1. Melquíades Andrés Martín in his lecture entitled "Reforma española y reforma luterana (afinidades y diferencias a la luz de los místicos, 1517-1536)" also believes that the Spanish reform is not necessarily a Counter-Reformation. He states: "Reforma española, no contrarreforma. Nacida en las últimas décadas del siglo XIV se desarrolla a lo largo de todo el siglo XV, principalmente en las observancias y reformas de los franciscanos, benedictinos, agustinos, dominicos y jerónimos" (published by the Fundación Universitaria Española, Madrid, 1975). Professor Andrés M. adds: "La reforma española se produce por vitalidad interior. Precede a la luterana casi siglo y medio. . .corre paralela a ella" (5).

2. Pedro Sainz Rodríguez in his study *Introducción a la Historia de la literature mística en España* (Madrid: Espasa-Calpe, 1984) lists these fifteenth century precursors of the religious literature of the sixteenth and seventeenth centuries in Spain. Sainz R. adds: "El volumen de la literatura místico-ascética abarca alrededor de 3.000 obras según la *Bibliotheca* de Nicolás Antonio." Sainz R. also explains that asceticism cannot be separated from mysticism: "Pero es imposible que en muchos casos se pueda separar el Ascetismo de la Mística" (222). Even works such as Santa Teresa's *Moradas*, according to Sainz R. are "ascéticas las tres primeras y místicas las cuatro últimas" (222). Sainz R. identifies four periods of Spanish mysticism: (1) "importacón e iniciación", its origins in the Medieval period up to 1500; (2) "asimilación", from 1500 to 1560 (this period includes writers such as Juan de Avila and Fray Luis de Granada; (3) "aportación y producción nacional",

1560 to 1600, this period includes the classical writers of Juan de la Cruz and Teresa de Jesús; (4) "decadencia o compilación doctrinal", one of the writers of this period would be Pedro de Nieremberg (222-23).

3. Cilveti stresses good works in his discussions on the spirituality of the Arabic Sufies and the Jewish writers of Spain. He writes that they place emphasis on the "obras en servicio de Dios y del prójimo" (17). He adds in the section on Jewish and Arabic mysticism in Spain that in their interpretation of the mystical experience, "la unión con Dios por semejanza y no por identidad" is an important factor. He continues: "El alma y Dios conservan su individualidad" with the obvious difference that ". . .el Dios con que se une el alma es la Trinidad" in the case of the Christian mystics (19). In his discussion of the Jewish *Zohar* the union is described in the following way: "El alma es recibida en el `templo de amor' y contempla la divina presencia a través de un 'Brillante Espejo'." He describes images such as "fuego de llama", "lámparas", "cauterios", "luz" and the image of the "ríos a la mar" (30).

4. Cilveti describes this humbling effect on the individual as he contemplates his own worldliness *vis-à-vis* God's as, "la pobreza espiritual" and the freeing oneself (divesting oneself) of the sensible appetites which he calls "desnudez de la voluntad o de los sentidos." He adds that the images of "desnudez del gusto" and "apetito de ellas deja al alma libre y vacía de ellas." He also describes the purity of the soul as a "desprendimiento" (18). The Spanish Arabist Asín Palacios considers Ibn Abbad de Ronda (1332-1399) as a precursor of Juan de la Cruz (Cilveti 89). See M. Asín Palacios *El islam cristianizado*, as well as I. W. Sweetman's *Islam and Christian Theology* (London: 1952). See also Luce López Baralt, *Islam in Spanish Literature: From the Middle Ages to the Present*. Trans. Andrew Hurley (San Juan: Ed. de la U de Puerto Rico, 1992).

5. García López in his study of Spanish literature in the section entitled "Mística y ascética: la prosa religiosa" also mentions the more than 3,000 titles produced during the Renaissance period in Spain. He describes the three phases of the spiritual journey to God in this way: "Ascética equivale al esfuerzo personal encaminado a lograr la máxima perfección del espíritu mediante la práctica

de las virtudes y el dominio de las pasiones. La mística aspira a un fin más alto: la íntima unión del alma con Dios, anticipando en lo posible la absoluta beatitud que sólo se alcanza con plenitud en la otra vida" (202). García López adds: "Nada vale aquí el propio esfuerzo puesto que todo depende de la voluntad divina" (202). According to García López "la vía iluminativa (*illuminatio*) corresponde ya a la mística. El alma libre de sus defectos anteriores comienza a participar-sin cooperación por su parte—de los dones del Espíritu Santo y a gozar de la presencia de Dios" (202). García López does not mention the spiritual dryness or sterility nor the temptations that take place in the second phase of the spiritual journey to God. He also lists the symbols and metaphors used by these Spanish writers of spirituality in their attempts to describe what the individual feels and experiences in the mystical way. These are: "noche oscura", "mariposa", "gozosa pena", "erizo", "tortuga", "cauterio", "noria", "fuente", "martirio-sabroso", "toques", "música callada", "rayo de tinieblas", "desposorio espiritual", "llama", and others. He also makes mention of the exaltation or divinization of sexual and common language (202-04). The inner way of Recollection and union many times led certain groups such as the *Alumbrados* to believe that since they had achieved such a state of perfection that they could not be capable of sin. Miguel de Molinos got into trouble with the inquisitorial authorities because he believed this very thing, or at least he was accused of this. However, classical Spanish literature of spirituality always maintains that individuals preserve their individuality and that they are responsible for their actions in this life. Because all individuals possess a physical body, they must continue to persevere and perform good works to keep from falling into sin. Contemplation and union perfect Christian life, but this does not mean that the individual is exempt from existing in the fallen nature of all humanity for it does not free him/her from the responsibilities to fellow human beings.

6. The gifts of the Holy Spirit are: fortitude, good counsel, intelligence, knowledge, wisdom, and fear of God.

7. There are various types of graces according to Catholic theology. Tanquerey identifies actual grace and habitual grace which make the individual similar to God. Actual grace illuminates our intellect and gives strength to our will.

The life of grace perfects and gives a supernatural substance to all of the elements of the soul, and it directs the soul to its ultimate end which is the possession of God through a type of beatific vision and the love which that vision engenders. Tanquerey defines grace as, "una cualidad sobrenatural, inherente a nuestra alma, que nos hace partícipes real, formal, pero accidentalmente, de la naturaleza y de la vida divina" (66-68). He adds that grace, "nos hace deiformes (semejantes a Dios). . .una vida semejante a la de Dios" (68-69).

8. The theological virtues are faith, hope and charity. The moral or cardinal virtues are prudence, justice, fortitude, and temperance.

9. Another theological term used by the ascetico-devotional-contemplative-mystical writers of Spain is *los carismas*, which are also gifts proffered by God with abundance to an individual. Several examples of these gifts are the art of preaching, discursive knowledge, the gift of performing miracles, the gift of prophecy, and the gift of speaking in tongues (Tanquerey 90).

10. The writers of spiritual literature in Spain categorize the different types of devotion according to the object of this devotion. These are: *dulia*, the cult that pays tribute to the angels; *latria*, which is the devotion that can only be offered to God; *hiperdulia*, the veneration of the Virgin Mary.

11. It must be stressed once more that the difference between the spirituality of Recollection (*recogimiento*) and the *alumbrados* or the *dejados* is the fact that these put all of their emphasis in the power of God's graces. They abandon themselves completely to God's power and in the process feel free from doing the good works and practicing the Christian virtues that are essential to the spirituality of Recollection. This is a long process that will lead to union with God, but it involves ascetical exercises, prayer, devotional reading, and, most importantly, good works and the practice of the Christian virtues. Many Illuminists in Spain actually believed that because they had abandoned themselves to God that they were above sin, and this led to many of their problems with the inquisitorial authorities.

12. The first (initial) or purgative stage of the spiritual ascent to God is perceived to be negative because it consists in recognizing our insignificance, and it involves the cleansing of the deadly sins and vices through self-abnegation. It

seeks to purge, cleanse, liberate individuals from their attachment to the material things of the world, as well as the vices such as sloth, arrogance, pride, idleness, lasciviousness, gluttony, covetousness, etc. In addition to the above, it seeks to eschew love of honor and position, fame, envy, anger, desire for money and earthly possessions, and the love of expensive clothing and fineries in addition to palaces. These are the things that weigh down the individual's soul and permit it to become attached to this world and thus prevent it from looking up to God.

13. The Franciscan reforms referred to these religious houses of retreat as *"recolectorios"*, *"conventos de retiro"*, and *"casas de oraciones y retiro."* These were one of the principle catalysts of the Spanish reform. The important protagonists include many of the writers that we shall be investigating in this study: Bernabé de Palma, Alfonso de Madrid, Bernardino de Laredo, Francisco de Osuna, Antonio de Guevara, Pedro de Alcántara, Juan de los Angeles, Diego de Estella, and Luis de Alcalá, in addition to many others. It is within these Franciscan communities that the practice of mental prayer became a common part of the monastic day. It consisted of reading, prayer, devotion, meditation and contemplation for a period of an hour and a half each day of the week (Andrés M., *Teologia esp.* I: 112-13). These practices led to contemplation and ultimately to union with God for a few members of the community. According to Melquíades Andrés M. all of these ascetical and devotional practices led to the spiritual renewal and reform of each member of the community as well as the entire community (*Teologia esp.* I: 114).

14. Miguel Cruz Hernández in his book *El pensamiento de Ramon Llull* writes on the need for reform in the Church during the thirteenth and fourteenth centuries: "Espirituales, beguines e iluminados, albigenses, valdenses y cátaros; personalidades como Joaquín de Fiore o Arnau de Vilanova, todos con evidentes diferencias pero sobre una base común, el clamor por la verdadera Jerusalén contra la Babilonia civil o eclesiástica, el retorno a una más imaginada que real simplicidad evangélica, la metodología del despojo radical de todo hasta la desnudez franciscana, la liberación de una jerarquía eclesiástica que en lugar de ser espejo de la divina, era interesada recaudadora

eñ las vías de acceso a la salvación eterna; el ansia de una nueva y definitiva cristianidad (Madrid: Castalia, 1877, 213-14).

15. Llull writes: "ofici de cavaller és mantenir e defendre la sancta fe catòlica per la qual Dèu lo pare tramès son Fill pendre carn en la verge gloriosa nostra dona Sancta Maria, e per la fe a honrar. . . soferí en este mon molts treballs e moltes ontes e greu mort" (47). Llull continues: "Per los cavallers deu esser mantenguda justícia. . ." (*Orde* 49). In other words, the profession of knighthood must maintain and defend the Catholic faith for whom God became man and suffered death. In addition, justice must be preserved by the knight.

16. After having been pope, Blanquerna retires to his hermitage. The emperor is looking for him and on the way finds a bishop who was on his way to Rome, where he would teach the *Arte abreviado de encontrar la verdad*. We cite from the Spanish translation of *Blanquerna*: "Gran gusto y placer tuvo el Emperador de la devoción del Obispo, y éste de la del Emperador, quien rogó al Obispo que en la corte de Roma fuese Procurador de la Virtud de Valor, la cual ha sido injuriada por tantas personas e impedidas en dar honor y loor a Dios: `y diréis al juglar de Valor, dijo el Emperador al Obispo, que cante estas coplas en la corte, para que el Señor Papa y los Señores Cardenales se acuerden mejor de los hechos y santa vida de los Apóstoles, en cuyos tiempos la santidad de la vida y la devoción vivían y reinaban en el mundo" (*Blanquera* 273). We now quote from the poem that is attached to the end of the *Blanquerna*. It gives us a good idea about the tone of religious reform which seeks to establish a return to a more pure and evangelical Christianity:

> *Ya en el mundo ha nacido*
> *Nuevo fervor hoy día*
> *Apostólico, puro y peregrino,*
> *La edad ha renacido*
> *En que la sangre hervía*
> *Inflamada de amor todo Divino:*
> *Luego el amador fino*
> *Vaya y publique osado,*
> *El gran Poder bendito,*

Y el saber infinito
De nuestro Salvador Dios encarnado:
A fin que el Mundo entero
Ame y sirva a Jesus Dios verdadero.
  Ya los Frailes menores
Recuerdan fervorosos,
De un Dios crucificado,
Los debidos Honores;
Ya en Miramar, dichosos,
Que el gran Rey de Mallorca hà destinado,
Y en Colegio fundado,
Se ocupan estudiando,
El idioma morisco;
Y en el Cristiano aprisco,
Recogerán al moro bautizado;
Con que de Africa el suelo,
Volverá a fecundarse para el Cielo.
  ¿Qué hacéis Predicadores?
Si tanto a Dios amáis,
Esta ocasión lograd, que es oportuna,
Abades y Priores,
Y obispos, ¿en qué andáis?
Dejad allá los bienes de fortuna;
Sin tardanza ninguna,
Servid a Dios que es justo,
Reyes y potentados,
  ¿Qué pensáis, regalados,
Con comer y beber sin pena o justo,
Largos sueños durmiendo,
Se logre estar Dios gozando y viendo?

. . . .

*(*Blanquerna *273-75).*

17. The book ends with these words: "Por gracia de nuestro Señor Dios, ha finido el *Libro de Evast, Aloma y Blanquerna*, su hijo, en el cual se ha tratado del

Matrimonio, de Religión, de Prelacía en los Obispos y Arzobispos y de sus oficiales en sus Obispados; del Apostólico Señorío que tiene el Santo Padre Apostólico y los Señores Cardenales en el régimen espiritual de la Universal Iglesia Santa, y de la vida eremética contemplativa, para dar doctrina cómo todos los hombres deban vivir en este mundo en servicio de Dios, y recibir su Divina gracia, y en el otro mundo la Gloria, a la cual por su Divina Bondad nos quiera llevar para más perfectamente entenderle, amarle y servirle y de todo darle gracias sin fin. Amén" (*Blanquerna* 275).

Chapter III
Endnotes

1. In fol. 8 of *Via spiritus* we read: "Este es el camino verdadero para desarraigar los vicios y plantar las virtudes. Enseñe, pues, quien quisiere a guardar la vista y hacer abstinencia y tener paciencia y cosas semejantes para ensalzar virtudes y bondades, que yo no quiero enseñar ese camino, mas que trabajen lo primero de recoger los pensamientos dentro de sí mismos, mirando con mucha diligencia qué se trata en sus entrañas, y examinar lo que puede hacer y no hacer. . . (Footnote 7, Book II: 185, in Andrés Martín's *Teología espiritual*).

2. The *Libro llamado Via spiritus, o de la perfección espiritual del alma* was first published in Sevilla in 1532. Subsequent editions were published in these localities: Flanders (1533-34), Salamanca (1541). Three abridged versions were published in Valencia (1546), Toledo (1550 and 1553) and in Barcelona (1549).

3. Ortiz writes: "Señor, el amor es atrevido y por eso, y a ayuda de la Buena Pascua, envío a vuestra merced dos *abecedarios*, el uno en muestra de las riquezas del niño Dios, que eternamente recibió de Dios Padre, y con propriedades que manifiestan quién es Dios. El segundo demuestra las penas y trabajos del mismo bendito Jesús. . .El primer alfabeto, que ayuda a pensar quién es Dios en sí mismo, es el siguiente: Amor infinito, Bondad dadivosa, Contentamiento seguro, Deidad escondida, Eternidad interminable, Fortaleza invencible, Grandeza incomparable, Hermosura indecible, Justicia inflexible, Liberalidad purísima, Majestad tremenda, Naturaleza incomprensible,

Omnipotencia indeficiente, Piélago de no limitada sustancia, Sabiduría inconmutable, Trinidad en unidad, Unidad en Trinidad. . .

El segundo alfabeto es para pensar qué quiso tomar y sufrir por nosotros un tan gran Dios en su humanidad salvatísima, que tan unida tenía El. . . (Footnote 12, 204-05 in *Teología espiritual* II).

4. Andrés Martín explains that Gómez García, in addition to following Augustine, the Pseudo-Dionysius and Bernard, also follows the teachings found in the writings of Richard of St. Victor, wherein he proposes three degrees ("grados") of contemplation: ". . .por delatación o ensanchamiento, sublimación y aliviamiento, exceso y arrebatamiento mental" (I: 373). Gómez García also dedicates a chapter to the definition and exposition of the *devotio moderna* and methodical prayer (I: 373).

5. Jaime de Alcalá, O.F.M., Libro de la caballería cristiana, compuesto por el muy reverendo padre fray Jayme de Alcalá dirigido a la Ilustrísima doña Mariana de Córdova, muger del Ilustre señor do{n} Fadrique Enríquez de Rivera (Alcalá: Juan de Villanueva, 1570). This text is found in the rare book section of the Bibiloteca Nacional in Madrid (BNM R255).

6. ". . .y así concluye que la gracia de la confirmación es necesaria, no absolutamente que sin ella no nos podemos salvar, mas que sin ella o por vía de recibir el sacrmamento de la confirmación o por otra vía alcanzar se pueda los que peleamos en esta vida contra sus espirituales enemigos no pueden alcanzar el reyno de los cielos" (Alcalá fol. 27). Leemos nuestro Señor Jesu Cristo aver sufrido dolores, aver llorado, aver passado fatiga andando camino a pie descalzo, aver sido escupido, azotado y crucificado. . .nunca leemos que se viesse ni aver escogido alguna prosperidad deste siglo de donde nace la verdadera esperanza de los escogidos de la gloria" (Alcalá fol. 29).

7. Melquiades Andrés M. makes this commentary concerning Alcalá's *Caballería cristiana*, which he classifies as the first *libro de caballería a lo divino*: "La espiritualidad del caballero es varonil, recia, casi diría áspera, camina como peregrino en un mundo poblado de enemigos. Alcalá recomienda la soledad, el recogimiento, el morar el caballero dentro de sí, como liberación del mundo y de los placeres terrenos (*Los recogidos 779).*

8. In Melguíades Andrés M.'s study *Los recogidos*, the professor outlines the various early writers of Spanish spirituality in the late fifteenth and early sixteenth centuries and the involvement of the whole person in the process of Recollection: this is based on an ascetical method that not only involves the practice of the virtues and mental prayer, but penance, austerity, frugality, readings, simplicity, and the development of the love for manual work and a responsibility to the community, the society and the state. These, added to scriptural meditations, the imitation of Christ and meditations on his life, contemplation and the practice of the theological virtues involve all of the functions of the soul as well as those of the body (ch. 23). Also of interest is Andres's discussion of the thrust of the different religious orders and the emphasis that these place in their respective writings. For example, Franciscan spirituality is classified by Fray Bruno Ibeas as "sentimental"; Augustinian spirituality is as would be expected, "voluntarista"; the Carmelites demonstrate a spirituality which is described as "emotivo-activista"; Dominican expression of their spirituality is "intelectualista", and the Jesuit is "sistemativa" (28).

9. Other writers of Spanish spirituality refer to this piling up of graces and virtues using the term *hacimiento*, which the *Diccionario de la Lengua Española* of the Real Academia Española relates to "acción de gracias." This word is not used today. The dictionary states, "acción y efecto de hacer" (764).

10. We read in Ann Benjamin's translation of Augustine's *De libero arbitrio* (*On the Free Choice of the Will*) (New York: Liberal Arts Press, 1964) the following: "Evil in man arises not from some evil principle embodied in his nature, but from the will's free determination to turn from higher things to lower, from eternal to temporal. Evil is to be found in man's free choice to pervert and corrupt his own will by turning aside from the good which is proper to it, the ultimate good that is God" (25). This is what Fray Alonso has been explaining in the last few chapters of the second part of the *Arte*. R. A. Markus in his book *Saeculum: History and Society in the Theology of St. Augustine* (London: Cambridge UP, 1970), also terms this same phenomenon as *amor frui* and *amor uti*: "Augustine often distinguishes two attitudes whose misdirection is the perversion of right order which we call vice,

"enjoyment" *frui*, the attitude we entertain toward things we value for themselves, and "use" *uti* the attitude we entertain toward things we value for the sake of something else" (67). In Fray Alonso's case, as well as in Augustine, this something else is God.

11. Although Osuna wrote his *abecedario* at the convent of La Salceda, he dedicated it to the Marqués de Villena. The *alumbrados, dejados, recogidos* and *quietistas* can all trace their origins to the Franciscan reform in central Spain. Antonio Márquez in his study *Los Alumbrados* writes: "El fenómeno se produce dentro de la reforma franciscana desarrollada por Cisneros y tiene estrecha vinculación con toda la tradición heterodoxa cristiana" (90). However, the art of Recollection, unlike the others mentioned above, although suspect, was never declared to be heretical.

12. Francisco de Osuna wrote a work called *Norte de estados* in which he writes, "se da regla de vivir a los mancebos, y a los casados, e a los viudos y a todos los continentes, y se tratan muy por extenso los remedios del desastrado casamiento " (Sevilla, 1531). Apparently, Cervantes was familiar with this work since it inspired several episodes in the *Quijote*, specifically, at least one scene in Sancho's experience as governor of Barataria. Several critics have written detailed studies of Francisco de Osuna and his works; one of these is Fidele de Ros's *Le pere Francoise de Osuna. Sa vie, son oeuvre, sa doctrine spirituelle* (Paris, 1936) (Andrés Martín, *Teología española*, 206-07).

13. Francisco de Osuna studied theology at the University of Alcalá. One of the important theological *Facultades* was that of Nominalism there. The nominalists who go back to William of Ockham and Gabriel Biel also emphasized the crucial role of the will, its freedom, and God's generosity in rendering graces (freely given grace). According to Andrés in his introduction to the *Tercer abecedario espiritual*, "otro aspecto de la teología nominal es la universalización de la perfección cristiana o su extensión a todos los bautizados. Dios no niega la gracia al que hace lo que le corresponde" (11-12). This leads to what Andrés Martín calls "individualismo y positivismo nominalista" (12). Nominalism devotes its attention to the problems of justification, merit, the giving of grace, the love of God above all things, and

God's assistance freely given to human beings. Nominalism "valora la experiencia individual, la espiritualidad afectiva, y el puro amor y la liturgia" (12).

14. These are Francisco de Osuna's major works: *Primer abecedario espiritual* (Sevilla, 1528; Burgos, 1537; Medina, 1544; Zaragoza, 1546; Sevilla, 1554; Venecia, 1583 (in Italian); *Segundo abecedario espiritual* (which treats different types of spiritual exercises), Sevilla, 1530; Burgos, 1545; Sevilla, 1559; Burgos, 1555; *Tercer abecedario espiritual* (Sevilla, 1530; Valladolid, 1537; Burgos, 1554; Sevilla, 1554; Burgos, 1555; Madrid, 1638, 1911; London, 1931 and 1948 (English translations); *Ley de amor o cuarta parte o cuarto abecedario espiritual: donde se tratan muy de raíz del amor y la teología que pertenece no menos al entendimiento que a la voluntad* (Sevilla, 1530; Burgos, 1536, 1542; Valladolid, 1551, Sevilla, 1554; Valladolid, 1556; *Quinto abecedario espiritual: consuelo de pobres y aviso de ricos* (Burgos, 1542; Sevilla, 1554; Burgos, 1554; *Sexto abecedario espiritual* (Medina del Campo, 1554; Sevilla, 1554; *Norte de estados: enseña qué tal ha de ser la vida del cristiano casado. Da regla de vivir a maridos y a los casados, y a los viudos y a todos los continentes y se tratan de los remedios del desastrado matrimonio* (Sevilla, 1551; Burgos, 1541, 1550, 1610?) (22-23). Once again, we are most grateful to Prof. Andrés M. who has contributed so much through his voluminous meticulously, and painstakingly researched studies of Spanish spirituality of the Renaissance, which also include his critical edition of the *Tercer abecedario espiritual*, his *Los recogios*, and his marvelous two volume *La teología española en el siglo XVI*. Without these sources a good portion of our own study would be missing.

15. Andrés Martín writes in the introduction to the *Tercer abecedario espiritual*: "A partir de 1537 Osuna se convierte en maestro espiritual de Santa Teresa. Incluye la vía de recogimiento San Juan de la Cruz, San Juan de Avila, San Francisco de Borja y algunos de los primeros miembros de la Compañía de Jesús" (61).

16. Andrés M. writes that, "la vía de recogimiento" is "buscar a Dios en el corazón sin salir de sí." In other words, person and spirit are not divided, neither is the body and the heart in this process (63).

17. These are the multifaceted meanings of the verb *recoger*: "levantar una cosa caída, juntar cosas dispersas, ir juntando, cosechar, encoger, acoger o dar asilo, ir a buscar, retirar de la circulación, obtener, captar, enterarse o valerse de algo, ensimismarse, abstraerse el espíritu de lo que pueda impedir la meditación o contemplación" (64-65).

18. Osuna advises his readers to also seek a physical recollection. He refers to, "la excelencia de un sitio apartado—celda o habitación, o ermita u otra cualquier parte escondida, donde se apartan los justos a orar" (100).

19. Osuna refers to the Augustinian image of the peregrine soul which must wander in this material world. The inner way of Recollection allows the individual to share in God's spiritual delights while yet imprisoned in the material body. God, according to Osuna, has given us this gift of the soul through which we can share and feel his spiritual sweetness (219).

20. We read in the 1574 edition published at Toledo: "libro espiritual que trata de los malos lenguajes del mundo, carne o demonio, y de los remedios contra ellos de la fe y del proprio conocimiento, de la penitencia, de la oración, meditación, y passión de nuestro Señor, Jesu Cristo, y del amor de los próximos" (51). In Psalm 45 we read: "Listen, daughter, pay careful attention / forget your nation and your own ancestral home, / then, the king will fall in love with your beauty.

21. Juan de Avila was cleared by the Inquisition since his *Avertencias* were sent to the Council of Trent. Here are some of the points that Sala Balust presents which made church officials suspicious of Avila: "Juan de Avila había dicho en confesión que los quemados por la Inquisición eran mártires. . .que el cielo es para los pobres y labriegos y que es imposible que los ricos se salven. . .; la oración debe ser mental; no había por qué maravillarse de las comunicaciones de Dios a mujeres, puesto que viene diariamente a manos de los sacerdotes; . . .era mejor dar limosnas que dejar capellanías. . .En Ecija y otros lugares había rumores secretos de gente en las que predicaba y luego hacía quitar la luz, quedando todos en contemplación. . .muchas veces se retiró en Ecija con una beata que tenía desmayos y arrobos" (Sala Balust, *Obras completas del Beato J. de Avila*, Introducción 44). Much of this activity had elements common to Illuminism as far as the Inquisition was concerned.

22. Avila uses the example of Mary Magdalen to make his point about how faith and love bring justification: ". . .y cuando el Señor habló de la fe y el amor, así en el negocio de la Magdalena, como en el que dijimos de sus discípulos nombró primero al amor que a la fe, dándole el primer lugar en la perfección al que es acto de la voluntad, que en cierta manera es postrero, cotejado con el acto del entendimiento, al cual pertenece la fe" (666). Love is more important for justification than faith, and love is a function of the will, just as faith is a function of the intellect.

23. Ludwig Pfandl suggests that the poem's spirit corresponds more to the sixteenth century even though it was published in the seventeenth. The fact that it is anonymous might be attributed to the fact that it originated in the environment of the inner spirituality of Recollection, and we believe that it is a literary product of this same mode of spirituality. We also believe that Juan de Avila or one of his disciples, Luis de Granada, Teresa de Jesús, or Diego de Mendoza composed it. It was most probably written when a cloud of suspicion hovered over all of the spirituality of Recollection. See Pfandl's *Historia de la literatura española de la edad de Oro.* Trans. Jorge Rubió Balaguer (Madrid: n.p., 1933).

24. Juan de Avila writes the following about the exercises that make up part of devotional reading: ". . .y como ya os he dicho, no ha de ser la lección hasta del todo cansar, mas para despertar el apetito del ánima y dar materia a pensar y orar (meditation and prayer) y los libros que para pensar en la pasión pueden aprovechar, entre otros, son las *Meditaciones* de San Agustín en latín, y las del padre fray Luis de Granada en romance, y el Cartujano que escribe sobre todos los Evangelios (743; ch. 74). We believe that *el Cartujano* is the author of the above cited work *Sol de contemplación* by Hugo de Balma.

25. See *De Civitatis Dei* I: bk 14, ch. 28. Osuna quotes from Augustine's masterpiece: "El amor de sí mimso, hasta despreciar a Dios, hizo a la ciudad terrenal, el amor de Dios, hasta despreciar a sí mismo, hizo la ciudad celestial" (806).

Chapter IV
Endnotes

1. Gomis, Juan Bautista, OFM. *Subida del monte Sión*. In *Místicos franciscanos españoles*. Biblioteca de Autores Cristianos. Madrid: Ed. Católica, 1948. For an excellent English translation see Edgar Allison Peer's *The Ascent of Mount Sion. Third Part* (New York: Harper, n.d.). Bernardino de Laredo was a medical doctor by training before he became a Franciscan brother; it is interesting that he never was ordained a priest. The word "redaño" in the dictionary means "prolongación del peritoneo." It is in fact a medical term which relates to peritonitis, an inflammation of the peritoneum or the membrane lining the walls of the abdominal cavity and enclosing the viscera. It's relation to "grosura", eating fat meat in opposition to fasting, seems to suggest gluttony and fat which weighs the body down and obstructs the spiritual ascent to God. We can only conjecture on this particular point.

2. Mount Sion, the place of contemplation, where the soul meets God: "está ladeada", it is skirted by the north wind because of its lofty position.

3. Cuando tañe a las horas, recoja en el pensamiento lo que aquella hora significa; la person en maitines, el discurso entre los jueces, prima, la columna (scourging), la tercia (terse), la cruz, la nona (none), el descendimiento de la cruz, las vísperas (vespers), la sepultura o monumento, las completas (compline) (Bernardino, *Subida* 32).

4. Bernardino also describes the whole person: "El ánima es el hombre interior, el cuerpo es el hombre exterior. Todo el hombre es el ánima y el cuerpo" (65).

5. We must keep in mind that the ascent to the mount of contemplation is accomplished on a horse, which in effect is the body. It is interesting that the soul ascends to this mountain riding on the body, and the virtues are the accouterments of this spiritual knighthood.

6. Bernardino identifies or describes the Trinity and the Virgin's womb with these words: "piélago", infinite sea, "fuente", fountain, "divinidad", eternal or divine substance, "tres ríos", triune essence, "río", also the assumed humanity of Christ. "Fuente" can also be the Virgin's womb, and the measured river may flow out of the fountain ("río medido") (155).

7. Bernardino uses these words to describe the point at which Christ as the Word takes on a human body: "el divino injerto, la divina potencia, la infinita bondad, sabiduría infinita, la potencia—Padre, la sabiduría, el Hijo, la bondad, el Espíritu Santo." In other words, when the Word became incarnate it did not separate for one instant from its equality with the Father and the Holy Spirit (Bernardino, *Subida* 161).

8. Bernardino had described God as "sustancia simplicísima": "Substancia es toda cosa que da ayuda a otra substancia a poderse conservar; tierra, yerba, carnero, hombre exterior. Sólo aquello se puede decir simple que nunca recibió alguna composición"; this privilege only belongs to God. This simple substance also sustains the rational soul of humans (167; ch. 7). Thus, all that God created is compound and is made up of contrary qualities.

9. Bernardino describes the process of contemplating God with the verbs, "gozar", to enjoy or to have possession of, "contemplar", to meditate on God, and "fruir", to enjoy the fruits of or live happily with.

10. Bernardino gives a detailed description of the mental image of the celestial city: ". . .que es tesoro de Dios el fuego de aqueste cirio. . .Es el muro cristalino, la clara virginidad que esclarece la ciudad; las diversas gemmas o preciosas piedras con la grande diversidad de los bienaventurados, doce torres, doce apóstoles, cuatro escudos con los cuatro evangelistas, y aun tenemos otra torre que es castillo, es fortaleza, casa fuerte, casa real, es aposento del rey, alcázar de la ciudad, está más cerca del cirio, es homenaje de Dios. Es fabricada por la mano de Dios, y es esposa de Dios, y es fundada sobre un muy fino cristal tan fuerte como diamante. . .de safiro y esmaragdo

son sus puertas fabricadas. . .las puertas de la ciudad celestial son edificadas de safiro y esmaragdo. La puerta por donde entramos a Dios nuestra muy gran Señora es. . .la torre principal de la ciudad soberana" (Bernardino, *Subida* 272-73).

11. Bernardino has three names for the soul according to the different operations of its powers: "ánima" involves the memory, and it is the part that needs to be purged in the first phase of the spiritual ascent to God; "espíritu", is the intellect and is involved in the illuminative phase of the spiritual journey; "mente" is the highest part or essence of the soul which contemplates God and shares in his life or unites with Him in the final stage of the *via mystica*.

12. Bernardino de Laredo calls this "ciencia escondida, ciencia infusa, sabiduría escondida o secreta o mística teología, o ejercicio de aspiración, súbito y momentáneo levantamiento mental" (Bernardino, *Subida* 324).

13. In this section of the *Subida*, Bernardino refers to the Psuedo-Dionysius's *Nombres divinos* wherein one of God's names is love. He also refers to the Areopagite's *Mystica Theologia*, where Bernardino translates: "En cada tocamineto que es hecho al ánima del amor increado es alumbrado el Entendimiento tan maravillosamente" (328). He also mentions the contemplative Enrique de Balma, where he has learned that through the bond of love the soul is made more capable to achieve union with God (327).

14. "Amor operativo nos hace andar cuidadosos y sirvientes por llegar a la virtud, y desechar nuestros vicios y tener vida ordenada. Amor desnudo, amamos a Dios por solo amigable amor, aparta de nosotros todo lo que no nos es favorable; tiene desnudo de todo nuestro interese. Amor esencial, cresce este amor hasta irse derecho a Dios, sin medio de las criaturas ni por vía de las potencias, sino por aspiración de afectiva, la cual súbito recoge el ánima en unidad de substancia. Amor unitivo, la dignación divina recibe este amor que en nuestras ánimas cría y ayunta nuestro amor criado en su amor infinito, porque ya está unido a Dios por la divina demencia" (Bernardino, *Subida* 368).

15. We present here these other *versos*:

> *En el inmenso secreto,*
> *sólo está su propio objeto (*Verso *12).*
> *El que es más enamorado,*
> *es de sí más descuidado (*Verso *13).*
> *La mansedumbre más quieta,*
> *es en amor más perfecta (*Verso *14).*
> *Y muy gran señal de amor,*
> *es padescer con fervor (*Verso *15).*
> *Quien no cesa de desear*
> *no puede cesar de amar (*Verso *16).*
> *La afición, con el deseo,*
> *da indulgencia y jubileo (*Verso *17).*

He explains "la afectiva", which is the lifting of the soul on the wings of love: "mas la afectiva considerámosla con su súbito o momentáneo levantamiento a se ayuntar con su Dios sin medio de cosa criada" (402). In *Verso* 19 we read: "El ánima enamorada siempre está necesitada" (Bernardino, *Subida* 425).

16. Thanks to Melquíades Andrés Martín's book, we found the 1541 Alcalá manuscript in the Biblioteca Nacional in Madrid. It is in the special collection area with the call numbers R.2233 and R.3826. There was a 1947 edition published in Madrid. Here are the editions: Alcalá, Juan de Brocar, 1541; Antwerp, 1556, Baeza, 1551, Alcalá, 1589.

17. Alcántara's treatise has been relatively popular in the English speaking world. G. Willoughby's translation *A Golden Treatise of Mental Prayer* was published in Brussels in 1632. There was a 1926 translation carried out by Dominic Devas and published in London in that same year and also a 1949 translation *A Golden Treatise of Mental Prayer* done by G. F. Bullock and published both in London and at Mowbray, N.Y. It was translated into Italian in 1583, into German in 1605, into Latin in 1607, and into French in 1622.

18. Devas informs us that it was in this final period of his life that he became acquainted with Teresa de Jesús. She acknowledges this often and in most generous terms all the help that he gave her both individually for her own spiritual guidance and in the great work of rebuilding Carmel (vi).

19. The seven last words on the Cross are the following: (1) Father, forgive them for they know not what they do; (2) This day thou shalt be with me in paradise; (3) Woman, behold thy son, son behold thy mother; (4) I thirst; (5) My God, my God, why hast Thou forsaken me; (6) It is consummated; (7) Father, unto Thy hand I commend my spirit (73).

20. It is important to keep in mind the crucial role of the spiritual guide, director or confessor in the spirituality of Recollection during the Golden Age. This is a vital ingredient in the religious climate of sixteenth century Spain in the attempt to avoid excessive individualism which might lead to heresy: Lutheranism, Illuminism, etc. The Inquisition was very suspicious of those who practiced this inner form of Catholicism, and most especially after the outbreak of the Lutheran reformation in western Europe. The main purpose of the spiritual director was to guide the individuals in their path to God within the parameters of Catholic orthodoxy.

21. It is important that what scholars have identified as Spanish mysticism is in reality part of the inner path of Recollection, which includes ascetical practices and vocal prayer in its first stage or purgative phase. Mental prayer, the imitation of Christ, the practice of the Christian virtues, contemplation and union simply are part of the latter stages of the spiritual ascent or journey to God and Christian perfection. Ascetical practices, self-knowledge, self-abnegation, and vocal and public prayers are encouraged in this spiritual process. We must also keep in mind that *mystica* implies secret or something hidden, which is also an integral part of the spirituality of Recollection.

22. Indeed, Melchor Cano, a theologian at the Council of Trent, and consultant to Phillip II and to the Inquisition, viciously attacked his fellow Dominicans, and most especially, Bartolomé de Carranza, Archbishop of Toledo. He also attacked Luis de Granada for promoting the practice of inner, mental prayer among the common people.

23. See the *Collected Works of St. Theresa of Avila*, translated by Kieran Kavanaugh, O.C.D. and Otilio Rodríguez, O.C.D. (Washington, D.C.: Institute of Carmelite Studies, 1980), 24. Among the Dominicans there were two camps; one was made up of scholastic, conservative theologians, such as Cano, Domingo de Soto, and Fernando Valdés; the other who contributed

with their works to the development of the inner path of Recollection with its mental prayer.

24. See *Obras completas*. 2nd edition (Madrid: Editorial de Espiritualidad, 1976), 661.

25. See *Confessions* X, ch. 27. In her *Libro de la vida*, chapter 40, Teresa writes: "Paréceme provechosa esta visión para personas de recogimiento para enseñarse a considerar a el Señor en lo muy interior de su alma, que es consideración que más se apega, y muy más fructuosa que fuera de sí, como otras veces he dicho, y en algunos libros de oración está escrito adónde se ha de buscar a Dios. En especial lo dice el glorioso San Agustín, que ni en las plazas, ni en los contentos, ni por ninguna parte que le buscaba le hallaba, como dentro de sí" (361).

26. Daniel de Pablo Maroto, the editor of *Camino de perfección* in *Obras completas* in a footnote to chapter 26 writes that Teresa uses various authorities when she treats the topic of Recollection, and one of these is Bernardino de Laredo and his *Subida del Monte Sión*. He cites *Vida* 23: 2 where we read: "Mirando libros, para ver si sabría decir la oración que tenía hallé en uno que llaman *Subida del Monte* en los que toca a unión del alma con Dios, todas las señales que yo tenía en aquél no pensar nada, que esto era lo que yo más decía; que no podía pensar nada cuando tenía aquella oración" (*Vida* 23: 12, 183-84). In *Vida* 4: 7 she refers to Francisco de Osuna's *Tercer abecedario espiritual*: "Cuando iba me dio aquel tío mío, que tengo dicho, que estaba en el camino, un libro. Llámase *Tercer abecedario* que trata de enseñar oración de recogimiento" (24). She admits that she considered that book as one of her mentors. She also refers to this inner prayer as "oración de quietud" (25).

27. Teresa alludes again to the image of the "delatamiento" or "ensanchamiento" of the soul in this prayer of Recollection. She adds: ". . .a manera de como si el agua que mana de una fuente estuviere labrada de una cosa que mientras más agua manase, más grande se hiciese el edificio; así parece en esta oración, y otras muchas maravillas que hace Dios en el alma que la habilita y va disponiendo para que quepa todo en ella. Así, esta suavidad y ensanchamiento interior se ve en el que le queda para no estar tan alada como

antes en las cosas del servicio de Dios sino con mucha más anchura, así en no se apretar con el temor del infierno, porque aunque le queda mayor de no ofender a Dios - el servil piérdese aquí—queda con gran confianza que le ha de gozar" (*Cuartas moradas*, 924).

28. We read in the Song of Songs:

> *Scarcely had I passed them*
> *than I found him whom my heart loves.*
> *I held him fast, nor would I let him go*
> *till I had brought him*
> *into my mother's house*
> *into the room of her who conceived me (3.4)*
> *How delicious is your love, more delicious than wine!*
> *How fragrant your perfumes,*
> *more fragrant than all other spices!*
> *Your lips, my promised one,*
> *distill wild honey.*
> *Honey and milk*
> *are under your tongue (4.10-14).*
> *His conversation is sweetness itself,*
> *he is altogether lovable.*
> *Such is my Beloved, such is my friend,*
> *O daughters of Jerusalem. (5.16).*
> *She is a garden enclosed,*
> *my sister, my promised bride,*
> *a garden enclosed,*
> *a sealed fountain; (4.12)*
> *I come into my garden,*
> *my sister, my promised bride,*
> *I gather my mirrh and balsam,*
> *I eat my honey and my honey-comb,*
> *I drink my wine and my milk (5.1).*

29. *Obras completas.* 2nd edition (Madrid: Editorial de Espiritualidad, 1980). This critical edition was prepared by José Vicente Rodríguez and Federico Ruiz Salvador.

30. This particular poem is famous:

> *Para venir a gustarlo todo,*
> *no quieras tener gusto en nada.*
> *Para venir a poseerlo todo,*
> *no quieras poseer algo en nada.*
> *Para venir a serlo todo,*
> *no quieras ser algo en nada.*
> *Para venir a saberlo todo,*
> *no quieras saber algo en nada (235-36).*

31. Spiritual lust is explained by Juan de la Cruz in this way: ". . .porque muchas veces acaece que en los mismos ejercicios espirituales sin ser en su mano, se levantan en la sensualidad movimientos y actos torpes, y a veces aun cuando el espíritu está en mucha oración, o ejercitando los Sacramentos de la Penitencia y Eucaristía. Los cuales, como digo, sin ser en su mano, proceden de una de tres causas. La primera procede muchas veces del gusto que tiene el natural en las cosas espirituales; porque, como gusta el espíritu y sentido, con aquella recreación se mueve cada parte del hombre a delectarse según su porción y propiedad; porque entonces el espíritu se mueve a recreación y gusto de Dios, que es la parte superior, y la sensualidad, que es la porción inferior, se mueve a gusto y deleite sensual, porque no sabe ella tener ni tomar otro, y tomas entonces el más conjunto a sí, que es el sensual torpe" (526). He also explains "gula espiritual": "Porque muchos de estos engolosinados con el sabor y gusto que hallan, en los tales ejercicios procuraban más el sabor que la pureza del espíritu y descreación de él, que es lo que Dios mira y acepta en todo el camino espiritual" (531). He continues: ". . .porque atraídos del gusto que allí hallan, algunos se matan a penitencias y otros se debilitan con algunos, haciendo más de lo que su flaqueza sufre, sin orden ni consejo ajeno" (531).

32. There are ten degrees or "grados." José Vicente Rodríguez, in a footnote in the critical edition of the *Noche oscura*, presents the ten degrees or "grados de la

escala divina", which San Juan outlines in various chapters beginning with chapter 19. These are culled from a spiritual treatise by a Dominican of the late thirteenth century and early fourteenth century, Helvicus Teudonticus, *De delectione Dei et proximi; de decem gradibus amoris secundum Bernardum.* These are:

1. enfermar provechosamente
2. buscar sin cesar
3. obrar y no faltar
4. subir sin fatigarse
5. apetecer impacientemente
6. correr ligeramente
7. atrever con vehemencia
8. apretar sin soltar
9. arder con suavidad
10. asimilarse totalmente

33. In the Prologue to *Llama de amor viva*, San Juan writes that the mystical union and the state of being transformed are the most perfect degrees of perfection that a person may attain. He adds: "esta llama de amor es el Espíritu Santo, el alma lo siente como fuego que consume y la diferencia que hay entre el hábito y el acto, hay entre la transformación en amor y la llama de amor que es la que hay entre el madero inflamado y la llama del que la llamó es efecto del fuego que allí está. . .De Donde el alma que está en estado de transformación de amor podemos decir que su ordinario hábito es como el madero, que siempre está embestido en fuego; (923).

34. Diálogos de la Conquista del espiritual secreto reino de Dios in Obras místicas del M.R.R. Fr. Juan de los Angeles, ed. Jaime Sala. Primera parte NBAE (Madrid: Bailly-Brailliere, 1912), which also includes Segunda parte de la Conquista del Reino del Cielo intitulada Manual de vida perfecta (1608).

35. Gomis in his introduction to the *Místicos franciscanos* describes the different types of this philosophy of love: "La filosofía de amor, hispánicamente sentida, es una sinfonía de amores que se levanta desde lo bajo y humilde de las criatures hasta lo alto, sublime y secreto de Dios. El amor pues, está en todos los seres y en todos resuena. . .El amor es la consonancia del ser y del

universo mundo. . .Siendo, pues, Dios amor y caridad, caridad y amor son sus obras, todas juntas y cada una de ellas. . .Dios es amor originario, fontal, los seres, amor participado, chispazo del divino amor" (I: 6). The manifestation of these types of loves are metaphysical love, cosmic love, anthropological love, and psychological love. In metaphysical love, love concatenates (connects) everything in the universe from God down to the lowest creature. It also involves what the Spanish spiritual writers call "ley de amor": "Todos los seres son y existen por la ley interna que los rige y orienta" (10). Cosmic love is also called "ley de naturaleza" or "inclinación natural", which is a natural appetite; it can be animal or rational (intellectual) (14-15) Anthropological love is love for all human beings. This type of love stresses the unity of humankind since everyone descends from Adam (17). This type of love involves what the Spanish writers call "ley social"; the love for one's neighbor. Psychological love is crucial to the understanding of the literature of Recollection, meditation, contemplation and union. It involves the governance of the natural appetites, the innermost part of the soul where union takes place, and the study of the three powers of the soul and their functions. All of these loves are important in the inner way of Recollection which leads to love and ultimate union (24-25).

36. See San Agustín, *Confesiones*. "Libro" I. Ed. Angel Custodio Vega, O.S.A. Séptima edición. BAC (Madrid: Editorial Católica, 1979), 73-111.

37. This is Fray Juan's description of these entrances: ". . .cuatro entradas o puertas, al Oriente, al Poniente, al Septentrión o Norte, al Mediodía; Oriente-humildad, Poniente, pasión y muerte de Cristo, Mediodía, abnegación de la propia voluntad; Norte, tribulación" (61).

38. See Angelo J. DiSalvo, *Cervantes and the Augustinian Religious Tradition* (York, S.C.: Spanish Literature Publications, 1989). In this book we discuss the influence that this ascetical-devotional literature had on Cervantes. It is important to keep in mind that Don Quijote himself battled to eradicate the giants which were the evils and vices of the society.

39. In this part of the eighth dialogue Fray Juan presents the reader with an interesting picture of the "beatas", who are especially scrupulous and extreme in their religious exercises, but do not necessarily possess the charity that can

assist them in their journey to God. They are in effect the negation of this affective form of Catholic spirituality. They tend to kill the spirit and are incapable of a loving union. This is what we read in regard to them: "Deprenden a andar por cosas ajenas, no solamente curiosas, mirando lo que hay en cada una, sino ociosas, porque no hacen nada, y verbosas, porque nunca cierran la boca, derramándose muchas veces en pláticas excusadas, todo lo cual las nace de poco espíritu y menos conocimiento del estado que tomaron, que al fin profesan alguna manera de religión y el hábito que traen es de mortificación y pentiencia" (*Conquista* 124).

Bibliography

Abellán, Luis. *Historia crítica del pensamiento español.* Volume 2. Madrid: Espasa-Calpe, 1980.

Alcalá, Jaime de, O.F.M., *Libro de la caballería cristiana, compuesto por el muy reverendo padre fray Jayme de Alcalá dirigido a la Ilustrísima doña Mariana de Córdova, muger del Ilustre señor do{n} Fadrique Enríquez de Rivera.* Alcalá: Juan de Villanueva, 1570.

Alarcón, Luis de, O.S.A. *Camino del cielo y de la maldad y ceguedad del mundo.* Ed. Angel Custodio Vega, O.S.A. Barcelona: Juan Flors, 1959.

Alcántara, Pedro de. Tratado de la oración y meditación. Madrid: Rialp, 1958.

- - - . *Treatise on Prayer and Meditation.* tr. Dominic Devas. Westminster, Md.: Newman, 1949.

Allison Peers, Edgar. *Book of Exercises of the Spiritual Life.* Monastery of Montserrat, 1929.

- - - . Spanish Mysticism. London: Methuen, 1924.

Andrés Martín, Melquíades. *Nueva visión de los alumbrados de 1525.* Madrid: Fundación Universitaria Española, 1975.

- - - . *Reforma española y reforma luterana: afinidades y diferencias a la luz de los místicos.* Madrid: Fund. Univ. Española, n.d.

- - - . *Los recogidos: nueva visión de los místicos españoles (1500-1700).* Madrid: Fundación Universitara Española, 1975.

- - - . *La teología española en el siglo XVI. Biblioteca de Autores Cristianos.* Madrid: Ed. Católica, 1977. 2 vols.

Angeleti, Carlo. *Il problema religioso del rinascimento.* Florence: Felice de Nommier, 1952.

Asín Palacios, Miguel. *El Islam cristianizado: Estudio del Sufismo" a través de Abenarabi de Murcia.* 1st ed. Madrid: Ed. Plutarco, 1931.

Aquinas, Thomas. *Summa Theologica.* Chicago: Encyclopedia Britannica, Inc., 1952.

Augustine, Saint. *City of God.* Trans. Marcus Dods. New York: Random House, 1950.

- - - . *Confessions.* Trans. I.G. Pilkington. New York: Liveright, 1943.

- - - . *The Happy Life.* Trans. Ludwig Schoff. New York: IMA Pub. Co., 1940.

- - - . *On Christian Doctrine.* Trans. D. W. Robertson, Jr. New York: Liberal Arts P, 1958.

- - - . *On Free Choice of the Will.* Trans. Anna S. Benjamin. Indianapolis: Bobb-Merrill, 1964.

- - - . *On the Trinity.* Trans. Stephen MacKenna, C.S.S.R. Washington: Catholic UP, 1963.

Avila, Juan de. *Obras completas.* Ed. Luis Sala Balust. Madrid: Castalia, 1952.

Balma, Hugo de. *Sol de contemplativos compuesto por Hugo de Balma de la Orden de los Cartujos nuevamente romanzado y corregido.* Toledo, 1513. In Biblioteca Nacional de Madrid R 20.511.

Bernard of Clairveaux. *The Love of God and Spiritual Friendship.* Portland, Or.: Mullnomah P, n.d.

- - - . *On Loving God.* Kalamazoo: Cistercian Publ.,Inc. 1995.

Bernardino de Laredo. *The Ascent of Mount Sion.* Third Part. Trans. Edgar A. Peers. New York: Harper, n.d.

Blarney, Raymond. *Meister Eckhard: A Modern Translation.* New York: Harper and Row, 1941.

Bonaventure, Saint. *The Mind's Journey to God.* Trans. L.S. Cunningham. Chicago: Franciscan Herald, 1979.

Bouyer, L. *Diccionario de teología.* Barcelona: Ed. Herder, 1972.

Bruyne, Edgar de. *Estudios de estética medieval. Biblioteca Hispánica de Filosofía.* Volume 1. Madrid: Gredos, 1958.

Canals Vidal, F. *Textos de los grandes filósofos: Edad Media.* Barcelona: Herder, 1979.

Castro, Manuel de, et. al. *San Buenaventura: Conferencias pronunciados en la Fundación Universitaria 4 feb. 11 y 13 marzo 1975*. Madrid: Fundación Universitaria Española, 1976.

Caterina da Siena, Santa. *Il dialogo della Divina Provvidenza*. Siena: Cantagalli, 1980.

Chew, Samuel. *The Pilgrimage of Life*. New Haven: Yale UP, 1962.

Cilveti, Angel. *Literatura mística española*. Madrid: Taurus, 1983.

Copleston, Frederick C. *A History of Philosophy: Greece and Rome*. Volume 1. London: Metheun, 1972.

- - - . *A History of Philosophy: Medieval Philosophy*. Volume 2. London: Methuen, 1972.

Cruz Hernández, Miguel. *El pensamiento de Ramón Llull*. Madrid: Castalia, 1977.

Díaz Borque, José M. *Literatura mística española II. Místicos franciscanos*. Madrid: Taurus, 1983.

Diccionario de la Lengua Española. Madrid: Real Academia Española, 1994.

Dionysius Areopagite. *The Works of Dionysius the Areopaguite*. Trans. John Parker. Merrick, New York: Richwood, 1976.

Eckhard, Meister. *The Book of Divine Comfort: A Modern Translation*. New York: Harper-Row, 1941.

Erasmus of Rotterdam. *Education of a Christian Prince*. Trans. Lester K. Born. New York: Farrar, 1973.

Fuensalida, Francisco. *Breve summa llamada sosiego y descanso del ánima*. Alcalá: n.p., 1541.

García Jiménez de Cisneros. *Exercitatiorio de la vida espiritual*. Montserrat, 1500.

García Oro, José, OFM. *Cisneros y la reforma del clero español en tiempo de los Reyes Católicos*. Num. XIII. Madrid: Consejo Superior de Investigaciones Científicos, 1971.

García Sánchez, don Julián. "Epítome de la vida de fray Juan de los Angeles." unpublished article.

Gilson, Etienne. *The Christian Philosophy of St. Augustine*. Trans. L.E. M. Lynch. New York: Randon House, 1960.

Gomis, Juan Bautista, OFM. *Místicos franciscanos españoles*. Biblioteca de Autores Cristianos. Madrid: Ed. Cat., 1948.

Gougaud, Don Louis. *Devotional and Ascetic Practices in the Middle Ages*. London: Burns, Gates and Washbourne, n.d.

Groult, Pierre. *Literatura espiritual española: Edad Media y Renacimiento*. Trans. Rodrigo A. Molina. Madrid: Fund. Univ. Esp., 1980.

Hatzfeld, Helmut. *Estudios literarios sobre mística española*. Madrid: Gredos, 1968.

Herp, Hendrik. *Directorio de contemplativos*. Trans. Juan Martín Kelly. Madrid: Fund. Univ. Esp., 1974.

Inge, William. *The Philosophy of Plotinus*. 3rd ed. Volume 1. Westport, Ct.: Greenwood P, 1968.

Juan de la Cruz. *Obras completas*. Madrid: Ed. de Espiritualidad, 1980.

Juan de los Angeles. *Diálogo de la Conquista de Dios*. Madrid: Aguirre, 1946.

- - - . *Lucha espiritual y amorosa*. Madrid, 1600.

- - - . *Místicos franciscanos*. Volume 3. Ed. Juan Bautista Gomis, OFM. BAC. Madrid: Ed. Cat., n.d.

- - - . *Vergel espiritual del ánima religiosa*. Nueva Bibilioteca de Autores Españoles 20. Madrid, 1912.

Kaulsky, Karl. *Foundations of Christianity*. Trans. Henry F. Mins. New York: Russell and Russell, 1953.

Kavanaugh, Kieran, O.C.D., and Otilio Rodríguez, O.C.D. *The Collected Works of Theresa of Avila*. Volume 2. Washington: Carmelite Studies, 1980.

Kempis, Tomás de. *Imitación de Cristo*. Introd. Francisco Montes de Oca. Mexico: Ed. Porrua, 1974.

Kempis, Thomas of. *Imitation of Christ*. Trans. P.G. Zomberg. Portland, Maine: Dunstan P, 1984.

Libro de meditaciones y soliloquios y manual. Antwerp: Martín Nucio, 1505 (Valladolid: Diego de Gumiel, 1511).

Llull, Ramon. *Blanquerna: A Thirtheenth Century Romance*. Trans. Edgar Allison Peers. London: Jaerolds, 1925.

- - - . *El libro del amigo y del amado*. 3rd. Madrid: Aguilar, 1981.

- - - . *Libre del Orde de Cavalleria*. Ed. Marina Gustà. Barcelona: El Garbell, 1984.

López Baralt, Luce. *Islam in Spanish Literature: From the Middle Ages to the Present*. Trans. Andrew Hurely. San Juan: University of Puerto Rico P, 1991.

Márquez, Antonio. *Los alumbrados: Orígenes y filosofía 1525-1529.* Madrid: Taurus, 1972..

Márquez Villanueva, Francisco. *Espiritualidad y literatura en el siglo XVI.* Madrid: Alfaguara, 1968.

Markus, R.A., *Saeculum: History and Society in the Theology of St. Augustine.* Cambridge: UP, 1970.

Monasterio, Ignacio, OSA. *Místicos agustinos españoles.* 2nd ed. San Lorenzo del Escorial: Ed. Agustiniana, 1929.

Moorman, John. *A History of the Franciscan Order from its Origins to the Year 1517.* Oxford: Clarendon P, 1968.

Morón Arroyo, Ciriaco. *La mística española: Antecedentes y Edad Media.* Madrid: Ed. Alcalá, 1971.

O'Connell, Robert J. "Art and the Christian Intelligence in St. Augustine." *St. Augustine.* ed. Martin D'Arcy, S. J. Cleveland: World, 1957.

Orozco, Alonso de. *Vergel de oración y Monte de contemplación.* Seville: 1544 and 1548. In BNM R/25.360.

Osuna, Francisco de. *Tercer abecedario espiritual.* Ed. Melquíades Andrés M. Bibioteca de Autores Cristianos. Madrid: Ed. Cat., 1972.

Pfandl, Ludwig. *Historia de la literatura nacional española en la Edad de Oro.* Trans. Jorge Rubió Balaguer. Barcelona: Gráfica Moderna, 1933.

Plato. *Timaeus and Critias.* Trans. Thomas Taylor. Bollingen Series 3. Washington: Pantheon Books, 1944.

Plotinus. *The Enneads.* Trans. Stephen MacKenna. London: Penguin Bks., Ltd, 1991.

Ricard, Robert. *Estudios de literatura religiosa española.* Madrid: Gredos, 1964.

Riccardo di San Vittore. *La preparazione dell'anima alla contemplazione: Beniamino Minore.* Claudio Nardini, ed. Firenze: Ed. Nardini, 1991.

Royo Marín, Antonio. *Los grandes maestros de la vida espiritual.* 2nd ed. Biblioteca de Autores Cristianos. Madrid: Ed. Católica, 1990.

Ruysbroeck, John. *The Spiritual Espousals.* Trans. Eric Colledge. New York: Harper, n.d.

Sainz Rodríguez, Pedro. *Espiritualidad española.* Madrid: Rialp, 1961.

Sanchís Alventosa, Joaquín. *La escuela mística alemana y sus relaciones con nuestros místicos del Siglo de Oro.* Madrid: Ed. Verdad y Vida, 1946.

Sanz Pascual, Atilano. *Historia de los agustinos españoles.* Madrid: Ed. Avila, 1948.

Schaff, Philip. *History of the Christian Church: Nicene and Post-Nicene Christianity.* Grand Rapids: Eerdmans, 1964.

Shahan, Robert W. and Francis J. Kovak. *Bonaventure and Aquinas: Enduring Philosophies.* Norman: U Oklahoma P, 1976.

Tanquerey, Ad. *Compendio de teología, ascética y mística.* Madrid: Ed. Palabra, 1990.

Teresa de Jesús, Santa. *Obras completas.* 2nd ed. Madrid: Editorial de spiritualidad, 1976.

Turnbull, Grace H. *The Essence of Plotinus: Extracts from the Enneads and Porfyry's Life of Plotinus.* Trans. Stephen McKennis. Westport, Ct.: Greenwood P, 1976.

Valdez, Juan de. *Valdez' two Catechisms: The dialogue on Christian doctrine nd the Christian instruction for children.* ed. Jose C. Nieto. Trans. William B and Carol D. Jones. Lawrence, Kan.: Coronado P, 1981.

Vinck, Joseph de. *The Works of Bonaventure I: Mystical Opúscula.* Paterson, New Jersey: St. Anthony Guild, 1960.

Wenley, Robert. *Stoicism and Its Influence.* New York: Cooper Square Pub. Co., 1963.

Workman, Herbert B. *The Evolution of the Monastic Ideal from the Earliest Times down to the Coming of the Friars.* Boston: Beacon P, 1962.

Wright, A.D. *The Counter-Reformation: Catholic Europe and the Non-Christian World.* New York: St. Martin's P, 1982.

Index

TEXTS AND STUDIES IN RELIGION

41. Aegidius of Rome, **On Ecclesiastical Power: De Ecclesiastica Potestate,** Arthur P. Monahan (trans.)
42. John R. Eastman, **Papal Abdication in Later Medieval Thought**
43. Paul Badham,(ed.), **Religion, State, and Society in Modern Britain**
44. Hans Denck, **Selected Writings of Hans Denck, 1500-1527,** E.J. Furcha (trans.)
45. Dietmar Lage, **Martin Luther's Christology and Ethics**
46. Jean Calvin, **Sermons on Jeremiah by Jean Calvin,** Blair Reynolds (trans.)
47. Jean Calvin, **Sermons on Micah by Jean Calvin,** Blair Reynolds (trans.)
48. Alexander Sándor Unghváry, **The Hungarian Protestant Reformation in the Sixteenth Century Under the Ottoman Impact: Essays and Profiles**
49. Daniel B. Clendenin and W. David Buschart (eds.), **Scholarship, Sacraments and Service: Historical Studies in Protestant Tradition,** *Essays in Honor of Bard Thompson*
50. Randle Manwaring, **A Study of Hymn-Writing and Hymn-Singing in the Christian Church**
51. John R. Schneider, **Philip Melanchthon's Rhetorical Construal of Biblical Authority: Oratio Sacra**
52. John R. Eastman (ed.), **Aegidius Romanus,** *De Renunciatione Pape*
53. J.A. Loubser, **A Critical Review of Racial Theology in South Africa: The Apartheid Bible**
54. Henri Heyer, **Guillaume Farel: An Introduction to His Theology,** Blair Reynolds (trans.)
55. James E. Biechler and H. Lawrence Bond (ed.), **Nicholas of Cusa on Interreligious Harmony: Text, Concordance and Translation of** *De Pace Fidei*
56. Michael Azkoul, **The Influence of Augustine of Hippo on the Orthodox Church**
57. James C. Dolan, **The** *Tractatus Super Psalmum Vicesimum* **of Richard Rolle of Hampole**
58. William P. Frost, **Following Joseph Campbell's Lead in the Search for Jesus' Father**
59. Frederick Hale, **Norwegian Religious Pluralism: A Trans-Atlantic Comparison**
60. Frank H. Wallis, **Popular Anti-Catholicism in Mid-Victorian Britain**
61. Blair Reynolds, **The Relationship of Calvin to Process Theology as Seen Through His Sermons**